Refugee Policy in Sudan, 1967-1984

REFUGEE AND FORCED MIGRATION STUDIES
General Editors: Dawn Chatty and Chaloka Beyani

Volume 1
A Tamil Asylum Diaspora. Sri Lankan Migration, Settlement and Politics in Switzerland
Christopher McDowell

Volume 2
Understanding Impoverishment. The Consequences of Development-Induced Displacement
Edited by Christopher McDowell

Volume 3
Losing Place. Refugee Populations and Rural Transformation in East Africa
Johnathan Bascom

Volume 4
The End of the Refugee Cycle. Refugee Repatriation and Reconstruction
Edited by Richard Black and Khalid Koser

Volume 5
Engendering Forced Migration. Theory and Practice
Doreen Indra

Volume 6
Refugee Policy in Sudan, 1967-1984
Ahmad Karadawi

Volume 7
Arguing and Justifying. Assessing Conventional Refugee Choices of Moment, Motive and Host Country
Robert Barsky

REFUGEE POLICY IN SUDAN 1967-1984

Ahmad Karadawi

Edited and with an introduction by
Peter Woodward

With a foreword by
Barbara Harrell-Bond and John Rogge

Berghahn Books
New York • Oxford

Published in association with the Refugee Studies Programme

First published in 1999 by

Berghahn Books

©1999 Estate of Ahmad Karadawi

Library of Congress Cataloging-in-Publication Data

Karadawi, Ahmad.
    Refugee policy in Sudan, 1967-1984 / Ahmad Karadawi ;
edited and with an introduction by Peter Woodward ; with a
foreword by Barbara Harrell-Bond and John Rogge.
      p. cm. -- (Refugee and forced migration studies ; v. 6)
    Includes bibliographical references and index.
    ISBN 1-57181-708-5 (alk. paper)
    1. Refugees--Government policy--Sudan.   2. Refugees--
Sudan--Social conditions.   3. Forced migration--Sudan.   4.
Sudan--Politics and government.   5. Sudan--Social policy.   6.
Sudan--Economic policy.
    I. Woodward, Peter, 1944- .   II. Title.   III. Series.
HV640.4.S73K35   1999
362.87'09624--dc21   99-19062
                                             CIP

British Library Cataloguing in Publication Data
A catalogue record for this book is available from
the British Library.

Printed in the United States on acid-free paper

REFUGEES

They approach me
In a halfhearted way – hesitatingly;
They eye me curiously – suspiciously?
Then tell a story.

To the question
How does it feel to be a problem?
I seldom say a word.

Ahmad Karadawi

Contents

List of Maps		viii
List of Tables		ix
Foreword		x
Author's Preface		xii
List of Abbreviations		xvi
Introduction		xviii
Chapter 1	Sudan, Its Eastern Region, and the Refugees	1
Chapter 2	The Emergence of a Centralised Refugee Policy during the Second Parliamentary Regime 1965-1969	30
Chapter 3	The Changing Nature of the Refugee Influxes 1970-1980	56
Chapter 4	Competing Interests within the Sudanese Bureaucracy and Their Consequences for Refugee Policy	88
Chapter 5	The Role and Limitations of Assistance to Refugees: UNHCR and COR, 1975-1978	137
Chapter 6	Refugees as an International Responsibility: The Sudanese Initiative of 1980 and Its Consequences	162
Chapter 7	The Active Role of UNHCR in the Development of Refugee Policy: The Promotion of Voluntary Repatriation as an Option	193
Chapter 8	Conclusion	216
Epilogue		223
Bibliography		228
Index		260

List of Maps

Map 1.1   Distribution of Refugees in Sudan   xxiv
Map 1.2   The Eastern Region and Surrounding Areas   14
Map 2.1   Border Area Affected by Congolese   35
Map 2.2   Refugee Influxes into the Eastern Region, 1967-1975   39
Map 3.1   Refugee Influx in the Nile Provinces   72
Map 4.1   Refugee Settlement in Eastern Sudan   113

List of Tables

Table 1.1 Modes of Living and Population Distribution by
Province in the Eastern Region   15

Table 3.1 Estimate of Numbers of Newly-Arrived
Refugees, 1975   68

Table 3.2 Refugees' Dates of Arrival in Kassala Area   80

Table 3.3 Percentage of Ethnic Groups among Refugees in
Gedaref   81

Table 3.4 Numbers of Refugees Registered in Khartoum,
1975-1978   84

Table 3.5 Date of Entry to Sudan among the Refugee
Population in Khartoum, 1974-1978   84

Table 4.1 Projections by COR for Relocation of Refugees
Evicted from Khartoum   112

Table 4.2 Distribution of Identity Cards to Refugees in
Khartoum by Category   117

Table 4.3 Distribution of Identity Cards to Refugees in
Khartoum by Nationality   117

Table 6.1 Summary of Project Type and Cost Estimates
for the 1980 Plan   167

Table 6.2 Pledges for the Refugee Assistance Programme
during the 1980 Khartoum Conference   169

Table 6.3 ICARA Pledges and Channel of Distribution   179

Table 6.4 Projects Proposed for the Consideration of
ICARA II by Region   184

Table 6.5 Projects Proposed for the Consideration of
ICARA II by Sector   185

Foreword

We are particularly pleased that the Refugee and Forced Migration Series is able to make available this valuable historical document, *Refugee Policy in Sudan, 1967-1984*. Social historians, students of refugee issues, Africanists, not to mention officials who continue to face the human drama of refugees – all of them deserve this rich documentation of the Sudanese experience.

Ahmad Karadawi was a pioneer among government officials in refugee-receiving countries during the 1970s and early 1980s. His dedication to the refugee cause was well known. The intellectual insights he cast on the development of policies towards refugees and the manner in which he promoted holistic and humane durable solutions for refugees are captured in this book. He was also a pioneer in having the vision to promote refugee studies as a field of academic concentration.

This book captures the hopes and failures of the 1970s and 1980s as African countries had to grapple with ever growing refugee numbers and increasing length of sojourn in countries of asylum. During this period, Sudan changed from a country with one of the most constructive and generous refugee policies and legislation, to one beset by growing economic, social and political problems, where the burden of supporting refugees became a further destabilising factor. The transition in government policy towards refugees is captured by Karadawi and analysed in a fair but forceful manner.

Both of us became acquainted with Ahmad Karadawi in 1982, when we began our research among refugees in Sudan. Having failed at the time to convince colleagues at the University of Khartoum to do research in this area, he rose to the challenge of helping to establish the Refugee Studies Programme at the University of Oxford. So many students learned from him during his years in Oxford in the 1980s. He was the one who always insisted that refugees must be at the centre of our work. It was his inspiration that led to the first international conference in Oxford in 1984, which was attended by as many refugees as aid workers and academics. As one journalist put it, 'Suddenly the silent ones get a voice'.

It was not only researchers that he influenced. As one UNHCR staff member has written:

> ...do mention the uniquely stimulating and convincing way Ahmad kept UNHCR (and all other foreign aid deliverers) on the right track, insisting in his inimitably clever fashion that refugees should be the first to be consulted about their needs and that they themselves were the most important resource to be tapped in meeting those needs, the next being the people and authorities in the countries of asylum. And he did this with a cool good humour even in the midst of the most dire emergencies. He was a rather blindingly bright light for many of us fumbling about on the messy humanitarian stage in Sudan in the 1980s.

In fact, it was his academic work on refugees that led to Ahmad Karadawi spending his last years as a *de facto* refugee himself in Addis Ababa. With colleagues at Juba University, an annotated bibliography of research and documents on refugees in Sudan was produced; the government at that time disapproved. He was able to leave Sudan by exchanging a pair of shoes for an exit permit from a policeman. He returned to Oxford from Addis in October 1995 to write up his research on Qala en Nahal refugee settlements in eastern Sudan. A few weeks later a death in his family led him to take the risk of returning to Sudan. On 20 November he died there. He is survived by his wife, Selma Mahmoud Maarouf, a son, Jehad, a daughter, Sarah, his parents, five brothers and three sisters.

John Rogge
United Nations Development
Programme, Geneva

Barbara Harrell-Bond
Refugee Studies Programme,
University of Oxford

Author's Preface

The refugee issue is politically loaded and involves many parties in complex sets of power relations. There are parties directly involved in the conflict that generates refugees, such as governments and opposition groups seeking to oust them. There are parties working to deal with the plight of the refugees and the consequences of the refugee exodus. Refugees themselves are characterised by ethnic and political diversity, which tends to influence patterns of conflict and cooperation with other parties, particularly the host government and populations. It is from this understanding that I present this analysis of government policy in the Sudan.

I worked for sixteen years with the government office of the Commissioner for Refugees in Khartoum. During these years, I was involved in policy issues relating to refugees and had extensive contact with 'liberation fronts', other government departments, aid organisations, refugees, and, not least, the Sudanese citizens themselves. Among all these I observed the complex relations which often worked to obscure what is conventionally recognised to be the humanitarian motive behind international legal protection and material assistance programmes.

However, neither in the general academic literature on Africa, nor in the mushrooming refugee research, has the complexity of the relationships between parties involved in the refugee phenomenon been sufficiently documented. One reason for this may be the lack of data and inaccessibility of information, as the different parties persistently guard and protect their organisations' interests. In studying the successive governments' policies, I have not faced these difficulties. In preparing the research material, I had access to all the government documents that I needed.

Sources

1. Government Documents

Government documents cited in this thesis consist of correspondence, reports and memoranda *(al Mudhakirat,* singular *Mudhakira).* All these documents are compiled in files *(Malaffat,* singular *Malaf)* kept by the different departments according to a standard system of classification. All issues related to government business are classified in subjects and each group of subjects is given a standard number. For correspondence, each department uses its first initials, then the number of the classified subject (the latter being also the file number) and the date. The filing system can be translated into English and the same pattern is followed for English correspondence. Thus, a Commissioner for Refugees' document relating to, for example, refugee education would be CR/17/A/1; CR refers to Commissioner for Refugees, 17/A to the classification number of the subject 'Education', and the last number refers to the number of the volume containing the subject.

The files relating to my research are located in various government departments in Khartoum and the Eastern Region. In Khartoum I consulted files in the Ministry of Interior, the Office of the Commissioner for Refugees, the Council of Ministers, and the Ministry of Foreign Affairs. For information from the technical ministries of health, education, agriculture etc., I concentrated on the issues related to refugees for which material was also available in the office of the Commissioner for Refugees.

In the Eastern Region, I had access to the documents of the offices of the Assistant Commissioner for Refugees in Gedaref, the General Project Management in Showak, and the Assistant Commissioner for Refugees in Kassala. In Kassala and Red Sea Provinces, I had access to valuable material, particularly in the provincial headquarters and the regional police offices in Gedaref, Kassala and Port Sudan.

A selected list of files is given in the bibliography. I have also listed particular memoranda that I found valuable. A memorandum is a document that deals with a specific issue in an analytical manner, either because the issue discussed has no precedent or rule to guide action, or because it simply contradicts existing rules. It is frequently used to seek advice or a decision from a higher authority. Memoranda constitute an important component in the documents of the Commissioner for Refugees, mainly because the management of a complex refugee phenomenon has no definite set of bureaucratic rules.

In relation to the security aspects of the refugee phenomenon, I had the opportunity to read the excellent monographs of the National Defence Academy. I include a list of the relevant material in the bibliography.

2. Conferences, Seminars and Aid Agency Reports

The diversity of parties and complexity of issues involved in the refugee phenomenon often make it necessary to hold meetings to clarify the issues. Conferences, symposia, and seminars, bringing together governments and refugee aid organisations, have been common practice. Some of these meetings have been instrumental in developing shared strategies for dealing with refugees among these different parties. Sudanese governments have invariably attended these exercises. Moreover, Sudan is a member of the Executive Committee of the United Nations High Commissioner for Refugees, and also a member of the Committee of Fifteen of the Organisation of African Unity. The Commissioner for Refugees acted as a national representative for the Bureau of African Refugees of the Organisation of African Unity.

During my career with the office of the Commissioner for Refugees, I had the opportunity to attend and contribute to several meetings. I have been particularly fortunate in contributing to the preparation of government documents for major conferences. Examples of these are the Pan-African Conference on Refugees held at Arusha, Tanzania in May 1979, the Khartoum International Conference, 1980, and the two International Conferences on Assistance to Refugees in Africa held in Geneva in 1981 and 1984. I have also been particularly privileged by being involved in organising the symposium on the Refugee Situation in the Sudan in 1982, the conference on Assistance to African Refugees held at Oxford in 1984, and the workshop on the Role of Indigenous Organisations in Provision of Assistance to Refugees held at Showak, Sudan in 1987. I have also been closely attached to the Refugee Studies Programme in Oxford. Its seminars, conferences and documents have provided additional information on the refugee situation in other parts of the world. I have benefited a great deal from all these sources as they improved my knowledge of the refugee phenomenon and provided me with valuable acquaintances with other involved parties.

3. Books and Other Published Material

Books and other published material on refugees in general and the refugee situation in the Sudan in particular provided a valuable secondary source. A selected list of books and articles is provided in the bibliography.

Dates and Themes

The dates 1967 to 1984 are intentionally selected for the scope of this study. In 1967 the government applied the OAU norms to the Eritrean refugees who arrived that year and who were generally referred to as the first Eritrean influx. The year 1984 marked the end of the phase when the government and aid agencies disagreed on the modalities of linking refugee assistance to development aid.

During the period under study, emphasis was given to the conception of refugees as a security threat and as a socio-economic burden. In my opinion, these two themes were of prime concern for government policy. Although the two themes are not mutually exclusive, I have divided the thesis into two equal parts: whereas Chapters 2, 3 and 4 stress how the refugee phenomenon was conceived as a security issue, Chapters 5, 6 and 7 discuss the attempts to deal with the socio-economic burden through material assistance.

Due to the nature and complexity of the refugee phenomenon in the period under study, there is an overlap between chapters regarding dates. This, I hope, is justified by my intention to elaborate the themes.

Transliteration

For names of people and italicised Arabic words in the text, I have followed the system of transliteration adopted by *Sudan Notes and Records.* However, I have omitted the diacritical marks on the names of people and places. In exceptional cases, I have used the conventional English form of well-known names, such as 'Nimeiry'. The names of some Sudanese authors appear as they wrote them in English, such as Mohamed Omer Beshir. In the cases where Arabic sources are quoted (e.g., Sudanese Government files), I have translated the source into English in order to make the text less cumbersome. I have, however, given the full Arabic names of sources transliterated in the bibliography. Names and places, towns and villages are spelled according to the pattern followed by the Sudan Survey Department.

Ahmad Karadawi
Oxford, 1988

List of Abbreviations

CCRR	The Central Committee for Rehabilitation of Returnees
COR	The Office of the Commissioner for Refugees
DUP	The Democratic Unionist Party
ECA	Economic Commission for Africa
EDU	The Ethiopian Democratic Union
ELF	The Eritrean Liberation Front
ELF/PLF	The Eritrean Liberation Front/Popular Liberation Forces
ELF/PLFRC	The Eritrean Liberation Front/Popular Liberation Forces Revolutionary Committee
ELF/RC	The Eritrean Liberation Front/Revolutionary Council
EPLF	The Eritrean People's Liberation Front
EPRA	The Ethiopian People's Revolutionary Army
EPRP	The Ethiopian People's Revolutionary Party
ERA	The Eritrean Relief Association
ERC	The Eritrean Relief Committee
ERCCS	The Eritrean Red Cross/Crescent Societies
EXCOM	The UNHCR Executive Committee
GPM	General Project Manager in Showak
ICARA	International Conference on Assistance to Refugees in Africa
ICF	The Islamic Charter Front
ICVA	The International Council for Voluntary Agencies
IGO	Intergovernmental Organisation
ILO	International Labour Organisation
INF	The Islamic National Front
LWF	The Lutheran World Federation
NCAR	The National Committee for Aid for Refugees in Sudan
NGO	Non-Governmental Organisation
NUP	The National Unionist Party
OAU	The Organisation of African Unity
OAU/BPEAR	The Bureau for Placement and Education of African Refugees
OLF	The Oromo Liberation Front
ORA	The Oromo Relief Association

PDP	The People's Democratic Party
PMAC	The Provisional Military Administration Council (Ethiopia)
RCS	The Refugee Counselling Service, Sudan
RRC	The Relief and Rehabilitation Commission (Ethiopia)
RSP	Refugee Studies Programme (Oxford)
RST	The Relief Society of Tigray
SCC	The Sudan Council of Churches
SCP	The Sudanese Communist Party
SSLM	The Southern Sudan Liberation Movement
SSU	The Sudanese Socialist Union
SUNA	The Sudanese News Agency
TPLF	The Tigray People's Liberation Front
UNDP	United Nations Development Programme
UNHCR	The United Nations High Commissioner for Refugees
UNHS	The United Nations Office for Human Settlement
WFP	The World Food Programme
£S	Sudanese Pound*

* Editor's note: During the period studied, the official rate of exchange of the Sudanese pound varied, being, for example, equal to US$1.10 in 1982, and US$0.77 in 1985. The official rate was kept artificially high while the black market rate was much lower.

Introduction

Ahmad Karadawi's D. Phil. thesis at Oxford, of which this book is an edited version, is a most revealing picture of policy making and implementation in an African context. Rarely does one see such an intimate portrayal of the inner workings of government, or relations with an international agency, in this case the United Nations High Commissioner for Refugees (UNHCR). However, because it is such a close-up, it needs some introduction. Karadawi had himself done much of this in his earlier (1977) unpublished M. Phil. thesis at Reading University, entitled 'Political Refugees in Africa: A Case Study from the Sudan, 1964-1972'. This brief introduction draws heavily on that thesis, as well as adding to the political context both in Sudan and its neighbouring countries.

The huge movements of refugees out of, as well as into, Sudan have their roots in the travails of African states, beginning virtually from the moment of independence. As Karadawi makes clear, the two-way flow of refugees greatly complicated the making of refugee policy, yet the story that follows is primarily concerned with the Sudanese Government side, and its international support. It is thus necessary to touch on the origins of the flows into Sudan with which the government was concerned, and in which Karadawi as a senior official was himself much involved.

The first to arrive were from the Congo (now Democratic Republic of Congo, formerly Zaire). It has been a byword for the misfortunes of African states since its independence from Belgium in 1960 and the assassination of its first prime minister, Patrice Lumumba, shortly after. In 1963 the Simba revolt, which claimed descent from Lumumba, led to the establishment of the People's Republic of Kisangani, but by 1964 it had collapsed and by 1965 an official total of over 6,000 refugees had entered southern Sudan. The leaders of the failed revolt were quite well off, arriving with looted gold (and arms, some of which fell into the hands of southern Sudanese rebels), but supplies soon ran out. The Simbas had arrived at a time when

Sudan was itself going through a short spell of radicalism, following a popular revolt of 1964 known as the 'October revolution'. There was thus some sympathy for the Simbas, and the first steps were taken in evolving a refugee policy.

A more serious, if less dramatic, build up of refugees was taking place in eastern Sudan. The incorporation of the former Italian colony and post-war United Nations Trust Territory of Eritrea into Ethiopia had been a matter of controversy in 1952. The Eritrean parliament had eventually voted for it, but there had not been wider consultation such as a referendum, and there were many critics. Over the subsequent decade it had become clear that the so-called federal incorporation was being eroded, with Eritrea brought ever more firmly under the centralised and personalised power of the Emperor, Haile Selassie. From 1962 a revolt began led by the Eritrean Liberation Front (ELF), which in turn was followed by a trickle of refugees that grew as the conflict increased, reaching about 45,000 by 1970.

Developments in Ethiopia in the 1970s were to bring a new chapter in the flow of refugees. There were hopes that the revolution, which began in 1974 and saw the overthrow of Haile Selassie, might herald the coming of peace, but instead the situation worsened. Not only did the war between the Eritreans and the new Ethiopian government intensify, but there were clashes among the Eritreans which saw the Eritrean People's Liberation Front (EPLF) replace the ELF as the leading group. The EPLF made much headway in the mid-1970s, only for the Ethiopian army, now strengthened by the Soviet Union, to inflict severe reverses at the end of the decade. At the same time a further revolt had broken out in Tigray, on the southern border of Eritrea, led by the Tigrayan People's Liberation Front, TPLF. By the mid 1980s there were over 600,000 refugees from Ethiopia in Sudan. Eastern Sudan had by far the largest concentration of refugees, and Karadawi selected the region as the focus of his thesis.

Uganda was another neighbour that contributed to the flow of refugees into the south. In the 1960s the flow had been mainly the other way, with thousands of southern Sudanese taking refuge in Uganda from the civil war in the south. However, in 1979, with the downfall of Idi Amin (whose regime had longstanding connections with southern Sudan), up to 200,000 refugees flooded into Sudan. They were taking refuge from the era known in Uganda as 'Obote II', which turned out to be of comparable violence to the Amin years.

In western Sudan as well, there was an intermittent refugee problem with regard to Chadians, though not on the same scale as in the south or east of the country. Chad was as unstable as anywhere in Africa, and groups from the north and east of the country were prominent in its years of conflict. In the 1970s it was primarily a case of northern and eastern groups fighting to take over the southern-dominated post-independence settlement of President Tombalbaye. And when that was finally accomplished the leading northern contenders, Goukouni Oueddi and Hussein Habre, struggled violently before the latter took power for the rest of the 1980s. As their fortunes waxed and waned, so there were cross border flows of refugees from Chad into Sudan.

While the refugee flows, particularly from Ethiopia, are central to Karadawi's thesis, its theme is government policy. As a background to that, it is necessary to consider briefly the changing character of government, and the agencies of the state responsible for implementing policy.

Karadawi's first work covers the second period of parliamentary government in Sudan (1965-1969), which followed the 'October revolution' a year earlier, and most of the second period of military rule under Gaafar Nimeiry which ran from 1969 until ended by a further popular uprising in 1985. Neither period was particularly stable.

An important aspect of instability was the civil war in the south which had begun in 1955 even before independence the following year, but which really developed from 1962. The inability of successive governments to end the conflict contributed much to instability, though it was not the only cause. Parliamentary government was dominated by two major political parties, the Umma and the Unionists, supported by rival northern Muslim sects, the Ansar and the Khatmiya respectively, neither of which was able to obtain an overall majority. The result was a series of unstable coalition governments, involving segments of the major parties, as well as a variety of smaller parties. Unstable government, combined with a costly continuing civil war, was a recipe for a fresh military intervention which duly came in May 1969.

Yet military rule was itself uncertain. War in the south continued and there were major confrontations, first with an armed Ansar uprising in 1970, and then between pro- and anti-communists in the armed forces one year later. But following that there was a concerted attempt by Nimeiry to create a new political order. A negotiated peace was made with the south in 1972, bringing the latter regional self-government, after which there was an attempt to establish a new secular constitution, build a single party, and establish a national parliament as well as devolved local government. But there were still serious intermittent challenges to Nimeiry's regime, and as a result he pursued 'national reconciliation' with his former enemies in the banned sectarian-based parties. His reconciliation in 1977 helped him to survive, but gave ground to Islamist forces in Sudanese politics, especially the growing Muslim Brotherhood, which Nimeiry sought to contain by placing himself at their head and introducing Islamic law in 1983. But in so doing he slowly lost the confidence of the south, and civil war developed once more from 1983. Once more political change was in the air and in 1985 Nimeiry fell from power, just after Karadawi's thesis concludes.

Sudan's domestic politics affected its external relations, including those with the neighbouring states which the refugees were fleeing. The brief sympathy for the Congolese Simba has been seen; that for the Eritreans was more widespread. In part this was because the Eritrean movement was perceived as associated with wider Arab containment of Ethiopia, especially since there is a substantial Muslim population in Eritrea. At the same time, eastern Sudan has ties with Eritrea reflecting common ethnic identity, while many on both sides of the border belong to the Khatmiya, which via the Unionist Party had a foot in national politics. Yet overt pro-Eritrean sentiment on the part of the Sudanese government damaged relations with Ethiopia. Thus for most of the period under consideration here, Sudan proclaimed itself bound by OAU resolutions on refugees, and not involved in political support. Following the restoration of liberal democracy in Sudan in 1965, successive governments sought to placate Ethiopia to check the latter's support to southern Sudanese insurgents. This continued after the coup of 1969, and Nimeiry appeared to offer a tacit deal with Ethiopia in 1972, at the time he made peace with the southern Sudanese in Addis Ababa. But it was hard to hold the line against the sentiments in Sudanese politics, and then came the Ethiopian revolution followed by much larger refugee flows. By now Ethiopia was linked to the USSR, while Sudan became allied with the USA, and possible cooperation on cross-border issues such as refugees once more diminished. Indeed, the years from 1976 to 1979 saw an ever more open rift between the Sudanese and Ethiopian leaders, as Karadawi makes abundantly clear.

In comparison, the situation on other borders with inward refugee flows was not so intense. There were few refugees either way while Amin was in power in Uganda, and in the 1980s the overwhelming issue in southern Sudan was the re-opening of civil war, not the question of refugees (though there was some annoyance in Uganda that Amin's henchmen found refuge in Sudan, and some sympathy and help for the new revolt in the south). Chad, meanwhile, was of even less significance, and refugees in western Sudan were linked as much to Libyan as to Sudanese politics.

The state machinery, in which Karadawi functioned for much of his working life, is another dimension of the thesis. Inherited from the

British, it expanded rapidly after independence, though not always with clarity or effectiveness. The Ministry of the Interior held central place in domestic security, and the office of the Commissioner for Refugees was established as a part of this ministry. Its problems with regard both to the ministry, and to the various security bodies established under Nimeiry in particular, are a running theme in the thesis. Decision-making often appears as confused. There are attempts to politicise the civil service, eventually including the top level of the Commission for Refugees itself. In the parliamentary period there were often attempts to accommodate party pressures; while under Nimeiry the emphasis moves towards his close allies in the security agencies, right up to the level of Vice-President.

There were other common problems right across the civil service. The growth in size did not mean greater capacity or efficiency, often the reverse. The growth itself, though underfunded, resulted in thousands of under-employed officials. Inadequate training for many officials contributed to widespread incompetence. There was political interference and sometimes nepotism, which worsened as the years passed. Opportunities for corruption increased in scale and blatancy. Such problems were encountered at all levels of government, and compounded the demarcation difficulties between central, regional and local government which are another strand of this thesis.

As mentioned, the thesis discusses the situation up to shortly before Nimeiry's downfall, and the return to a third period of parliamentary democracy in 1986. But the same circumstances prevailed as in the two previous attempts – unstable coalition government at the centre and civil war in the south – and a military coup occurred once more in 1989. The new military regime was unlike its predecessors in that it firmly espoused a radical ideology – Islamism – with the strong backing of the Muslim Brotherhood/National Islamic Front. It also took a firm grip on the state, especially the armed forces: doubters were purged and a 'popular' militia established. Similar treatment was accorded the civil service and education; and there was a programme of privatisation, generally to the advantage of Islamist businessmen. (Karadawi was one of the many forced out who left the country, in his case residing mainly in Addis Ababa.) The war in the south was more vigorously prosecuted, and now presented as *jihad.*

Throughout the period 1984-1991, the broad picture had not changed dramatically as far as the question of refugees was concerned, particularly in eastern Sudan. There was a considerable upsurge in numbers and media exposure with the famine of 1984-1985, but that in the longer term did little to change the basic situation. Potentially much more significant was the victory of the

Eritrean and Tigrayan movements over the Ethiopian president, Mengistu Haile Mariam, in 1991. Since the EPLF and the TPLF had had good relations with Sudan, there were hopes that the refugee problem in the east could now be solved by repatriation. The task, however, proved difficult. Relations between Eritrea and Ethiopia on the one hand, and Sudan on the other, deteriorated steadily, partly as a result of fears that Sudan saw itself as flag bearer for Islam across Northeast Africa. Allegations were made that Sudan was delaying the return of refugees and using them as pawns in its machinations. However, research among the refugees also suggested that there were complex social, environmental and economic factors delaying voluntary repatriation. For many, it seemed, the situations that they had been able to carve out for themselves in eastern Sudan over the previous decade and longer were more attractive than returning to a war-ravaged Eritrea. In part the continuing preference for Sudan was a result of the work of Ahmad Karadawi and his colleagues, a debt that is readily attested by many Eritreans amongst whom he was a most popular figure. His death has been widely mourned in the areas in which he worked, as well as among his many friends and colleagues around the world.

Peter Woodward
Department of Politics, University of Reading

Map 1.1 *Distribution of Refugees in Sudan*

1

Sudan, Its Eastern Region, and the Refugees

Since independence in 1956, successive governments of Sudan have been challenged by flows of refugees from the neighbouring countries of Zaire, Ethiopia, Uganda and Chad. By 1984 there were 700,000 refugees in the country compared to 35,000 in 1967. Problems have arisen not only because of the size of the influxes but also because of the complex political background against which these refugee movements have occurred. All these refugee situations result from domestic conflicts which are often prolonged and which inevitably bring political repercussions for neighbouring countries. Similarly, refugees arrive in a dynamic political and economic situation in the country of asylum itself. The conditions in the country of origin and the host context are equally important in understanding a refugee crisis.

Facing an abnormal influx of people, Sudanese governments have invariably considered refugees as a threat to their security and as an unwelcome burden on their resources. An underlying suggestion in the governments' responses has been that refugees are a political problem. As politically active groups or as popular constituencies with which active groups are associated, refugees are symptoms of conflicts which threaten to spill over into Sudan. Similarly, the presence of large numbers of refugees is likely to influence the domestic situation in Sudan, particularly when resources are scarce and when a regime is already suffering from economic and political upheavals. Governments have sought to stabilise the consequences of the refugee phenomenon by adopting international conventions and by seeking material assistance from international organisations.

However, international organisations have their own policies, mandates and interests which may not be compatible with those of host governments. This study attempts to show the complexity of the issues raised by the refugee phenomenon, and the diversity of actors involved at the local, central and international levels. By tracing the responses of Sudanese governments in the period between 1967 and 1984, it shows how these actors, from their different positions, often worked to resolve the refugee crisis as competing interests rather than as partners. The study draws on the special case of eastern Sudan which, over the period covered, received refugees from Ethiopia who were fleeing from the conflict in Eritrea, and to a lesser extent from parts of Ethiopia proper such as Tigray where armed conflict erupted after 1975.

Sudanese Governments and the Refugees

Due to its geo-political location, Sudan has been destined to receive considerable numbers of refugees. Although refugee migrations have occurred throughout the history of the area comprising today's Sudan, the emphasis will be on more recent decades.

According to the 1983 census, Sudan then had a population of 21.5 million. As well as having the largest area in Africa (2,505,813 km²), Sudan is a neighbour to eight African countries.[1] It is bounded by Egypt and Libya in the north, Chad in the west, and the Central African Republic, Zaire, Uganda and Kenya in the south, while the eastern border as a whole is shared with Ethiopia. The historical links forged with the border areas of neighbouring countries are a result of natural extensions and cultural relations. The movements of refugees from the areas of danger into the border regions of Sudan usually occur with ease as there are no physical hindrances, and people are often received with a great deal of hospitality by the local Sudanese communities. This has been particularly the case since the 1960s, as mass movements of refugees entered Sudan from Eritrea, western Ethiopia, northeastern Chad, and northern Zaire and Uganda. However, this apparent ease of movement is affected by the nature of the conflicts and by the actions taken by the governments involved to intervene as tension arises between states.

The massive movement of refugees in the region has not been confined to Sudan's neighbours. Civil war and power struggles within Sudan have forced its citizens to flee abroad as refugees, notably to the neighbouring countries of Ethiopia, Uganda and Zaire. This was particularly the case during the war in the South (1955-1972), and during the confrontations between Nimeiry's regime and the Sudanese National Front (1970-1977) and the Sudan People's

1. Editor's note: Since Eritrea gained independence in 1993, there are nine.

Liberation Front (from 1983 on). This is an important factor as the conflict causing the flight of refugees has also constituted a serious challenge to the legitimacy of the regime in power and to the territorial integrity of the country as a whole. Consequently, the presence of the Sudanese refugees in the neighbouring countries has been as threatening to successive governments in Sudan, as refugees present in Sudan are to the governments of their respective countries. For states affected by domestic conflict, therefore, refugees are not only a symptom of conflict but also a likely source for the perpetuation of that conflict. Moreover, the presence of refugees is likely to become a source of tension between the neighbouring states themselves.

Refugee policy has therefore been concerned primarily with containing the real or perceived threats to national security posed by the refugees. Affected states feel vulnerable to the presence of refugees and are aware of their role in threatening internal stability and interstate relations. While it is open to a country like Sudan to pursue a policy of supporting opposition groups from neighbouring countries, the advantages have to be weighed against the possibility of the neighbouring countries doing the same. Another possibility is to resort to interstate bilateral and multilateral agreements, or policies to deter opposition groups from engaging in any activity that may constitute a threat to the stability of the states and their incumbent regimes, or that may jeopardise harmonious relations between states. The latter option has usually been preferred, and it is this option that gained continental support when it was approved by the OAU. As far as Sudan is concerned, the policy of prohibiting refugees from conducting political or military activities against countries of origin has been officially adopted since 1967.

Government Response to Refugees 1955-1985

Since independence in January 1956, Sudanese politics alternated between multiparty parliamentary government and military regimes. Sudan has had three parliamentary periods dominated by the two main traditional parties, the Umma and the Democratic Unionist Party (formerly the NUP and the PDP). The first parliamentary regime ended in November 1958 in a military coup. The military continued to rule until they were overthrown by a popular uprising in October 1964. The second parliamentary government from 1965, was again ended by a military intervention in May 1969. This second military regime lasted for sixteen years under President Nimeiry until it was overthrown, also by a popular uprising, in April 1985.

On only two occasions did Sudanese regimes show unconditional support for exiled groups from neighbouring countries. The first was under the first transitional government of the 1964 'October Revolution'. The second was during the confrontation that erupted between President Nimeiry and Chairman Mengistu of Ethiopia between 1976 and 1979. However, both instances of support were ended by a change of direction resulting in a more conservative policy with forms of restraint. Most of the time the official policy was to adhere to the principles of the OAU and the related resolutions regarding respect for the sovereignty and integrity of member states.

The First Parliamentary Government 1956-1958

During the first parliamentary regime after independence, the refugee phenomenon did not constitute an important factor in either internal or interstate politics. However, towards the end of the 1950s, the outbreak of the rebellion in southern Sudan against the northern hegemony, and the simultaneous dismantling of the Eritrean federation by the imperial regime in Ethiopia, resulted in the exodus of small groups of refugees from both areas. The movement of these groups became significant as the exiles helped the growth and organisation of political and military resistance against the governments in both Sudan and Ethiopia.

The refugee exodus from southern Sudan began in earnest during the first military regime (1958-1964) which opted for a military solution to the southern Sudan question. By May 1964, 85,000 refugees had fled from southern Sudan to Uganda and Ethiopia. At the same time, the Eritreans began to conduct armed resistance against the imperial regime in Ethiopia. In the ensuing years, refugees assumed a growing importance in the domestic as well as the external affairs of Sudan, particularly as the southern Sudan problem escalated.

The Genesis of Refugee Policy 1964-1969

General Abboud's military regime was overthrown by a popular uprising on 21 October 1964. The uprising was orchestrated by an alliance of progressive groups comprising the trade unions, a group of young officers who called themselves the 'Free Officers', and the Sudanese Communist Party. In the period between October 1964 and June 1965, Sudan was governed by a caretaker government dominated by these radical groups. The resistance groups from Eritrea and the Congo (Zaire) were received with great enthusiasm. The government not only tolerated their presence but also helped with military training and allowed the sending of arms shipments to the Congolese Simba and the Eritreans (*Africa Report* 10 [7] 1965:30). The Congolese and the Eritreans were treated as liberation movements on an equal footing with the other African liberation movements struggling against colonial and racist regimes in southern Africa. However, this policy of support for liberation movements paralysed the government's attempt to resolve the ongoing conflict in southern Sudan. The arms supplied to the Congolese were passed to the southern Sudanese rebels and thereby helped the nascent movement to intensify its resistance to the government, so that the whole war witnessed a new phase of escalation. The policy also contributed towards the development of antagonistic feelings in both Zaire and Ethiopia, which also received Sudanese exiles.

When the general elections were held in June 1965, the traditional political parties were reinstated in power and the progressive mood of the transitional government was brought to an end. The coalition governments of the Umma and the DUP which dominated the second parliamentary regime (June 1965 to May 1969), worked systematically to dismantle the policy of support for the exiled groups of Eritreans and Congolese. The alternative policy over this period was articulated by Mohammed Ahmed Mahjoub, who was Prime Minister for the whole period with the exception of the twelve months of Al-Sadig Al-Mahdi's premiership, June 1966 to June 1967. Mahjoub believed that a restrictive policy against the Congolese and the Eritreans was an indispensable complement to any policy towards southern Sudan. He was convinced that such restriction was necessary to ensure the success of the military action that would decisively put an end to the rebellion. Diplomatic initiatives with the neighbouring countries were also necessary to quell the southern resistance thought to be operating from them.

It was at this stage that the OAU began to develop its norms for the treatment of refugees. Thus, the government policy of intensive diplomatic efforts to restrict the opposition occurred roughly at the same time as the efforts of the OAU to achieve the same end. This suggests that, at least in the case of Sudan, there was no difference between the emerging government policy and the OAU prescriptions. Actually, Sudan was particularly active in formulating the OAU strategy due to its participation on the first committee which was assigned the task of advising the organisation on ways to address the refugee problem. By 1967, therefore, Mahjoub's policy had taken shape and at that time the term 'refugee' was applied to exiled groups with the very specific meaning of dispossession of political rights.

To ensure that the refugee problem was treated as a non-political issue, the special office of the Commissioner for Refugees (COR) was established in 1967 to execute government policy. COR's role was to obtain material assistance for refugees and to implement a policy based on the OAU norms. In order to meet the needs of the refugees, special links were forged with the United Nations High Commissioner for Refugees (UNHCR) to ensure the provision of material assistance for refugees already in Sudan, and for those who were likely to come. The Eritreans and the Congolese who persisted in their attempts to uphold their political cause and to resist regimes in their countries of origin were treated as separate cases and were subject to arbitrary treatment whenever the Sudanese Government deemed it necessary and was able to achieve it. The new refugee policy worked in complete harmony with the political priorities of the government.

Refugee Policy under President Nimeiry 1969-1984

The second parliamentary regime was terminated in May 1969 by a military coup which brought Nimeiry to power for sixteen years. The new regime preserved the refugee policy designed by its predecessors. It even helped to consolidate this policy by accession to the UN Convention Relating to the Status of Refugees (1951) as well as to the 1969 OAU convention. In 1974 Sudan enacted its own law, the Regulation of Asylum Act, which incorporated the principles of the two international conventions in national law. In its attempts to achieve national unity, the regime succeeded in negotiating a peaceful settlement to the seventeen years' conflict in southern Sudan in 1972, after which the majority of the Sudanese refugees returned home (Akol 1987:146). The ending of the conflict in the south relieved the regime from a problem which had constantly threatened the territorial integrity and the internal stability of Sudan. This also meant that Sudan became primarily a host for refugees: that is, the number of refugees in Sudan became larger than the number of Sudanese in exile.

In fact, the regime continued to have a close relationship with Ethiopia even after the overthrow of Emperor Haile Selassie in September 1974. When Ethiopia's new Provisional Military Administration Council (PMAC) recognised the need to find a political solution to the Eritrean question, Nimeiry offered to provide help as a mediator. However, the ideological changes in the orientation of the Nimeiry regime towards the West, accompanied by radical changes in the region, particularly in Ethiopia which aligned with the USSR from 1977, came to have a direct influence on the nature of the refugee phenomenon.

As far as Nimeiry's regime was concerned, the nature of the opposition and the politics of those who were exiled had changed dramatically. Exiled groups emerged from northern Sudan for the first time since independence as a result of the power conflict in Khartoum. After an abortive uprising in 1970, armed followers of the Umma Party, the DUP, and the Muslim Brothers went to Ethiopia to try to organise a comeback and overthrow Nimeiry. After five years of training in Ethiopia and Libya, the National Front contingent infiltrated into Khartoum in July 1976 and almost succeeded in their aim. This attempt provoked responses from Nimeiry particularly against the Ethiopian regime, which was considered the major force behind the attack. In retaliation he offered to help all the opposition groups whose aim was to overthrow the regime in Ethiopia.

In the meantime, Ethiopia itself was witnessing extreme political changes as a result of the 1974 coup. The power struggles within PMAC eclipsed any hopes for a peaceful solution in Eritrea and a military approach to suppress the resistance was resumed. Moreover, opposition groups emerged, based on nationalities and political parties, and for their different reasons rose in arms against the Ethiopian military regime. By February 1977, Mengistu Haile Mariam had emerged as the unquestionable leader, who determined the Marxist-Leninist course of the revolution. The Soviet Union's support from 1977 overturned the close traditional relationship between Ethiopia and the West. These developments had extreme and dramatic effects on the nature and size of the refugee exodus from Ethiopia. The access to large amounts of Soviet weapons and their use against the rebels in Eritrea and Tigray led to the escalation and proliferation of fighting within Ethiopia.

What happened in Sudan was actually a similar change but in the opposite direction. Sudan, which had severed its relations with the Soviet Union in 1973, formed a military pact with Egypt and sought alliance with the West. From 1976 onwards, political support was provided by Nimeiry's regime for the Eritrean fronts and the Ethiopian Democratic Unionists (EDU), who launched successful offensives against the Ethiopian forces in 1977 and in the first half of 1978. However, the intensive military offensives by the Ethiopian army in mid-1978 led to the eventual retreat of the Eritrean fronts and the demise of the EDU. Simultaneously, Nimeiry's success in achieving national reconciliation with the National Front (the exiled northern Sudanese parties) helped to ease the way towards rapprochement with the Ethiopian regime. As a consequence of the attempt to improve relations with Ethiopia, the policy of support for the Eritrean fronts and the EDU had to be modified.

The Ethiopian military offensives in Eritrea and Tigray brought to Sudan 300,000 refugees whose hope of return was eclipsed by the failure of the resistance groups and their breakdown into warring factions.

The refugees came from different ethnic, cultural, and political backgrounds. This large number of refugees accumulated at a time when refugee policy was marginalised not only by Sudan's political adventures but also by drastic administrative reforms which neglected the position of COR. On another level, refugee policy was influenced negatively by the detached stance of UNHCR which adopted a wait-and-see attitude. This policy seemed to be justified by hopes for the repatriation of the refugees, which were raised first by the brief interlude after the change of government in Ethiopia, and later by the remarkable success of the Eritrean fronts in 1977 and 1978. Another reason in reality behind UNHCR's inaction was its growing doubt about the ability of COR to execute the UNHCR-financed projects.

From mid-1978, some of the municipal and local government authorities in eastern Sudan began to perceive the presence of the refugees as a liability. With the beginning of the signs of decline in the national economy, signalled by the failure of ambitious plans for agriculture and the intervention of the IMF, the authorities called attention to the contribution of the refugees to the economic crisis. Moreover, the refugees were considered partly responsible for the rising rate of crime, and the rise of violence in local communities through smuggling and sales of arms. The internecine fighting between the factions of the refugee political fronts was seen as a direct threat to internal order in the areas where they resided. The situation was further exacerbated by the arrival of new influxes from wars in Uganda and Chad during 1979 and 1980. In short, by 1980, the refugee problem coincided with a deteriorating situation in Sudan and there was little consensus about ways to deal with the negative consequences of the refugee presence. In the face of overwhelming pressure from other government actors to apply restrictions to refugees, COR struggled to maintain the standards of treatment of refugees advocated in refugee laws and conventions. Despite its marginal position within the government, COR was left alone to conjure up a solution to the voluminous problems bequeathed by the refugee crises, crises which had changed both in terms of size and the declining sympathy of the hosts.

Faced with UNHCR's reluctance to engage itself in a large assistance programme, COR opted for an ambitious campaign to reach the financial donors directly and to seek large sums to meet the needs not only of the refugees but also of the Sudanese population in areas affected by the presence of the refugees. COR's argument that Sudan was a specific case was undermined by the fact that other countries were making similar demands on the donors. Consequently, donors questioned the feasibility of COR's plan and demanded more concessions from Sudan to guarantee a durable solution to the refugee problem.

Almost two decades after the refugee policy was launched in Sudan, the refugee situation had reached a crisis level. The domestic conflicts in neighbouring countries were endemic, and continued to produce more refugees. Assistance for refugees continued to be a palliative, treating only the symptoms. As a result, not only were the life chances of hundreds of thousands of refugees endangered, but also the economic survival of the host country itself.

The Scope of the Study

This study focuses on the case of the Eastern Region of Sudan, which received refugees exclusively from Ethiopia. The period from 1967 to 1984 was selected to illustrate the evolution of refugee policy in Sudan. The specific selection of both the time and the region needs explanation. This is particularly important as refugees were known in Sudan before 1967 and continued to arrive after 1984. Similarly, refugees were present in the other Sudanese regions of Darfur and Equatoria from the neighbouring countries of Chad, Zaire and Uganda.

However, between the refugees who arrived in the other regions and the refugees who arrived in the Eastern Region there are major differences. In a previous study I differentiated for conceptual purposes between two main types of conflict that generate refugees (Karadawi 1977:7). Firstly, there is the type which results from a sub-national group's demand for secession or at least the right of self-determination. Such conflict, I argued, is likely to become protracted, involving large numbers of the population in the contested areas, and is therefore more likely to produce a mass exodus of refugees over time. The refugee movement will continue to be uni-directional and refugees will not return home as long as the cause of the conflict remains unresolved. The resolution of the conflict needs either agreement between a sovereign state and the rebels, or an outright victory by one of the parties. An example of this type of conflict is the case of Eritrea.

In contrast to this, I identified a second type of conflict arising out of a power struggle between a certain regime and its opponents, without claims to alter state boundaries. In the absence of an institutionalised relationship between government and opposition, the losers opt for exile. As these exiles are usually political parties with ideological or ethnic orientations, their exodus involves smaller numbers and their stay in exile may be shorter if, as in some African countries, governments continue to be unstable: today's rulers are tomorrow's exiles and vice versa. Such situations are exemplified by the refugee movements from Chad, Uganda and Zaire. If the opposition stays long in exile it is likely to lose its ability to overthrow a regime, as was the case with the Zaireans in Sudan.

Unlike the refugees from the protracted conflict in Eritrea, the Chadian and Ugandan influxes have had a pattern of irregularity and reversibility. In the case of Chad, exiled groups arriving in Sudan in 1960 formed a liberation front, Frolinat (the *Front de Libération Nationale du Tchad*), and returned to conduct an armed struggle inside Chad in 1966. New waves of refugees arrived in Northern Darfur in 1979 and 1980. Five hundred Chadian government soldiers who arrived after the downfall of Felix Malloum returned to Chad in September 1980, and in December of that year 22,000 refugees arrived after the retreat of Hussein Habre's forces into Darfur. However, the same group returned in 1983 after Hussein Habre seized power once more.

The refugee influxes into Sudan from Uganda also followed a similar pattern of intermittent and reversible movement. The exile of 4,000 Ugandans who arrived in Sudan during Amin's regime (1971-1979) ended with the overthrow of his regime and the return of the refugees. However, the changes of government and the ensuing chaos, particularly in 1982, led to the movement of 300,000 from northern Uganda into Equatoria. But by 1984 there were clear signs that repatriation was in progress.

The irreversible refugee inflow from Eritrea from 1967 onwards and from other parts of Ethiopia since 1974 on the one hand, and the specific characteristics of the Eastern Region on the other, have predominated in shaping Sudan's national policy towards refugees.

The year 1967 was selected as a starting date for this study as the government had by then developed and institutionalised a policy that was basically one of restitution of the principles of state sovereignty, integrity and non-intervention in the internal affairs of other countries. Over the period under study this policy became the norm according to which the responses of successive Sudanese governments can be judged. In addition, the policy considered the refugees as objects of humanitarian material assistance from international donors. The year 1967 itself was the year when the new policy was applied to a sizeable influx of 30,000 Eritreans. By 1984 there were more than half a million refugees from Ethiopia in the Eastern Region, and the limitations of the refugee policy had become evident. While controversy continued over how to overcome these limitations, a new and overwhelming situation arose as another wave of refugees entered Sudan from areas affected by drought and famine. Because the new challenges were different, the definition of the term refugee became confused and the main concern shifted back to crisis management.

Although the experience of the Eastern Region influenced the national policy towards refugees, the region has specific characteristics which are derived from three factors. Firstly, refugees did not spread evenly over the different parts of Sudan. The Eastern Region is the only one that continued to receive refugees without substantial repatriation. As it was the point of entry, a popular conception developed among Sudanese authorities in other regions that those refugees should normally remain in the Eastern Region. The concentration of refugees in this region led to a crisis.

Secondly, the Eastern Region contains the Sudanese section of the Red Sea coast and part of the international borders with Egypt and Ethiopia. It adjoins areas of strategic importance which have been characterised by protracted conflict. This factor has made the position of the Eastern Region of prime concern for state security under successive Sudanese governments.

Thirdly, the Eastern Region has its own ethnic and environmental characteristics; the availability of resources and their distribution among different social groups are a potential cause of social and political discord. Historically, the region has been predominantly occupied by nomadic groups who have used its vast areas as pastures. The arrival of additional pastoralists in the last century and the recent development of irrigated and rainfed commercial farming have created pressures on the land and consequently changes in land use. Immigration from other depressed parts of Sudan, especially the south and the west, became a common pattern over the years, particularly to towns and labour-hungry agricultural schemes. The refugee influx is particularly significant as the flows are not spread evenly even within the Eastern Region. The pattern of settlement, spontaneous or planned by external assistance, is concentrated either in towns or in agricultural lands.

The Geopolitical Factor

The Eastern Region has a total area of 338,756 km^2 and comprises the two provinces of the Red Sea (212,490 km^2) and Kassala (126,266 km^2). The region borders Khartoum province and the Northern Region in the west and the Central Region in the southwest. Its border with Ethiopia covers 1,680 km of the 2,210 km long Sudanese–Ethiopian border. The significance of the long border lies in the historical differences on demarcation and conflict over certain areas between the different powers that have ruled in the two countries since the 1890s. The border itself was divided into different sectors which became subject to separate agreements. For example, the most northern part was subject to agreements between Egypt and Italy (December 1898), Britain and Italy (November 1908), the colonial administrators in Sudan and Eritrea (1907, 1922) and later between Sudan and Ethiopia in July 1972. The middle and southern parts were subject to different agreements between Britain and Ethiopia and later between Sudanese governments and Ethiopia (El Nour 1983).

The length of the border also constitutes a security problem. While the absence of major physical impediments facilitates the movement of refugees, it also allows antagonistic forces, such as the Ethiopian army, to penetrate. Sudanese authorities argue that this factor raises more problems for Sudan than for Ethiopia due to the small size of the Sudanese army (Fadl al-Sid 1984:99) and the direction of the slope from the highland of the Ethiopian plateau to the low flat lands of Sudan. However, Ethiopia, of course, likewise sees the free passage of armed opposition across the border as a security problem.

The contiguity of the Eastern Region to the western parts of Ethiopia constitutes a natural extension. This is particularly the case in the northern part that adjoins Eritrea. The Red Sea Hills and Kassala are a continuation of lowland Eritrea (ibid.). They share a similar climate, and a land formation which stretches into the Eritrean hinterland rising until it reaches the highland plateau of Eritrea. The geographical and historical links between lowland Eritrea and eastern Sudan have been viewed by successive Ethiopian governments as a source of threat, as the link between Eritrea and eastern Sudan is seen as one of Arab–Muslim encirclement. The source of the Eritrean conflict itself has been dismissed as an Arab–Muslim plot to threaten the regime in Ethiopia. Consequently, apart from the contention over the border demarcation, the refugee influx frequently invited border tension. In 1967, 1979, 1982 and 1984, the influx of refugees was accompanied by Ethiopian military penetration into Sudanese territory.

The historical significance of the Red Sea assumed a particular importance in the events that were unleashed by the overthrow of Emperor Haile Selassie in Ethiopia in 1974. The subsequent change of superpower positions by the United States and the Soviet Union led to the growth of regional military pacts in which Sudan and Ethiopia were placed in polar positions. Long before these ideological shifts, Ethiopia's intransigent opposition to the attempts to separate Eritrea was motivated by its need for access to the sea. The attempts by Sudan, North Yemen and Saudi Arabia to make the Red Sea an 'Arab lake' were taken as a direct threat to Ethiopia. On the other hand, Sudan believed that the intervention of the Soviet Union in Ethiopia in 1977, the escalation of war in Eritrea and the establishment of the Aden Pact in 1981, comprising South Aden, Libya and Ethiopia, amounted to a direct threat to Sudanese national security.

As a result the Eastern Region became the scene of military activity, and the Sudanese army was deployed in border areas. During the years of confrontation between Sudan and Ethiopia, the armed opposition groups from the latter were able to move freely in and out of the Eastern Region. After the defeats suffered by the Eritrean and Ethiopian movements in 1978, the Eastern Region became the scene of skirmishes between warring factions. This generated frustration in the Sudanese army in the Eastern Region as it was made to face the consequences of the influx of armed bands as well as to guard the long border (Fadl al-Sid 1984).

The Indigenous Population of the Eastern Region

The region has a population of 2,208,198 divided between Kassala province, which has the larger population of 1,512,325, and the Red Sea which has 695,873. Population settlements are concentrated mainly in the areas of Gedaref, Kassala, New Halfa and al-Fau. In Red Sea Province the population is mainly concentrated in Port Sudan and Tokar (DRS 1985:1) (see Map 1.2). According to the official statistics, the region has an annual rate of population growth of 3 per cent, which is higher than the national average of 2.8 per cent (Mills 1985:13).

The population distribution and modes of living are closely related to the climatic conditions. Climatic zones of the region range between desert in the north, arid and semi-arid areas in the centre and a wet monsoon climate in the south. The rainy season (mid-June to September) is characterised by variations in the amount of rainfall and its distribution over the different zones. The vegetation is consequently influenced by the pattern of rainfall. The areas north of latitude 14°N, which receive an average of less than 200mm per annum, are dominated by a varying mixture of grasses usually with scrub bushes. This area includes the larger part of the Red Sea and parts of northern Kassala arid zones where agriculture is practised only in the irrigated flood plains of the Atbara, Gash and Tokar rivers (NCAR 1980:2). South of the 200mm line, where the rainfall reaches 400–600 mm, the vegetation is of the savannah type composed of trees and shrubs which in the most southern parts of the region form tall grasslands interspersed with tree thickets. South of the line linking Khartoum with Kassala, the land becomes part of the central clay

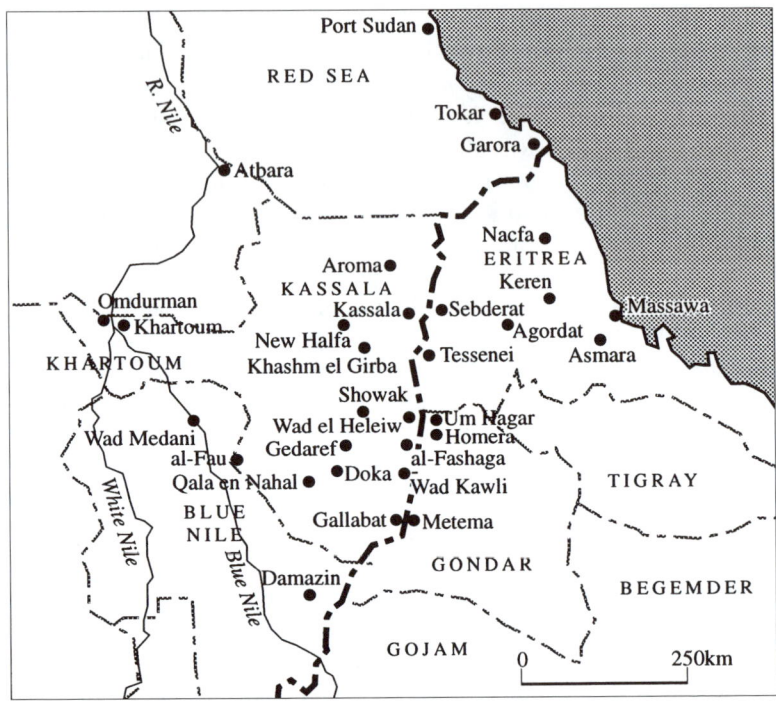

Map 1.2 *The Eastern Region and Surrounding Areas*

plains which extend from the White Nile to the Ethiopian foothills. It is in this area that the bulk of the irrigated schemes as well as the vast areas of rainfed agricultural farms have been established.

The modes of living vary significantly between the two provinces of the region. In the whole region 29 per cent of the population live in urban areas whereas 71 per cent live in rural areas, of whom only 25 per cent are nomads. However, the Red Sea has a higher percentage of urban population (35 per cent) and a higher percentage of nomads (55 per cent) due to the arid nature of the province (see Table 1.1). The high percentage of urban population is explained by the fact that when the nomads are affected by drought, the only alternative in the Red Sea province is to move to towns, particularly to Port Sudan. By contrast, Kassala Province has a larger settled population who depend on agriculture or are semi-nomadic (Ahmad and Harir 1981:166-71). It is estimated that 80 per cent of the 3.1 million *feddans*[2] of land cultivated is under mechanised farming. The

2. 1 *feddan* = approximately 0.4 hectares.

Table 1.1 *Modes of Living and Population Distribution by Province in the Eastern Region*

	Kassala	%	Red Sea	%	Total Region	%
Mode of Living						
Urban	395,187	26	243,646	35	638,833	29
Settled Rural	938,940	62	71,750	10	1,010,690	46
Nomadic	178,198	12	380,477	55	558,675	25
Total	1,512,325	100	695,873	100	2,208,198	100

Source: COR-FINNIDA, 1987.

development of mechanised farming has resulted in severe pressure on the land. Rainfed agriculture, sometimes reaching 1,000 *feddan* leaseholds, has claimed grazing lands and forest areas, eliminated the grass cover and led to a deterioration in soil fertility. The large irrigated schemes of New Halfa (1960-1964) not only claimed land but were also required for the resettlement of 68,000 Halfawis who had been displaced by the construction of the Aswan High Dam. The Rahad scheme, a World Bank financed agricultural project, was also established in an area which had been the traditional grazing land of the nomadic groups of Shukriya and Rufaat al-Sharq (Ahmad and Harir 1981:186).

It was in Kassala Province that the bulk of the refugee population arrived (with the exception of some 55,000 in Port Sudan). Various factors contributed to the uneven distribution of refugees over the Eastern Region. These relate to the entry points at the border which lie predominantly in Kassala Province, the aridity of the northern parts of the region which makes it unsuitable for settlement, and the economic attractions offered by the agricultural lands of Kassala and the towns. In addition, the government policy of establishing refugee settlements also led to the concentration of refugees in the province. Policies pursued in the neighbouring Central Region and Khartoum persistently discouraged the presence of refugees and led to the general trend to confine refugees to the Eastern Region. Thus the 26 refugee villages established as settlements were deployed in the area that extends from South Gedaref northwards to Khashm al Girba district. It is estimated that in 1984 the land allocated for refugees was 167,524 *feddans* (al-Amin 1984:15) with an additional 6,663 km² in residential areas (Kursany 1985:181).

The geopolitical location and the resource capacity of the region have had a direct influence in shaping its ethnic composition. Historically the dominant groups have been the Beja in the north and the Shukriya in the south. The Beja occupied all the area from the Red Sea to the River Atbara; the Shukriya occupied the Butana, an area bounded by the River Atbara, the main Nile and the Blue Nile. Both groups claimed exclusive rights over their respective areas. However, from the mid-nineteenth century other groups moved to live in the area. The Rashaida nomads, for example, moved into the area in the 1840s from the Arabian peninsula. The Beja allowed them to use their territory on a usufructory basis while retaining the original right of ownership over land (Salih 1980:122). Similarly, nomadic groups of al-Lahawiyin and al-Kawahla moved to the Shukriya areas at the turn of the century. *Jellaba* (traders) also migrated from northern Sudan to commercial centres.

The process that eventually led to sedentarisation and urbanisation occurred against a background of a long history of external intervention and natural disasters. These factors contributed to the shrinking of land traditionally used by the nomadic groups and the marginalisation of nomadism. On the other hand, the large scale commercial farming resulted in production relations that were biased against small farmers in favour of farmers with large holdings. The immigrants formed the source of wage labour.

The intervention of colonial powers in Sudan generated complex processes of conflict and co-operation between the local groups of the Eastern Region. For example, the Hadanduwa had been active supporters of the Mahdists against the Turco-Egyptian rulers in the late nineteenth century, and later showed close sympathy with Sayed Abdel-Rahman al-Mahdi's call for an independent Sudan in the mid-1940s. This was contrary to the traditional position of the other Beja groups – the Bisharin, Amaraar and Milhitkinab – who were staunch supporters of the Khatmiya and therefore called for union with Egypt (Ohaj 1986:100). However, the fact remains that these groups have been moulded by the experience of being part of the modern Sudan and as such they have continued to seek active participation as Sudanese national groups. In 1958 the Beja formed a special political organisation, the Beja Congress, which aimed at rallying support from the Beja people and articulating their demands at the national level. The group was a federation of various autonomous groups of the Hadanduwa, Bisharin, Amaraar, Arteiga, Habab, Milhitkinab, Kemeilab, Beni Amer, and the Ashraf (ibid.:12). This process of integration was of great significance for the refugee factor as there are historical ethnic and religious links between the groups living in the Eastern Region and those living in Eritrea.[3] The emergence of refugees as a separate category needs an explanation.

Linkage of Eastern Sudan to the Protracted Conflict in Eritrea

The ethnic and religious affinities across the border constituted a positive factor for those who were forced to leave their home areas. However, the separate experiences of people under the domination of different powers often obscured those affinities. In this sense, the particular experience of the ethnic groups in Eritrea under Italian rule (1890-1941) and the period that followed moulded them towards what may be called 'Eritreanisation', rather than towards immediate identification with their kin in Sudan.

Groups in Eastern Sudan and Eritrea did have common beliefs and ethnic affinities. Of specific importance is the allegiance to Islam, particularly to the Khatmiya sect established in Mecca by Sayed Mohammed Osman al-Mirghani (1793-1853). After his first visit in 1817, the Khatmiya gained strongholds among the Beja tribes in eastern Sudan and in the north. However, this sect has two main characteristics. Firstly, it strongly opposed the Mahdiya, and therefore forged links with the Egyptian rulers until the Mahdist state was defeated by the Anglo-Egyptian occupation in 1898. Moreover, its association with Egypt continued until today and the Khatmiya has constituted the core of an organised political party in Sudan. Secondly, the Khatmiya has never had a monolithic organisation under one paramount leader. It has been organised in regional spheres of influence (Trimingham 1949:231-35). The Mirghani family spread into the different regions. Kassala and Eritrea have developed as separate regions of equal status. The dominance of Khatmiya in both eastern Sudan and western Eritrea is demonstrated by the settlement of the descendants of the founder of the sect in Keren (Eritrea) and Kassala (Sudan).

Another feature in common was the ethnic affinity across the border as a result of the presence of the same communities in both countries. Like the Beja of Sudan, the Beni Amer of Eritrea developed as a confederation of tribes which included 21 subgroups. The Hadanduwa, Amaraar, and Habab of Eritrea were members. The number of Beni Amer in Eritrea was estimated to be 60,000 by Nadel (1977:23). The Beni Amer confederation, however, was more of a political alliance of diverse groups than of people who claimed common descent. The nature of this alliance has changed over time as new groups have joined and old members seceded. Moreover, the Beni

3. Editor's note: Thus, for example, in the late 1890s the territory of the Beni Amer was split between the de facto British colony Sudan and the Italian colony Eritrea, with two thirds in Eritrea.

Amer's traditional territory covered the western lowlands of Eritrea extending from the Red Sea hills in the north to Um Hajar in the south. It includes a section in Sudan whose numbers were estimated by Nadel to be 30,000 in 1944. This Sudanese section developed close links with the Sudanese Khatmiya and gained considerable political weight in Sudan after the Mahdiya. For example, on the dissolution of the Mahdiya, Sayed Mohammad Osman Taj al-Sir headed the Beni Amer and the Shukriya against the Ansar. Their concentration in Kassala and their association with the *jellaba* from the northern region who settled in Kassala and who also follow the Khatmiya sect, reinforced their position. Thus, the Khatmiya and Beni Amer factors seem to offer favourable conditions for members of these communities to join their co-believers and kin in response to stressful events. However, these factors have to be assessed against the background of Italian rule (1890-1941) and its aftermath in Eritrea.

The Rise of Eritrean Nationalism

The experience of the western Eritrean lowlands under Italian rule led to the growth of a wider Eritrean nationalism. It is believed that the Beni Amer confederation maintained itself because of the class divide, by which it was dominated by the 'nobles' of the Nabtab. The Nabtab claim common descent from Nabit who was born of a marriage between a Jaali from the Nile and a Bellou woman. They claim superiority and purity of origin over the other Beni Amer groups who joined, over time, for protection or simply subjugation. This noble class acted as a ruling elite over a lower class: the Hadareb (i.e., the other Beni Amer tribes who constituted the serfs) (Nadel 1977). During Italian rule the position of the Nabtab was severely shaken due to the reduced dependence of the Hadareb on their protection (Trevaskis 1960:51). As this amounted to emancipation of the serfs, the role of the Nabtab as an aristocracy was also undermined. The serfs, who were not restricted by tradition from accumulating wealth, prospered and benefited from the protection and the services of the colonial authorities. By 1941 the defeat of the Italians in the war, the improved position of the serfs, and the simultaneous decline of the nobility, created conditions conducive for rebellion. When rebellion broke out in 1946, it coincided with other factors that encouraged other groups in lowland Eritrea to steer the course of the rebellion towards a wider national struggle (Gebre-Medhin 1984). These external factors relate particularly to recruitment into the colonial armies. Recruitment and training in modern warfare improved the relative capacity of soldiers (Paul 1954:150); while after the war, thousands of soldiers returned to their home areas often with arms. This had a particular significance for the Eritreans who worked for the Italians and who, after the defeat of the Italians, found themselves in a difficult position once the British occupied Eritrea. Moreover, the British helped to create a liberal atmosphere in which nationalist ideas gathered momentum as the returning soldiers became aware of the tide of nationalism in other parts of Africa.

Amid the controversy between the great powers over the fate of Eritrea after 1945, Ibrahim Sultan, a Muslim, organised a political party called the Muslim League. He considered it a step towards the emancipation of the serfs from the nobility. As some of the nobility in Eritrea moved to join a rival party which called for unification of Eritrea and Ethiopia (the Unionist Party), the Muslim League shifted towards a more nationalist line calling for the independence of Eritrea. The Muslim League, which was chaired by Sayed Abu Bakr al-Mirghani (a descendant of the Khatmiya family), defined its objectives as the preservation of the territorial unity of Eritrea before 1935, including certain parts of Sudan.

This process of transforming lowland Eritrea's ethnic politics into a stream of Eritrean nationalism is indicative of the profound changes that occurred during colonial rule in Eritrea. The presence of the Beni Amer and the Khatmiya did not lead to a simple integration with Sudan, but worked as a springboard to strengthen the national struggle in Eritrea. After the disposal of Eritrea by the UN in 1952, the eventual dismantling of the Eritrean Federation by Emperor Haile Selassie in 1962, and the banning of political parties, the leaders of the Muslim League went into exile. Leaders such as Ibrahim Sultan and Idris Mohamed Adam launched another phase of resistance in cooperation with other Eritrean nationalists such as Woldeab Wolde Mariam and Tedla Bairo. In exile, Kassala offered the most appropriate place to organise political and eventually military resistance. This explains why the Eritrean Liberation Front (ELF) considered it useful to open one of its first offices in Kassala in 1962. Eastern Sudan was to provide momentum for the struggle, rather than absorbing it.

The association of the nascent nationalist movement with the Muslim Eritreans and the Arab cause helped the movement at a particular stage. By the mid-1960s it was no longer composed simply of lowland Eritrean Muslims of the Beni Amer. Sudanese political parties in general, and the groups in Eastern Sudan in particular, saw the movement as a nationalist movement which was not simply composed of their kith and kin seeking to re-establish themselves in Sudan.

However, the Eritrean nationalist movement passed through a stage which made it readjust its course from one of exclusive association with the Muslim/Arab cause. This was not only because the Haile Selassie regime succeeded in isolating the Eritrean liberation front, but also because other non-Muslim Eritreans were getting involved in the struggle against the Ethiopian hegemony. The process of divisions among the Eritrean groups led eventually to the establishment of organisations based on Eritrean identity rather than on religious or ethnic identities.

After 1977 the expansion of organisations such as the Eritrean People's Liberation Front (EPLF) is significant. The Eritrean political and military movement began to include wider ethnic and religious representation and the improved political and military capacity exported the 'Eritreanisation' process to the whole of Eritrea. Moreover, after 1977 the escalation of fighting brought into eastern Sudan groups of refugees from places in Eritrea with no cultural, religious and ethnic affinities. The process of 'Eritreanisation' and the resulting incompatibilities with the Eastern Region in Sudan led to the emergence of the refugees as a separate group. These processes were encouraged not least by a refugee policy that attempted to isolate them as a socio-legal category for its own purposes. In spite of the fact that both the process of Eritreanisation and the development of refugee policy in Sudan led to the emergence of the refugees as a separate category, it is arguable that the two processes were contradictory. While the Eritreanisation process aimed at linking the exiled Eritreans to their political struggle, the refugee policy evolved out of the government's perspective that linked the influx of refugees to Sudanese national security. The objective of government refugee policy was to prohibit the refugees from turning into a political constituency, and to defuse any threats to national security.

Refugees as a Threat to Security and a Socio-Economic Burden: the Origins of the OAU Norms

The traditional definition of national security involves the protection of vital national interests against possible external threat or challenge, and entails the extension and promotion of national values, independence, sovereignty, territorial integrity and political and economic life (Orwa 1984:203). However, when applied to African countries this definition requires further elaboration.

Firstly, the concept of national security is largely contextual as it varies from one country to another. Due to the specific characteristics of each situation, the concept of security becomes dependent on the degree of political cohesion and the environment within which a ruling regime functions. Secondly, the concept of security is subjective, and therefore depends on whose security is at stake and what threatens that security. In Africa, as elsewhere, threats to national security may arise from within the state as well as from outside it (ibid.:203). Domestic factors such as legitimacy, integration, and the capacity of the government to manage internal dissent peacefully, play equally important roles in shaping national security.

In the context of this study, therefore, the term is used to mean state security as it is less ambiguous and places emphasis on the state as a centralised governing organisation and less on individuals and social groups existing within the state (Azar and Moon 1988:12). Where threats to the state come from internal challenges, the principles of national security may be invoked to justify arbitrary measures to impose control and hegemony from the centre. Challenges to state security may come from pressures organised by internal groups as well as external powers. Moreover, state security may also be influenced by factors like the state of the economy, ecological pressures and the dependence of the population on the resources of the physical environment. But the concept of threat itself is ambiguous as it is highly subjective, and reflects the political leadership's particular assessment of the situation. As Buzan argues: 'Each state exists, in a sense, at the hub of a whole universe of threats. These threats define its insecurity and set the agenda of national security as a policy problem' (Buzan 1988:284).

The perception of refugees as a threat to state security offers a very useful platform for an explanation of government responses to the refugee phenomenon. The threat to security raised by the refugees is not confined to the territory of the state concerned, since refugees also become a source of external threat. As most refugees move across the border from one country to the neighbouring one, the presence of refugees in another state's territory leads to reciprocal threats between the two countries. Therefore, although the outflow of refugees is caused by domestic conflict in one country, the exodus brings the refugees themselves, the country to which they flee and the country from which they have fled, into a new set of relationships. As the results of the conflict spill over and the countries themselves face domestic problems, the tendency is to see the refugee problem in a wider context and to ignore the specificity of each situation. In the case of African countries the urge for a collective response was promoted by the OAU.

What was the process whereby the refugee issue was reconciled with the cardinal principles of the OAU: sovereignty, territorial integrity and non-intervention in the internal affairs of member states? This process is composed of two elements: firstly, the internalisation of the refugee phenomenon, whereby refugees are brought within the sovereign control of a member state; secondly, the externalisation of responsibility for the welfare of the refugees as the member state fails to cope with the additional population of refugees.

The OAU Approach

The Process of Internalisation of the Refugee Threat

Internalisation refers here to the process whereby refugees are brought under the control of the host country through specific decisions and laws. Refugees are not given the status of 'aliens' or of 'citizens', but are placed in a category between the two. The internalisation process is complemented by interstate agreements which urge the host government to prohibit the refugees from undertaking any acts that may threaten stability in the country of origin. It is, therefore, a process whereby the will of the country of origin is indirectly extended over the refugees through interstate agreements.

Theoretically, the domestic conflict in a particular country that causes a refugee exodus is considered to be an internal affair of that country according to the principle of sovereignty. However, the exodus of some of the people influenced by the conflict to another country is likely to raise the wrath of the government of the country of origin. For one thing, they are seen categorically as members of opposing and outlawed sections of the population, whose *raison d'être* is to threaten the established order. More seriously, the exodus of refugees means that these people are under the sovereign domain of another country. They are no longer within easy reach of the government of the country of origin. For the home government, refugees are enemies across the border.

Whether the country to which the refugees flee is directly involved in offering support for active groups, or is merely unable to control the influx, is immaterial. The government of the country of origin, at least theoretically, considers that the host country is offering sanctuary for subversive groups. The host country therefore becomes suspect and the presence of refugees is likely to worsen relations between the two countries. These assumptions are based on the fact that most African refugee situations occur as a result of armed conflict in the peripheries bordering other states. Since 1961, African countries have adopted the principles of good neighbourly relations and peaceful coexistence expressed in the draft charter of the Union of Africa and Malagasy States. Article 2 of the OAU Charter of 1963 affirmed the principles of independence, sovereignty, territorial integrity and non-intervention in the internal affairs of member states. In spite of the fact that the refugee problem in Africa resulted from domestic conflicts, in which the legitimacy and/or the territorial integrity of member states were challenged from within, the OAU approach was to give complete support to the member states according to these principles.

Seven months after the birth of the OAU, the refugee problem was introduced for consideration by the OAU Council of Ministers. The OAU Council of Ministers resolved that a committee comprising ten member states be formed in order to recommend how to solve the problem and how to maintain the refugees in their countries of asylum (OAU/CM/Res. 19[II], Lagos, Nigeria, February 1964). The OAU developed the norms by which the refugee problem was seen primarily as one that resulted in a heavy charge on the countries of asylum, as it constituted a burden and a source of tension between states. The Committee then ensured that discussion of the internal politics of countries that expelled refugees was not possible. The committee comprised representatives of Rwanda, Burundi, Congo, Uganda, Tanzania, Sudan, Senegal, Nigeria, Ghana and Cameroun. All of these countries were either ones from whose territories refugees originated or ones which had had to receive them. The OAU did not intend to establish its own political authority to arbitrate or interfere in conflicts generating refugees.

In its meeting of July 1964, the OAU Council of Ministers requested the Committee of Ten to continue its work and to draft a convention covering all the specific aspects of the refugee problem in Africa. But more significantly it urged member states which had refugee problems to continue discussion on a bilateral basis so as to find a solution to these problems (OAU/CM/Res. 36[III] para. 2. Third ordinary session, Cairo, 13-17 July 1964). A process was already developing in which state integrity was respected and member states were to decide for themselves what should happen to the refugees. From the beginning the OAU resolutions emphasised the integrity of the member states and denounced any activity undertaken by the refugees to threaten it. The resolutions by the Heads of States and Government and the OAU Council of Ministers constantly stressed the link between refugees and the potential for threatening the stability of member states and governments. In 1965 this link was addressed in two resolutions which were crucial to the OAU's conception of refugees. In the Declaration on the Problem of Subversion, the OAU Heads of State and Government pledged not to tolerate 'any subversion originating in our countries against another Member State of the Organisation of African Unity' (OAU/AHG/Res. 27[II] para. 1, Assembly of Heads of State and Government, Second Ordinary Session, Accra, Ghana 21-25 October 1965). Referring to the refugees, the African leaders promised to observe the principles of international law with regard to all political refugees (ibid. para. 6). The potential destabilising role of refugees was the subject of another resolution at the same OAU summit. It reaffirmed that the member states pledged to: 'prevent refugees living in their own territories from carrying out by any means whatsoever any acts harmful to the interests of other states, members of the Organisation of African Unity' (OAU/AHG/Res. 26[II] para. 2, Assembly of Heads of State and Government, Second Ordinary Session, Accra, Ghana, 21-25 October 1965).

The meeting requested member states never to allow the question of refugees to become a source of dispute between them (ibid. para. 3). New definitions for refugees, the nature of asylum, and strategies were carefully designed. 'Refugees' accordingly became a universal category and were divorced from their political context. In the Convention Governing the Specific Aspect of the Refugee Problem in Africa, the OAU introduced a widely acclaimed definition of the term 'refugee' that not only endorsed the definition stated in the UN 1951 Convention Relating to the Status of Refugees but also added that:

> The term 'refugee' shall also apply to every person who owing to external aggression, occupation, foreign domination or events seriously disturbing public order in either part or the whole of his country of origin or nationality is compelled to leave his place of habitual residence in order to seek refuge in another place outside his country of origin or nationality. (ibid. Article 1 para. 2).

However, this wide definition was qualified by a condition that made it equally restrictive. It made its own distinction between 'a refugee who seeks a peaceful and normal life and a person fleeing his country for the purpose of fomenting subversion from outside' (OAU Convention Governing the Specific Aspects of Refugee Problems in Africa, Addis Ababa, September 1969, Article 1, para. 2). The convention stated that its stipulations 'shall not apply to any person (who) has been guilty of acts contrary to the purposes of the Organisation of African Unity' (ibid. Article 1, 5[c]). Furthermore, the convention stipulated that the signatory states should undertake to prohibit refugees residing in their territories from 'attacking any state, Member of the OAU, by any activity likely to cause tension between Member States, and in particular by use of arms, through the press, or by radio' (ibid. Article 3[2]).

In order to safeguard against any possible attacks, the refugees were put under the control of the member state. The state would reserve the right to determine whether a person was a refugee. However, the granting of asylum was considered 'a peaceful and humanitarian act' and was not to be regarded as an unfriendly act by any member state (ibid. Article 2[2]). The Convention meant to oblige the contracting state as well as the refugees not to endanger the security of other countries. On the one hand, countries of asylum were required for reasons of security to 'settle refugees at a reasonable distance from the frontier of their country of origin' (ibid. Article 2[6]). On the other, the refugee was obligated by the stipulation that 'every refugee has duties to the country in which he finds himself, which requires in particular that he conforms with its laws and regulations as well as with measures taken for the maintenance of public order' (ibid. Article 3[2]).

Through these stipulations the OAU helped member states to regain control over the refugee issue. It reinforced the demand for sovereignty and integrity of its member states. However, in so doing, the OAU practically transformed the refugee phenomenon by making it entirely the responsibility of the state of asylum. Due to the fact that domestic conflict in member states was outside the OAU's concern, the causes of the refugee exodus were persistently avoided. The OAU resolution instead shifted to interpret the refugee phenomenon as 'one of a complex and purely humanitarian nature' (OAU/CM/Res. 88[VII], OAU Council of Ministers Seventh Ordinary Session, Kinshasa, 4-10 September 1967).

Externalisation of Responsibility as a Way to Deal with the Refugee Burden

Separated from their political context, the refugees were made to acquire new characteristics. For their hosts, they become a 'burden', for in the OAU's view, refugees created considerable socio-economic, financial, cultural and security problems (OAU/CM/Res. 104[IX], OAU Council of Ministers Ninth Ordinary Session, Kinshasa, 4-10 September 1967). It was therefore believed that it was a moral and political obligation of the international community to find adequate solutions to this problem, in view of the potential threat to peace and stability in Africa and throughout the world (OAU/UNECA/UNHCR Conference on the Legal, Economic and Social Aspects of African Refugee Problems, Recommendation 1. Addis Ababa, 9-18 October 1967).

The perception of refugees as a socio-economic burden derived from, and was complementary to, the attempt to depoliticise the refugee phenomenon. There was already a popular assumption that the refugee threat to stability could be avoided if refugees were helped to establish new roots in new havens. The alleviation of the burden on host countries was considered necessary and complementary to political stability and economic prosperity. This assumption, drawn from the European experience, was readily accepted in Africa in the 1960s. The OAU attempt to emulate the European approach was not only evident in its resolutions but also in its inviting organisations which were either European or whose perception derived from the European experience. For the Europeans themselves, support for the OAU concept was also motivated by the need to maintain friendly regimes and to combat the infiltration of new powers such as the Soviet Union into Africa.

The portrayal of the refugees and their problems in a universal context helped further to obscure and isolate the domestic politics of member countries. The OAU resolutions after 1964 urged that member states should act within the UN system with intergovernmental and nongovernmental organisations to elicit more assistance for the refugees in Africa. Although the UN had recommended and provided assistance since 1957 for specific categories of refugees in particular countries, in 1965 a special resolution was made to help all African refugees, realising that substantial aid was needed for 'immediate assistance and constructive aid' (UNGA Res. 2040 [XX] 7 December 1965). After that, the OAU prescription for the refugee burden was that member countries should seek assistance from external sources. Major conferences which contributed guidelines for policy were held in 1967, 1979, 1981 and 1984. Over these last three decades, the African states have used the OAU and different international forums to highlight the plight of the refugees in order to gain assistance and to emphasise the principle of international responsibility (Mazzeo 1984:1).

However, this persistence in externalising the responsibility sharply contradicted the policy of internalising the politics behind the refugee phenomenon. Seeking assistance from external sources invited intervention and often worked to undermine the sovereignty of individual states (Jackson and Rosberg 1986:24). The provision of assistance brought new standards and laws which were not necessarily compatible with the specific local situation. Of more significance, however, was the arrival of foreign organisations specialising in refugee assistance, to work inside the territory of individual countries. As the concept of provision of assistance to solve the refugee problem made the refugees an issue of government public policy, such policy was bound to be influenced by these organisations. The specific mandates of these organisations and the values of their representatives were not necessarily compatible with those of the governments. Here I cite particularly the case of the United Nations organisations whose agencies have had a pervasive influence over government policy. Despite the fact that states are granted juridical sovereignty within the UN system, UNHCR has its own specific mandate, bureaucracy and authority over its finance independent of its founding body, as it earns most of its funds from voluntary contributions. Conferring benefits in the form of material assistance to needy governments offers it a discretionary power comparable to that of the leading treaty-based agencies like the IMF and World Bank (Buehrig 1981:227). 'The basic nexus between international administrative agencies and domestic policy is the conditional benefit: the strategy, in other words, of dangling the carrot' (ibid.). But while refugee aid agencies work hard to prod governments and to influence refugee policy for their own purposes, the governments themselves work hard to influence the agencies and donors in order to gain extra assistance. These cross pressures often result in competitive situations.

The relationships between assistance organisations and a government must be understood within the context of a constantly changing refugee situation and an equally dynamic political and economic situation in the host areas themselves. Increasing demands are made both on governments and on assistance agencies, demands which result from the refugees and also from the local populations. The more these demands increase, the more conspicuous appear to be the limitations of the refugee aid regime. This leads to fragmentation and conflict of interests within a government, and between it and aid agencies.

Refugees are defined and labelled by policies which are inevitably drawn up under the exigencies of maldevelopment and scarcity. Refugees are seen as a security threat and as a socio-economic burden. The label firstly severs refugees from previous links. Secondly, it severs links with the new context in which they arrive. Refugee policies function through the imposition of interests and values represented as universally valid. The complexity of issues that result in (and from) such labelling and the power relationships arising from the diversity of actors involved at local, national and international levels are the subject of this study.

References

Ahmad, A. G. M. and Harir, S. A. (1981) *The Rural Community in Sudan* (Arabic), Development Studies and Research Centre, Khartoum.

Akol, J. (1987) 'Southern Sudanese Refugees: Their Repatriation and Resettlement after Addis Ababa Agreement' in Rogge, J. R. (ed.) *Refugees: A Third World Dilemma*, Rowman and Littlefield, NJ.

Al-Amin, B. (1984) 'Agriculture in Refugee Settlements: Its Past, Present and Future' (Arabic), memorandum, COR, Khartoum.

Azar, E. E. and Moon, C. (eds.) (1988) *National Security in the Third World: the Management of Internal and External Threat*, Edward Elgar House, Aldershot.

Buehrig, E. H. (1981) 'The Resolution-Based Agency', *Political Studies* vol. 29 no. 2.

Buzan, B. (1988) in Azar, E. E. and Moon, C. (eds.) *National Security in the Third World: the Management of Internal and External Threat*, Edward Elgar House, Aldershot.

COR/FINNIDA (1987) 'The Project for Mechanisation of Agriculture in Refugee Settlements in Eastern Sudan: A Study of Context and Beneficiaries' (Mikels, G. and Hassan, Y.), a COR/FINNIDA Evaluation Report, COR, Khartoum.

DRS (Democratic Republic of Sudan) (1985) *Population of the Sudan and its Regions*, Third Population Census, Project Document No. 1, Population Studies Centre, University of Gezira (Medani) and Department of Statistics, Khartoum.

El Nour, T. H. (1983) 'The Ethiopian Sudanese Boundaries: A Study in Political Geography', Ph.D. Thesis, University of Durham.

Fadl al-Sid, O. A. (1984) 'The Eritrean Question and its Effects on the Sudan' (Arabic), National Defence College, Khartoum.

Gebre-Medhin, J. (1984) 'Nationalism, Peasant Politics and the Emergence of a Vanguard Front in Eritrea', *Review of African Political Economy* 30: 48-57.

Jackson, R. H. and Rosberg, C. G. (1986) 'Sovereignty and Underdevelopment: Juridical Statehood in the African Crisis', *Journal of Modern African Studies* vol. 24, no. 1.

Karadawi, A. (1977) 'Political Refugees in Africa: A Case Study from the Sudan', M.Phil. Thesis, Reading University.

Kursany, I. (1985) 'Eritrean Refugees in Kassala Province of Eastern Sudan: An Economic Assessment', *Refugee Issues*, BRC/QEH working papers, vol. 2(1), October.

Mazzeo, D. (ed.) (1984) *African Regional Organisations*, Cambridge University Press.

Mills, R. (1985) *Population Policy, Trends and their Implications in the Sudan*, Population Studies Centre, University of Gezira.

Nadel, S. F. (1977) 'The Demographic Composition of Eritrea' (Arabic), translated by Joseph Safeer, Dar al-Masira, Beirut.

NCAR (National Committee for Aid to Refugees) (1980) *Background and Project Summary*, Documentation for the June 1980 Conference Volume II, Khartoum.

Ohaj, M. A. (1986) *From the History of the Beja* (Arabic), Khartoum University Press, Khartoum.

Orwa, D. K. (1984) 'National Security: An African Perspective', in Bruce, B. and Arlinghaus, E. (eds) *African Security Issues*, Bowker, Epping.

Paul, A. *The History of the Beja Tribes of the Sudan*, Oxford University Press.

Salih, H. M. (1980) 'Hadanduwa Traditional Territorial Rights and Inter-population Relations within the Context of Native Administration (1927-1970)', *Sudan Notes and Records* vol. 61.

Trevaskis, G. (1960) *A Short History of Eritrea*, Oxford University Press.

Trimingham, J. S. (1949) *Islam in the Sudan*, Oxford University Press.

2

The Emergence of a Centralised Refugee Policy during the Second Parliamentary Regime 1965-1969

This chapter discusses the process by which the governments of Sudan's second parliamentary regime (June 1965 to May 1969) endeavoured to assume control over the refugees. The genesis of the refugee policy applied in 1967 dates back to 1965, particularly after the election of Prime Minister Mohammed Ahmad Mahjoub. The policy which evolved was necessarily centralised and institutionalised. Several factors came into play to shape it.

First was the arrival of sizeable influxes of refugees from areas of conflict in neighbouring Ethiopia and the Congo (subsequently Zaire). These influxes occurred at the same time as Sudanese were fleeing from areas in southern Sudan to neighbouring countries, particularly the Congo and Ethiopia. The conflict in southern Sudan had developed considerably and most of the southern organisations were founded in exile (Beshir 1975: 45-77; Karadawi 1977: 34-44). Second was the election of conservative governments dominated by the traditional parties of northern Sudan which rejected any substantial concessions to the south. In fact, the emerging policy towards refugees was part of a wider policy to suppress the radical elements, led by the Sudan Communist Party, which had dominated the Transitional Government (October 1964 to June 1965). In contrast to the position of the traditional parties, the transitional government had called for a nonviolent and just solution to the southern Sudan problem, organising the unsuccessful Roundtable Conference of 1965. At the same time, it had provided support for the dissident groups from Ethiopia and the Congo, as these were considered to be justly struggling against neo-colonialism. However, the governments of the second parliamentary period treated the southern problem as one of rebellion. They considered the support for dissident groups from neighbouring countries as counter-productive and contradictory to the attempt to crush the rebellion in the south. Consequently, the imposition of restrictions on political activities by refugees in Sudan was complementary to establishing order. Thirdly, an opportunity was offered by the emerging OAU standards for the treatment of refugees while supporting preservation of the *status quo* in member states. Thus, despite the differences between the causes of the three separate problems of southern Sudan, the Congolese Simba rebellion, and the Eritrean question, the governments treated them as being linked.

The elections of June 1965 brought to power the coalition government formed by the Umma and the Nationalist Unionist Party, ending the phase of radicalism which followed the revolution of 21 October 1964. Immediately after he assumed office, Prime Minister Mahjoub began to design his policy to contain the problem in the south. He believed that the southern problem was mainly a security problem. In his first address to parliament, he pledged to end the policy of appeasement and leniency in dealing with the outlaws and those who supported them. He promised that the government would 'order the army to follow the criminals, return the state of law and order and punish the mutineers' (Salih 1971: 180; Beshir 1975: 26). The growing presence of the Anya-Nya[1] and the unwillingness of southern Sudanese politicians to settle the issue was thought to be mainly caused by external involvement and support for dissidents channelled through the neighbouring countries (Mahjoub [1973] makes particular reference to Israel). Any attempts at peace would be obstructed unless the neighbouring countries could be persuaded to desist from allowing their territories to be used against Sudan. This was considered to be a priority because, inside Sudan, the government planned to re-equip its forces, as well as to isolate the 'rebels' from the population (ibid.: 216). A ministerial committee was formed to propose economic reforms in the South. Later, it suggested the formation of peace villages in areas under government control. Although this policy was originally intended to deal with a problem within Sudan, it came to have a direct effect on the refugees from other countries.

---

1. Editor's note: The Anya-Nya was formed in 1963 with the aim of achieving independence, or at least regional autonomy, for southern Sudan through military action.

Responses to the Congolese Influx

The rebellion which broke out in the Congo in September 1963 and which was crushed with the support of Belgian and American troops, was at first hailed as an authentic movement for real independence. Support for the leaders came in the form of military supplies from Algeria, Egypt and Ghana. The rebellion was considered a continuation of the struggle led by Patrice Lumumba who had been assassinated in 1961.

Contact between the Sudanese Government and the Congolese insurgents was made some time before the latter's withdrawal into Sudan in March 1965. Government reports refer to requests to allow the supply of arms across Sudan from Egypt from the end of September 1964. A positive response was only made after the 'October Revolution' which brought the radical Transitional Government into power. On his visit to Khartoum on 13 November 1964, Gaston Soumaliot, one of the leaders of the Congolese, met Mubarak Zarroug, then Minister of Finance and Secretary General of the National Unionist Party, who promised to meet the demands of the Congolese revolutionaries after consultation with the Prime Minister (Soumaliot 1966). Egypt, on the other hand, had had a relationship with Lumumba since 1958 and Nasser believed that the Congolese revolution should be supported, as a war against neo-colonialism. Also, the position of the Congo had a special significance for both Egypt and Sudan. The security of the Nile sources was a major concern for Egypt, while the position of the Congo was of vital importance to the ongoing conflict in southern Sudan. Foreign intervention and the activities of the southern Sudanese insurgents were dependent upon the regime in Leopoldville (Fai'q 1984: 146). Consequently, the Transitional Government of Sudan agreed to secure road transport from Juba to the areas where the Congolese insurgents were conducting their fighting in Northeast Congo. The fears expressed among Sudanese Government circles that the large quantities of arms might fall into the hands of the Sudanese rebels were quietened by constant assurances from Nasser (Fai'q 1984: 192) and the radicals in Sudan (particularly Communists). The government's fears later proved to be justified.

The acquaintance with and even support for the Congolese rebellion had an obvious effect on the way in which the Congolese Simba were received in Sudan. The Transitional Government considered the Congolese to be the standard bearers of the African revolution and gave the leaders official recognition. After their arrival, the leaders were received in the government guest house, allowed freedom

of movement, the right to maintain their military organisation, to conduct their own affairs and to administer the resources they had
brought with them. The Prime Minister, Sir al-Khatim al-Khalifa,
appointed a special envoy to liaise between the Congolese Revolution
and the Transitional Government. A special account was opened in
the Bank of Sudan for the cash and gold brought by the Congolese;
the Ministry of the Treasury released funds for cheques signed by any
two of the three Congolese leaders – Soumaliot, Gbenye and Olenga.

Arguably, the characteristics of the Congolese were such that the
group could hardly be seen simply as 'refugees'. The demographic
composition of the group was determined by the nature of the conflict
and the military organisations involved. The group largely consisted
of former fighters who had been members of the various organisations
that came together in Kisangani. The popular army had comprised the
Bembe, the Tutsi refugees and rural young men mainly in the age
group of 12 to 20 years. The only skills that these young, able-bodied
Congolese exiles had were those of a military and political nature, neither of which qualified them for gainful employment in Sudan. Again,
unlike the usual image of refugees, the Congolese of March 1965 were
not impoverished or powerless when they first arrived. The period of
their triumph in Congo had enabled them to be acquisitive; wealth, in
cash or in kind, was collected from local banks and merchants, and a
large quantity of arms was supplied by sympathetic governments, or
seized from the government forces (*Armée Nationale Congolaise*). Even
before their retreat into Sudan, reports referred to thousands of kilos
of gold being transferred to Cairo, Uganda and Sudan in exchange for
arms supplies.[2] However, the Congolese rank and file were paid
extremely high salaries in exile, and this contributed to a rapid exhaustion of these funds. The minimum salary paid to a private soldier was
250,000 Congolese francs (equivalent to £212 sterling). Eight colonels
at the top of the hierarchy received one million Congolese francs each.
Such an expenditure indicates that the total for salaries alone was
£1,184,000 per annum.

In the ensuing months from late 1965 to mid 1966, the Congolese
revolutionaries rapidly lost their credibility and popularity. The
rivalries which led to the split between the leaders proved to be irreconcilable. On 25 April 1965, Soumaliot left for Cairo to form the

2. Two Commissions of Enquiry held in Sudan and Uganda revealed the huge
amounts of resources which were abused in both countries, and officials in both
countries were implicated. Even in Cairo, Fai'q (1984: 173) confirms that Congolese gold was deposited in the Central Bank in 1961. When Cairo decided to
send back the gold after the brief reconciliation of 1962, it was found that it had
already been exhausted.

Conseil Suprême de la Révolution, which denounced Olenga and Gbenye and excluded them from its leadership. The rivalry between these two leaders remaining in Sudan embarrassed the Sudanese Government and pushed it to take sides. Recognition was confined to Christopher Gbenye, allegedly because he had earned the support of the radical African states of Ghana and Algeria and, as one minister stated, the government did not wish to bear the responsibility for burying the Congolese Revolution.[3] Two practical implications also led to a general decline in sympathy on the part of the Sudanese Government.

Firstly, the money which the Congolese had deposited and continued to depend on, dried up. The government in Khartoum recognised only the quantity of 49 kilos of gold, valued at £45,000. By October 1966, the government claimed that this sum was already overdrawn and an additional sum of £25,000 from the government purse had been spent on the Congolese leaders in Khartoum. In the south, the Congolese influx had injected the local war-affected economy with sudden flows of cash and commodities which, in the absence of any system of accountability, were quickly siphoned off by local merchants and corrupt politicians and bureaucrats.

Secondly, the influx of Congolese had had a direct impact on the military struggle in the south. The Sudanese army in Equatoria was particularly strained by the presence of the Congolese. As they were situated in border areas, the Sudanese army found itself responsible not only for protecting them against the incursions of the Congolese government forces (CR/MI/35/G/2/B/Vol. 1, Ministry of Interior, p.82), but also for preventing them from launching attacks across the border. A report from Equatoria showed that these additional responsibilities cost £250,000 during the period March 1965 to February 1967 (ibid., Military Intelligence Report, p.47). Simultaneously, the trade in arms was already beginning to show with reports indicating that Congolese weapons were being passed to the Anya-Nya as early as September 1965. The Congolese government retaliated by offering favourable treatment to the southern Sudanese by allowing them to organise and by facilitating access to arms.

Change of Policy towards the Congolese

The special treatment afforded to the Congolese revolutionaries by the Transitional Government proved to be disastrous for the Sudanese Government's security strategy in Southern Sudan. The

3. Statement by Mohammed Jubara al-Awad to the Commission of Enquiry on the Congolese, Government Report, Ministry of the Interior, Khartoum 1966.

Congolese government had responded by contributing to the proliferation of the Anya-Nya; the arms brought in by the Congolese had begun to be passed to the southern Sudanese fighters as early as September 1965 (CR/MI/35/G/2/B/Vol. 1, p.48). It should be remembered that the presence of, and treatment extended to, the Congolese in Sudan occurred at the time when the number of southern Sudanese refugees in the Congo was rising from 8,000 in January 1965 to 22,000 in January 1966 (Hamrell 1967: 14-15). This aspect of the conflict, whereby the Congolese Government assisted the Anya-Nya, became a major cause for concern for the government in Sudan (Beshir 1975: 53).

Another problem was caused by the fact that the government allowed some of the Congolese in Equatoria to acquire arms, on the pretext that they needed to protect themselves when they gathered their food from the jungle. (This involves a delicate issue in North-South relations where successive governments often armed local militias.) Such an action proved to be fatal, whatever the motives of the authorities might have been. On at least one occasion, an embarrassing situation arose whereby the Congolese used their arms to force a Sudanese community to flee to exile in the Central African Republic. An excerpt from a letter from the UNHCR Representative in Bangui confirms that:

...information submitted officially indicates that the new influx of Sudanese refugees in Bambuti (CAR) is basically due to the extortions by

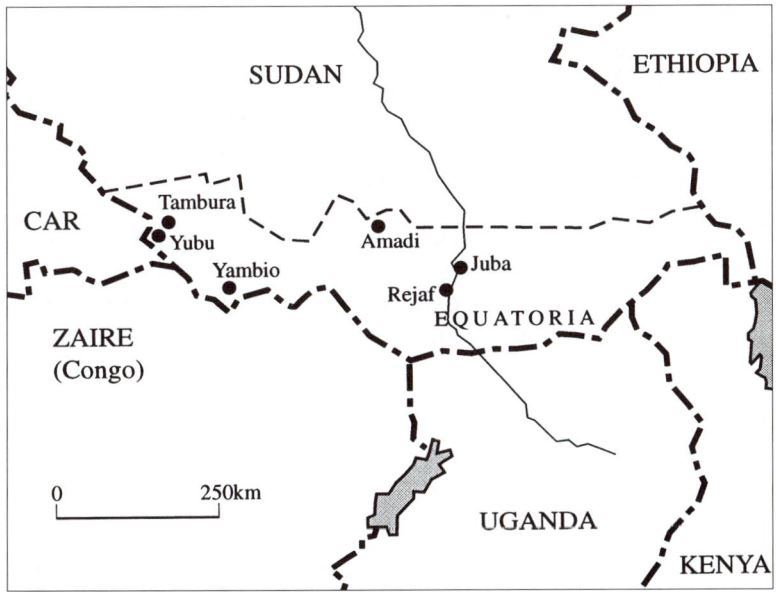

Map 2.1 *Border Area Affected by Congolese*

the Simbas tolerated, or not, by the Sudanese authorities. According to statements made by the refugees, the Simbas move freely in the region of Tambura carrying arms, looting villages and committing acts of violence against the population. According to certain information, a military post of Simbas equipped with firearms from the Sudanese army, has been installed half-way between Youbu and Tambura to protect the road link between the two towns.[4] (See map 2.1)

An additional decisive factor which led to the change of policy towards the Congolese was Joseph Mobutu's rise to power in November 1965, just after the OAU leaders had made their declaration on the prohibition of subversion in October 1965. From then on Mobutu was accepted by all member states as the unquestionable leader of the Congo.

Applying the Label 'Refugees' to Congolese Exiles

With this convergence of national and continental interests, the fate of the Congolese revolutionaries in Sudan was sealed, and the Sudanese policy towards the Congolese in Sudan became unequivocal. In the meeting held at the Sudanese Prime Minister's office on 29 September 1966 it was decided that:

1. the Congolese were to be officially considered as refugees and not *thuwar* (revolutionaries);
2. their stay should be restricted to Equatoria Province, where essential needs of food, shelter, and means to support themselves were to be provided by the government;
3. those who wanted to leave the country would be allowed to do so on condition that they should not return.[5]

These three elements of the policy had obvious implications. The treatment of the Congolese as refugees rather than as a revolutionary group meant that political support was withdrawn and that activity from Sudan against the Congo was no longer considered legal or legitimate. The decision to restrict the stay of the exiled Congolese to Equatoria, and to end the policy of helping them to support themselves, meant an end to their freedom of movement, and a growth in their dependence

4. A copy of this letter from the UNHCR representative to HQ in Geneva, dated 23/3/68, was found in File No. 1 CR/MI/35/G/2/Vol. 1 (Arabic), Ministry of the Interior, Khartoum.
5. Circular issued by the Secretary for the Council of Ministers, 29 September 1966, in CR/MI/35/G/2/B Vol.1, p.1. The circular on policy indicates great disaffection. In later resolutions, more refined wording replicated the OAU resolutions.

on government or external organisations for handouts. As a result of the third element of the policy, the political activists became unwanted.

Consequently, the government initiated moves to transfer refugees away from the border and to regroup them in the refugee settlement in Rejaf, for which UNHCR provided assistance. A few of the Simba leaders left for Algeria and Libya; others left for Europe. Those who remained behind had to forget the illusion of the revolution, and either opted for repatriation arranged between the two governments or learned to work on the land and support themselves. The group was eventually transferred to the Rejaf refugee settlement, including an additional 2,000 who had arrived in January 1968.

It was through this experience of dealing with the Congolese that the government first employed the term 'refugee' to restrict political or military action against another country. Consequently, when the Eritrean influx arrived in March to May 1967, the government was ready to develop the treatment of refugees as a domestic rather than an international issue.

The Eritrean Mass Influx: March to May 1967

When 25,000 people reached the outskirts of Kassala town in 1967, both the official and popular responses were affected by the relationship between Sudan and Ethiopia. The protracted nature of the conflict in Eritrea, dating back to the defeat of the Italians in 1941, had resulted in the politicisation of the Sudanese people, particularly those who had historical links across the border. Furthermore, the political organisations representing the Eritreans which were present in Sudan before 1967 had cultivated popular sympathy for the Eritreans. When official policy changed, and a decision was made to suppress exiled dissident groups, the government needed not only to intensify inter-state accord, but also to suppress popular feeling inside Sudan.

The size of the influx came as a great shock for the Sudanese, particularly in the town of Kassala. Between 5 and 13 March 1967, 8,883 men, women and children drifted towards the outskirts of the town. By the end of May, the number had grown to 25,503. The refugees brought new revelations about the nature of the conflict. The Provincial Commissioner reported that as a result of:

> ... the sweeping operations against the Beni Amer and Baria villages near the borders of Kassala, large numbers of Eritreans crossed the border in order to escape the looting and the destruction caused by the Ethiopian Army. (Report by Commissioner, Kassala, File No. MI/35/G/4, p.4, Ministry of Interior, Khartoum)

The refugees described the atrocities and produced as proof circulars distributed by the Ethiopian army ordering villagers to move to government security posts and police stations: 'So that the army could differentiate between the good and the evil'.[6]

As a result of these revelations, there was heightened sympathy for the refugees on the part of their kin and co-believers (such as the Beni Amer and Khatmiya). This support was particularly charged by the claim that:

> ... the Ethiopian military offensive was directed against the Muslims in general and leading personalities in particular, with the aim of replacing them by Christians who are sympathetic to the regime in Addis Ababa. (Report of the Minister of the Interior on his visit to Kassala, 12-18 March 1967, Ministry of the Interior, Khartoum)

The immediate response in Kassala was the establishment of the 'National Committee for Relief for the Eritreans', which raised voluntary donations from the public. At a meeting with the Minister of Interior on 12 March 1967 in Kassala, the committee demanded support for a national campaign for fundraising and immediate help for young Eritreans in order to defend the Eritrean cause. They also demanded official approval for the training of Sudanese who wished to fight on the side of the Eritreans. However, the minister's view, and certainly the view of his government, was completely at variance with the wishes of the committee. He made it clear that military training in Sudan was governed by law, which could not endorse the committee's demand. He also persuaded the committee to confine its fundraising to Kassala Province. He assured them that local donations, added to government and UN contributions, would be enough to cover the relief needs of the Eritreans.

In fact, the government was most concerned to suppress this popular reaction which had begun to threaten relations with Ethiopia. A balance was therefore needed between acknowledging the humanitarian concerns of the people, and responding to the pressure exerted by the Ethiopian Government. The minister made it clear to the Nazir (traditional ruler) of the Sudanese Beni Amer:

> ... we will treat these people as refugees and [therefore] as non-Sudanese. We will allow them to choose between returning home with guarantees of safety and amnesty, or remaining among us on condition that they will

6. The circular, which was issued by the Governor General of Eritrea, was shown by the refugees to the Minister of the Interior during his visit to them (MI/35/G/4, p.4). See also, *Africa Confidential* 10, 12 May 1967, p.7.

be subject to the regulations concerning refugees. As we are bound by agreements on refugees with the neighbouring countries, we are obliged to remove the refugees who are unwilling to return home, 150 miles away from the borders. We have to disarm them and send the political activists away from the country. (Ibid.)

However, the Eritrean influx, unlike the Congolese, was typical of people who were caught in the fighting at home. They moved as whole villages representing different Eritrean ethnic groups from the Muslim lowlands. Their plight was described by Louise Holborn: '... refugees were clustered in nine square miles of baked sand surrounded by mountains' (1975: 1337), and in the words of Thomas Jamieson, UNHCR Director of Operations, 'the only things they have in abundance are sand, dust and despair' (ibid.). The minister had in the back of his mind the Ethiopian protest against UNHCR involvement on the grounds that the Eritreans were considered as 'rebels and not refugees' (ibid.: 1338). The influx also coincided with a border dispute in al-Fashaga area (see map 2.2), leading to growing tension between the two countries.

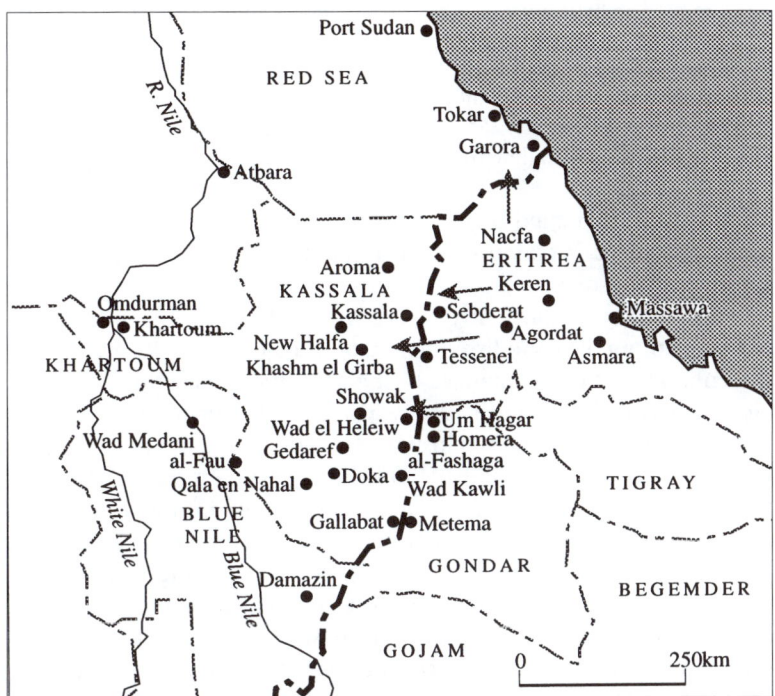

Map 2.2 *Refugee Influxes into the Eastern Region, 1967-1975*

Diplomatic Contacts with Ethiopia

In July 1965, Prime Minister Mahjoub paid a four-day visit to Ethiopia with the intention of sealing the border between the two countries to prevent aid filtering through to the southern Sudanese rebels. The joint communiqué resulting from the friendship mission strongly advocated the new trend:

> The two parties agreed that neither party should engage itself, or its nationals, or nationals of the other party or institutions within its jurisdiction, in any type of activity that was harmful or designed to harm the national interest of the other party. (O'Ballance 1977: 77)

Reports at the Ministry of the Interior in Khartoum (in the aftermath of the visit) provided ample evidence of the serious intention of the Sudanese Government to implement its new policy. After the return of the 'friendship delegation' from Ethiopia, the politically active Eritreans were subjected to relentless harassment. One report stated that the Ministry of the Interior:

> ... immediately began to implement all the procedures that would prohibit subversion against the sister Ethiopia from the territories of the Republic of Sudan ... Letters explaining the new policy were circulated among the security authorities in the different provinces with orders to ban any form of anti-Ethiopian activity. (Memorandum: 'Problems between Sudan and Ethiopia', Police Headquarters, Ministry of the Interior, 6 March 1968, p.1)

The letters were issued by the Director of Police to his subordinates in the provinces. Procedures were applied in Khartoum, Kassala and Blue Nile Provinces.

The leaders of the Eritrean Liberation Front (ELF) in Kassala were summoned by the Provincial Commissioner and briefed about the content and consequences of the agreement with the Ethiopian Government. They were also warned that any activity against Ethiopia would lead to the closure of the ELF offices and the expulsion of its leaders. Eventually, '150 Eritreans who used to reside in 36 houses in Kassala town were evicted and moved into the interior of Eritrea' (Letter from Commissioner, Kassala to Under-Secretary, Ministry of Interior, No. KP/SCR/66/F/4/3/ll 26 August 1965).

The reports also revealed that the political activists were listed and declared *personae non gratae*. At least one leader was deported direct to Ethiopia as a sign of commitment to the new policy (Memorandum: 'Problems between Sudan and Ethiopia', Police Headquarters, Ministry of the Interior, 6 March 1968).

On several occasions, the Sudanese security authorities accepted help offered by the Ethiopian Embassy in Khartoum. In addition to keeping a close eye on the Sudanese Government's efforts to implement the agreement, the Embassy was able to detect the movements of the dissidents. Consequently, as sources at the Ministry of the Interior in Khartoum admitted:

> The Ministry of the Interior has frequently moved without delay to apply the prohibition of activities against Ethiopia on the information provided by the Ethiopian Embassy's private informants. (Ibid.)

From then on, the new line of policy was emphasised in all bilateral arrangements. In August 1965, one month after the Prime Minister's visit, the Minister for Foreign Affairs announced that the Sudanese Government would undertake to prevent refugees living in Sudan from engaging in subversive activities against their country of origin (ibid.). Both countries were party to the Declaration on Prohibition of Subversion issued at the OAU Summit in Accra, October 1965 (OAU, AHG/Res. 27(II)). Later communiques began to emphasise the principles of the OAU. Sayyid al-Sadig al-Mahdi, premier from June 1966 to July 1967, continued with the same policy designed by Mahjoub. On 28 July 1966, the communiqué issued in Khartoum after the visit of the Ethiopian delegation headed by the Minister of Defence declared that:

> ... both parties enumerated, in detail, incidents of subversive activities detrimental to friendly relations and national interests. In accordance with the principles enshrined in the UN and OAU charters, and the previous agreements concluded between the two parties; the two governments agreed to co-operate, in a spirit of goodwill and brotherly relations, to eliminate these activities.

The same message was reiterated during the visit of the Sudanese Minister of Foreign Affairs on 4 January 1967 to Addis Ababa. Between 23 and 26 February 1967, Emperor Haile Selassie paid a visit to Sudan at the end of which both governments announced their wish to conclude a treaty on refugees which would establish mutual obligation either to encourage voluntary repatriation of refugees or to transfer them away from the borders. This bilateral arrangement was intended to complement the strategy of wiping out the ELF in western lowland Eritrea; the Ethiopian Government was keenly aware of the dangers which might arise if the Eritreans found the opportunity to strike back from Sudan. In April 1967, during the continuing flow of refugees, the Sudanese Minister of the Interior ordered the evacuation of all villages near the border in Kassala and the transfer of

Eritreans into areas within reasonable reach of police and military posts (Memorandum: 'Problems between Sudan and Ethiopia', Police Headquarters, Ministry of the Interior, 6 March 1968).

Arguably, however, these bilateral arrangements were not only an attempt to tackle the immediate threat, but were also part of a wider strategy to suppress both internal and external opposition.

Although the bilateral arrangements between Sudan and Ethiopia apparently accepted restraint in their attempts to suppress opposition, their actions sometimes belied this. While the democratic Sudanese Governments could only be as conciliatory to Ethiopia as public opinion would allow, Imperial Ethiopia tried to force Sudanese Governments to restrain those who were actually sympathetic to Ethiopian and Eritrean exiles. Military attacks across the border were an important component of Ethiopian Government action. In March 1967, the military offensive extended to Sudanese border villages which were suspected of harbouring and protecting the 'rebels'. On 15 March 1967, the village of Id Guba was reported to have been attacked by 50 Ethiopian soldiers. The village of Debre Sultan was also attacked. In Id Guba, the village was inspected, arms were confiscated and three people were kidnapped and taken back into Ethiopia. One of them, a Beni Amer, was shot dead (Ministry of the Interior, 'Report of Police Headquarters', March 1967, Khartoum).

In addition to using physical force, the Ethiopian Government also employed the weapon of official protest: it blamed the Sudanese Government for its unwillingness to ban public support for the Eritreans. It even alleged that the influx of the Eritreans was carefully planned by some Sudanese leaders in order to establish a base for the Eritrean dissidents. Their aim, the Ethiopian Government contended, was eventually to allow the Eritreans to undergo training and to have military equipment, to enable them to secede from Ethiopia.[7] Good neighbourliness, argued the Ethiopians, dictated that the Sudanese Government should have prohibited this plan; instead, it should have policed the common borders against the dissidents:

> Since this action was not taken, the Sudanese Government should be held responsible for deterioration in relationships and for any steps Ethiopia might take to safeguard its interests. (El Nour 1971: 218)

This blend of bilateral arrangements and the intense pressures of militant refugees between the two countries explains the confronta-

---

7. In March 1967 the denial of support for the ELF by the Sudanese authorities was not helped by the announcement by Tedla Bairu (ex-Prime Minister in Eritrea) in Damascus that the Sudanese supported the ELF both officially and privately. *Africa Confidential* 10, 12 May 1967.

tions which ensued. None of the other sources of tension, such as undemarcated boundaries, disputed water resources, and ideological differences, produced tension comparable to the refugee problem. This was, as argued, a direct consequence of the inability of the governments to suppress internal and external threats of dissent. The failure of the agreements between governments to impose control over citizens living in exile, made the government representatives in both countries seek explanations.

The Sudanese authorities believed that they had tried as hard as they could. The previous declarations to prohibit subversion were reinforced by the Sudanese Government's decision of 6 July 1967, to ban ELF activity (Resolution 1408, Council of Ministers Extraordinary Session, No. 241, 6 July 1967). Assistance was requested from the international community on humanitarian grounds for those refugees who were not politically motivated. An Ethiopian delegation was invited to Kassala to ascertain the reasons for the refugees' reluctance to return home. Simultaneously, UNHCR was called upon to carry out its own investigation. Both gestures were attempts to prove that the Eritreans who arrived in 1967 were simply refugees, that they were not willing to return, and that the Sudanese Government was acting on humanitarian principles (Memorandum No. SG.MI/CONF/28, Ministry of the Interior, Khartoum, 11 April 1968).

However, reports of the Sudanese Ministry of the Interior suggest that Ethiopia was still not happy with the manner in which the Sudanese Government was handling the refugee influx of 1967, and that it saw the appeal for international aid as an attempt to arouse world opinion and to encourage Arab and Muslim countries in particular to intensify their support for the Eritreans. The Sudanese Government, on the other hand, claimed that the Eritrean refugee problem was taken to international bodies only in good faith and without the intention of undermining the image of the Ethiopian Government or propagating the cause of the ELF. The Sudanese Government affirmed that it had been acting according to the principles laid down by the OAU and the UN, both of which stipulated that humanitarian treatment of refugees need not threaten the integrity or the sovereignty of the country of origin (Allan 1968).

According to a Sudanese Minister of the Interior,[8] speaking in retrospect, the failure of the two countries to implement the agreements can be attributed to the inability or the unwillingness of both parties to contain the conflict. In the case of Sudan, inconsistencies could be attributed to the frequent changes of governments. As for Ethiopia, the minister

8. Hassan Awad Allan was an NUP Minister whose party (later DUP) had been a partner in all the coalition governments from June 1965 to May 1969.

cited the consistent reluctance of the government to comply with the agreements. He accused Ethiopia of expansion into Sudanese territories and of 'turning a blind eye to the flagrant subversive activities of the Southern Sudanese rebels and their foreign missionary sponsors' (ibid.).

The Ethiopians had their own explanations for the failure of the agreements, blaming the Sudanese Government. According to the Ethiopian Minister of Foreign Affairs:

> We are complaining about the Eritrean outlaws who took the Sudanese territories as bases for attacking Ethiopian soil ... we have met time and again in Ethiopia and in Sudan, but unfortunately we have not achieved any improvement. It is my personal conviction that what has been accorded in the joint communiques and bilateral arrangements before hardly needs to be added to ... what more can we do? (Quoted in ibid.)

Arrangements with Other Countries

What emerges clearly from these exchanges is that there were no differences between the official lines towards refugees in the two countries. Officially, refugees were seen as objects of policy; their role in determining events was barely recognised. The problem was how to bring them under government control; the host government must act to safeguard its own interests even if this involved indirectly acting on behalf of the government of the country of origin.

The same kind of pattern is reflected in the actions of the Sudanese Government towards refugees from the neighbouring countries to the south. Diplomatic arrangements with Uganda (1964, 1966), Kenya and Tanzania (1965, 1966), Zaire (1966, 1967), and with the Central African Republic (1965) were made with a strong emphasis on restricting 'subversive activities' by exiled elements. The need to encourage the repatriation of refugees, or to assist them to live peacefully in host countries, was generally recognised as the optimum approach.

Centralisation of Decision-Making as a Response to the Incompatible Views of the Provincial Authorities

As noted, there were attempts by the Sudanese Governments after 1965 at intergovernmental *rapprochements* with the aim of establishing standard treatment for nationals living in exile. The aim was to depoliticise Sudanese exiles, and at the same time to quieten sympathy and support for the Eritreans and Congolese among certain sectors of the Sudanese public.

However, in the case of both the Congolese and the Eritrean influxes, the views of the provincial authorities as articulated by the Provincial Commissioners reflected a deep rift between the local and the central authorities as well as among central authorities, that is, between ministries of central government.

Conflict between Provincial Commissioner in Kassala and Central Government: Phase I

The Provincial Commissioner in Kassala reacted strongly against the central government's plans to deal with the refugee influx. His position derived from a tradition where the local government, similarly to the civil service, prided itself on acting independently of political influences of partisan governments. The Commissioner of Kassala had a series of exchanges with the central government in Khartoum during the period of the latter's agreements with the Ethiopian Government. For example, after his return to Khartoum from his week's visit to Kassala in March 1967, the Minister of the Interior made a series of recommendations to the Council of Ministers (Nugdalla 1967). On the basis of the report, the Council of Ministers produced Resolution No. 1225 in its 212th session of 15 March 1967. The content of the resolution was that:

1. refugees unwilling to return home should be transferred into the interior parts of Kassala Province in a location to be decided by the Provincial Commissioner; and
2. UNHCR should be contacted by the Ministry of the Interior to assist with relief aid and resettlement of the refugees.

The Commissioner of Kassala who was entrusted with the implementation of the Resolution at the provincial level objected to it. Two weeks later he wrote:

> The government should immediately enter into negotiations with the Ethiopian Government to send the refugees back home with their safety guaranteed. (Commissioner of Kassala to Under-Secretary, Ministry of Interior, Letter No. KP/SC/66/F/5/11, 29/3/67, Ministry of the Interior, Khartoum)

The Commissioner even expressed his doubts about the genuine motives of at least some, if not all, the refugees. He stated that:

> The first newcomers who entered from the Tessenei sector of the border facing Kassala have really suffered from the excesses of the Ethiopian army,

but the waves that followed are composed of people who were not subjected to measures on any scale that justifies their flight into Sudan. (Ibid.)

He argued that the sympathy shown to the first arrivals spurred the
others to follow, particularly 'if we take into consideration the economic scarcity and shortage of food crops suffered in Tessenei after
we suppressed contraband activities across the border' (ibid.).

The Commissioner of Kassala also referred to the designs of some
political groups in Sudan:

> We were informed that some of the Sudanese Beni Amer were sent
> [across the border] to urge their Eritrean kith and kin to move into
> Sudan. Firstly, because of the abundance of food which is given freely.
> Secondly, in order to increase the number of the Beni Amer in Kassala
> Province. (Ibid.)

Of relevance here is that the emergence of the Beja Congress as a
political bloc in 1965, taking votes from a traditional Khatmiya base,
undermined the power of the PDP in all Eastern Sudan, as the Congress won three seats in the 1965 elections and ten in the 1968 elections. So, according to the Commissioner: 'The People's Democratic
Party has more than one reason for sympathising with the Eritrean
insurgents and refugees. The Beni Amer in Eritrea are, after all,
Khatmiya followers' (ibid.).

However, the attempts by the Commissioner to disqualify the
Eritreans from the legal status of refugees could not veil the stark and
objective reality of the Ethiopian military campaign against the
Eritreans or the extreme suffering among those who fled into Sudan.
That reality was enough to warrant the granting of refugee status
which was, in any case, decided by the Council of Ministers two
weeks before the Commissioner wrote his letter. Knowing this, the
Commissioner changed his tactics by stressing his fears of the consequences of admitting the refugees to stay in Sudan. 'We do not
need them,' he warned, 'we do not have the resources to keep our
citizens and we do not want to have additional factors which exac-
erbate instability or inflame political feelings which will consequently influence our relationship with Ethiopia' (ibid.).

According to the Commissioner, the presence of the refugees
would not only have an adverse effect on relations with Ethiopia, but
it would also bring local political interests into play. 'The Communists
are happy with the influx and are trying every means at their disposal
to get the government [Umma-NUP coalition] in trouble with the
Ethiopian Government' (ibid.). According to the Commissioner, the
Islamic Charter Front believed that support for the Eritreans against

the Imperial Government was a duty because Eritreans were fighting against religious persecution. Support for the Eritreans was also seen as commendable, as being a practical step towards the triumph of Islam against its enemies (ibid.). However, as we have seen, even these arguments did not change the views of central government.

Phase II: Planning of the Refugee Settlement

The next phase, which involved planning for the resettlement of the refugees, brought similar conflicts. This time the provincial authorities were supported by some of the central departments, most notable among which were the Ministry of the Treasury and the Ministry of Local Government. Now that the pressure exerted by the Ethiopian Government was defused by the mutual submission to the OAU principles, another pressure was generated by the demands of UNHCR. UNHCR responded to the Sudanese Government's request for assistance by allocating a sum of US$150,000, but this was 'pending the elaboration of a long-term solution to the Eritrean refugee problem' (UNGA, A/Ac/96/UNF-78 Res. 1, 31/10/67). Until then, 'the government should temporarily remove the refugees from their present location' (ibid.). Meanwhile, the local Committee for Relief was pressing for the removal of the refugees from their shabby camps which would not stand up to the vagaries of the rainy season. A delegation travelled to Khartoum to demand the approval of a transfer of the refugees to a drier site in Al Adirgawi on the River Atbara some 32 km west of the town of Aroma. They also requested a contribution of £13,380 to cover expenses (Acting Commissioner of Kassala to Under-Secretary for Local Government, Letter KP/CONF/66/F/4/5/11 25/5/67. Copy to Under-Secretary for the Interior).

The Commissioner again raised objections, citing technical reasons why the suggested site was unsuitable. He argued, quoting a special report (Report by Chief of Eye Diseases and Filariasis Division, Ministry of Health, Khartoum, 25/6/67), that the area of the River Atbara was an endemic onchocerciasis zone. As long as there were 'disease carriers' among the refugees, the Commissioner objected to resettlement in any area along the River Atbara. The policy of resettling the Eritrean nomads in Kassala was questioned by the Commissioner in principle. The ecological balance in Kassala was precarious and because of the marginality of grazing resources, the Sudanese nomads needed vast areas for the practice of transhumance as the only way for them to manipulate the inhospitable environment (Dafalla 1975). The nomads had already come under pressure as government schemes had encroached on their traditional land. The large settlement scheme of

Khashm al Girba (Ahmad and Harir 1981: 162-96), **and the prolifera-tion** of large-scale mechanised rain-fed agricultural projects, claimed areas traditionally used by the tribes of Kassala. Objections along these lines were echoed in the meeting organised by the Commissioner with the Nazirs of the Shukriya, the Bisharin and the Rashaida (Report on the Meeting with tribal Sheiks and Nazirs File No. MI/SC/35/G-4, pp.112-114, Min. Interior, Khartoum 6/6/67). In the Commissioner's view, additional population pressure on the limited resources would certainly have a negative impact on public order. In the particular case of the Eritrean tribes, this view was partly justified. Animosities did exist between Sudanese and Eritrean communities, particularly the groups to which the refugees belonged: the Beni Amer, the Baria and the Maria. The Commissioner argued that it was because of these animosities that the British in 1947 had changed their minds about the Bevin-Sforza pro-posal of annexing the western lowlands of Eritrea to Sudan after the 'lib-eration' of Eritrea from the Italians (ibid.).

Even the possibility of settling the Eritreans among their kin, the Sudanese Beni Amer, was ruled out by the Commissioner. The Sudanese Beni Amer lived in border areas and any resettlement of the refugees there would be a clear violation of the arrangements between Sudan and Ethiopia. He also dismissed the idea of resettling the refugees in another area in Sudan outside Kassala. He argued:

> I doubt that the refugees themselves will abide by any decision to transfer them from their temporary settlements. They, unequivocally, refused to live among the Beja, the Shukriya or the Bisharin, and their transference into the interior of the country will make it difficult to look after their herds which are now grazing along the banks of the Setit in Ethiopia. (Ibid.)

The Commissioner ended his report to the central government by reminding it of the impasse. The alternative might have been to allow the refugees to stay where they were, but this, he argued, was also 'a violation of the government's previous decision' (reference to CM. Res. 1225 of 15/3/67).

In my view, the uncompromising and xenophobic attitude of the Provincial Commissioner was not, in fact, due to lack of compassion. It stemmed mainly from a professional insight which foresaw and feared the administrative, security and economic burdens that would result from an open-ended commitment to resettle refugees. There was a fear that compassion and charity would turn into an unsup-portable obligation.

Despite his efforts, the Commissioner was finally overruled by the central government. He was asked by the Under-Secretary of the Interior:

To leave matters of national policy to the appropriate top authorities in Khartoum who, being conscious of the principles which govern the treatment of refugees, are bound to put them into practice as a sign of respect for those principles, which are shared by other African states which are equally burdened by the refugee problem. (File No. CR/MI/35/A/6/2 13/2/68)

Conflict between Central Departments over the Cost of Settlement of the Refugees

As a result of Resolution 1408 of the Sudanese Council of Ministers, the Shukriya tribe, which had already been made to accept the resettlement of the Nubians of Wadi Halfa, was again persuaded to accept the resettlement of the Eritreans as a move dictated by 'national interest' (Resolution 1408, 6 July 1967). The site proposed near Khashm al Girba was soon discarded because a high incidence of tuberculosis among refugees raised fears about the spread of the disease among the local population. There was also some doubt about the possibility of peaceful coexistence between the Sudanese and the Eritreans, in view of the shortage of drinking water and arable land. The newly established Commissioner for Refugees of the Ministry of the Interior negotiated an alternative site with the Mechanised Farming Corporation. This site, at Sam Sam–Um Seinat Salient, was also deemed to be unsuitable because of its heavy clay soil, which prevented the use of the refugees' traditional tools (Commissioner for Refugees to UNHCR Representative in Khartoum MI/CR/35.A/6/A Letter 6 November 1968). When a decision was at last taken to establish the settlement at Jebel Sam Sam, the Commissioner for Refugees was asked to prepare a comprehensive plan and budget for the construction of the settlement. The area selected was part of Dar Bakur administration which was largely uninhabited and unexploited, although the tribes of Rufaa Sharq did use it for pasture during the rainy season.

This time, the objection came from the Ministry of Local Government. In a Memorandum to the Council of Ministers, the Minister of Local Government wrote:

> I do not support the approach adopted by the Ministry of the Interior [of allotting 100,000 *feddans*] for refugees south of Gedaref for the following reasons: first, being good arable land, part of which is cultivated by Sudanese farmers, it seems irrational to confiscate this land from those who have the right to use it and give it to the refugees. Second, the establishment of a land settlement would invite other Ethiopians to come and settle in Sudanese lands. Third, the majority of the refugees are old people and young children who cannot manage the tough farming operations. ('Resettlement of Eritreans in Kassala Province', memorandum by

the Minister of Local Government to the Council of Ministers, File No. CR/MI/35/A/6/2, 6 March 1968)

When the Ministry of the Interior submitted its plan and budget for the settlement, another objection came from the Ministry of the Treasury. The government contribution to the plan was estimated at £S275,000. The Ministry of the Treasury rejected the whole proposal on the grounds that 'the resettlement of the refugees should not take priority over the pressing demands of the Sudanese population in the different parts of the country' (Under-Secretary of the Treasury to Under-Secretary of the Interior, letter 9 May 1968). Instead, the Ministry of the Treasury proposed an alternative strategy. It suggested breaking the refugees into small groups and helping them to settle in different parts of the country where they could make the maximum use of their skills without impairing the capacity of the receiving communities to accommodate them. However, the Under-Secretary of the Treasury argued 'If this proves too difficult to achieve, there will be no alternative but to postpone the implementation of the resettlement project and to continue the provision of relief assistance' (Minister of Interior to Council of Ministers, Memorandum 24/3/68 CR/MI/35/A/6/2. The same argument was the subject of a memorandum by the Minister, 11 April 1968).

In the face of these objections, the Minister of the Interior exerted exceptional efforts to convince government departments of the need to comply with the bilateral, regional and international agreements dealing with refugees. Assessing the costs of not supporting the resettlement project, the Minister of the Interior argued '… the country is going to face security risks and loss of material assistance which is provided by the international community' (ibid., and the Commissioner for Refugees' memorandum of 26 May 1969, in CR/MI/35/A/6/2).

This argument was important in two respects. Firstly, it suggested that refugees are a threat to security if left unattended. Secondly, it suggested the link between aid and defusing that threat. As a result of the constant appeals to the Council of Ministers, the latter finally endorsed the project on condition that the Sudanese Government would contribute only the land. The Ministry of the Interior was entrusted with responsibility for coordinating the contribution of the government technical departments with assistance provided by UNHCR.

Building Central Institutions for the Refugees

The creation of a special institution was seen as an important part of the emerging centralised policy towards refugees. The Central Committee for Rehabilitation of Returnees (CCRR) was originally conceived by Prime Minister Mahjoub as part of his strategy to isolate the southern Sudanese dissidents. The CCRR was formed by the Council of Ministers' Resolution 840 of 12 June 1966, 'to cater for Sudanese as well as other non-Sudanese refugees and to act as a coordinator with other concerned authorities'. It was attached to the Secretariat of the Council of Ministers with membership representing the Ministries of the Interior, Local Government, the armed forces, the Treasury, Foreign Affairs, and Communications. The CCRR was conceived as an autonomous body with full control over its budget. It had a full time chairman who was responsible directly to the Prime Minister (MC/CM/35/A/1 CM/Res.840, 12 June 1966).

The functions of the Committee were defined as 'humanitarian and patriotic' (Statement of the Chairman of the CCRR, First Meeting, 29 June 1966) and these terms were to be complementary. Through repatriation, rehabilitation and resettlement of returnees, the CCRR was supposed to lay the foundation for a lasting solution to the political problem which had caused the refugee exodus. To achieve its functions, the duties of the CCRR were enumerated as follows:

1. to initiate the repatriation of Sudanese living in other countries;
2. to construct peace villages for the reception of Sudanese returnees in provincial areas of Southern Sudan;
3. to establish subcommittees to supervise the operations of repatriation and resettlement of Sudanese returnees;
4. to cater for non-Sudanese refugees, residing in Sudan;
5. to facilitate bilateral agreements for the above-stated purposes. (Ibid.)

As it seems that the CCRR was mainly concerned with the Sudanese abroad, paragraph (4) relating to the function of looking after non-Sudanese refugees was invoked only after the fate of the Congolese was decided on 29 June 1966. In October 1966, the CCRR was asked to become responsible for catering for the Congolese refugees and hence for implementing general policy directives that all Congolese should be confined to Equatoria Province (CCRR 7th Meeting, 20 October 1966. File MC/CM/35/A/1).

By January 1967 representatives of the CCRR had visited neighbouring countries to pursue and implement agreements between them and the Sudanese Government. In Sudan it had made projections for the rehabilitation of an estimated 100,000 returnees. The sums required for the plan of resettlement for both returnees and persons displaced inside Sudan had been estimated at £S1.5 million. However, criticisms began to mount soon after the CCRR began work, and came to a head during the brief premiership of al-Sadiq al-Mahdi, July 1966 to June 1967. Most of the people who were resettled in the peace villages in the three southern provinces were internally displaced persons. They were completely disappointed. As the Minister for Irrigation, Jervase Yak, pointed out: 'No policy of resettlement can succeed unless it rests on a secure economic foundation to better the lot of the inhabitants. It is true that no one, however poverty-stricken, would like to remain a permanent charity case' (Yak 1967). He reported further that 'the only thing that came out in our discussion was the question of the effectiveness of the Commission in persuading them [refugees] to return. For months now both members of the public and the press have been dwelling on the failure of the Commission' (ibid.).

Convinced of the inefficiency of the CCRR, Prime Minister al-Sadiq al-Mahdi declared that it had achieved nothing during its term in office.

> The number of refugees who returned through official channels was only 430 out of the total of 125,000. Even the return of that tiny number was facilitated by the Sudanese Embassies rather than the CCRR. At the external level the Commission did not show any spirit of initiative. Inside Sudan its responsibilities were performed by the provincial authorities. (Memo to the Council of Ministers No. CM/16/C-19, 28 January 1967)

Consequently, it was recommended that the CCRR should be dissolved and its activities for promoting repatriation should be delegated to relevant Sudanese embassies. Rehabilitation and resettlement of returnees and displaced persons were to be delegated to the provincial authorities in the south and a special office with full-time staff was to be established as part of the Ministry of the Interior.

The failure of the CCRR can be attributed to the fact that it was entrusted with a programme for repatriation which was impossible to achieve, due to the security situation in the South. Repatriation could not be promoted by simple administrative facilities when the political conditions militated against it.

The Commissioner for Refugees and the Change of Approach to Refugee Assistance

The office of the Commissioner for Refugees (COR) was established as a subdepartment of the Ministry of the Interior by the Council of Ministers Resolution 840 of 1 March 1967. Its creation was indicative of the significant shift from the government's emphasis on repatriation to assistance for refugees in host countries.

Sudanese Governments had in principle been against the provision of assistance to Sudanese refugees abroad. Material assistance was considered a negation of the principle of repatriation which was seen as the only solution to the refugee problem. The provision of material assistance to Sudanese refugees abroad was considered to be tantamount to supporting dissident groups and a means of evoking antagonistic foreign interests.

The attitude towards provision of material assistance to Sudanese refugees had been reinforced by mistrust of foreign agencies, which were seen as perceiving the problems in the South as North/Arab/Muslim against South/Negro/Non-Muslim. The involvement of Western agencies, particularly church agencies, was seen as part of the problem, and this led to the government's decision in 1964 to expel the foreign missionaries from southern Sudan (Ministry of the Interior 1964). Government reports subsequently alleged that the expelled missionaries played a role in exacerbating conflict and delaying voluntary repatriation. According to one report by the Commissioner of Equatoria on the situation in the Central African Republic:

> A few of the refugees who want to return to Khartoum are confronted with considerable obstacles from the local authorities, the outlaws, the missionaries, UNHCR, the World Council of Churches and a company which exploits the refugees in growing silkworm trees which tend to make refugees forget their homeland. (Bilal 1969)

The author of the report also commented that these agencies had vested interests in prolonging the refugee situation: '...the people working for the Red Cross and UNHCR and those who are looking after the welfare of the refugees are interested parties' (ibid.). UNHCR and Red Cross staff had, after all, very highly paid jobs.[9] The government's point of view was that international aid would be more constructive if it were invested in southern Sudan. Such investment would encourage the refugees to return from the bush or from neighbouring countries. This view was expressed even within the UNHCR Executive Council annual meetings which invariably called for the widening of the UNHCR mandate to provide for long-term projects for the returnees in the country of origin (e.g., UNGA A/AC.96/376 p.15 'Statement by the observer from the

---

9. These arguments were sustained even as late as 1971 when the late Joseph Garang reported after a visit to the Central African Republic: '... we sensed the concern of the settlement authorities and members of the interested international agencies, perhaps for personal reasons, to perpetuate and develop the settlement project' (Joseph Garang, Minister of State for Southern Affairs, 'Report on a visit to the Central African Republic, 5-13 July 1971', Ministry of the Interior).

Sudan', 17th Session of the UNHCR Executive Committee, May 1967. Also in Al-Bashir 1978: 264).

With the adoption of the new policy towards the Congolese in September 1966, the arrival of the March-May 1967 Eritrean influx, the failure of the government to achieve repatriation of the Sudanese refugees, and the established consensus over the OAU approach, the policy of the government towards refugee aid agencies began to change. In 1967 a new phase was launched when UNHCR was invited to come and help.

In late 1966 the new UN High Commissioner, Sadruddin Agha Khan, visited the country and was able to restore the image of UNHCR as a nonpolitical UN organisation which was willing to help host governments and refugees, irrespective of race or creed. The UNHCR Director of Operations, Thomas Jamieson, visited Sudan in May 1967 and September 1968, when he was able to sign an agreement with the Sudanese Government to open a UNHCR branch office in Khartoum. At that stage UNHCR considered the OAU standards (i.e., disarming the refugees and transferring them away from the border) as appropriate conditions for the provision of assistance. Since then UNHCR has been welcomed as a complementary partner in the implementation of government policy towards refugees.

COR was designated as its main government counterpart, and therefore was the executive and implementing agency for programmes of refugee assistance. The refugee projects executed by COR with UNHCR involved the establishment of two settlements for Eritrean and Congolese refugees in Qala en Nahal District, Eastern Region, and in Rejaf respectively.

Conclusion

As I have explained in this chapter, the policy towards refugees that took shape in 1967 was originally intended to contain the threat posed by the refugees. The restrictive measures imposed through Council of Ministers resolutions were eventually complemented by the involvement of the international organisation concerned with provision of material assistance to refugees. COR was established to coordinate government policy and to act as counterpart for UNHCR. Consequently the refugee problem and the duty to seek solutions to this problem became the joint responsibility of the host government and the international community. The two-tiered policy of prohibiting political activity and seeking external assistance for refugees seemed to provide a suitable approach to the refugee problem. However, it remained to be seen whether such a policy would be able to contain the refugee problem in the ensuing years.

References

Ahmad, A. G. M. and Harir, S. (1981) *The Rural Community in the Sudan* (Arabic), Khartoum: Development Studies and Research Centre.

Al-Bashir, A. R. (1978) 'Problems of Settlement of Immigrants and Refugees in Sudanese Society', D.Phil. Thesis, St. Antony's College, University of Oxford.

Allan, H. A. (1968) 'Report on Mission to Uganda and Ethiopia' (Arabic), Ministry of the Interior, Khartoum, 3 June.

Beshir, M. O. (1975) *The Southern Sudan: From Conflict to Peace.* Khartoum: The Khartoum Bookshop.

Bilal, C. A. (1969) 'A Brief Report of my Journey to the Central African Republic', 1 September.

Dafalla, H. (1975) *The Nubian Exodus*, Khartoum, Khartoum University Press.

Fai'q, M. (1984) *Abdel Nasser and the African Revolution* (Arabic), Beirut: Dar al Wuhda.

El-Nour, T. H. (1971) 'The Ethiopian/Sudanese Boundaries: A Study in Political Geography' Ph.D. Thesis, Durham University.

Hamrell, S. (ed.) (1967) *Refugee Problems in Africa*, Uppsala: SIAS.

Holborn, L. (1975) *Refugees: The Problem of our Times*, Methuchen NJ: The Scarecrow Press.

Karadawi, A. (1977) 'Political Refugees in Africa: A Case Study from the Sudan', M.Phil. thesis, University of Reading.

Mahjoub, M. A. (1973) *Democracy on Trial*, Beirut: Dar al Nahar.

Ministry of the Interior (1964) *Expulsion of Foreign Missionaries from the Southern Provinces*, Khartoum, March.

Nugdalla, A. A. (1967) 'Report on a visit to Kassala, 12-18 March 1967' (Arabic), Ministry of the Interior, Khartoum.

O'Ballance, E. (1977) *The Secret War in the Sudan 1955-1972*, London: Faber & Faber.

Salih, M. A. M. (1971) 'The Round Table Conference and the Search for a Solution to the Problem of Southern Sudan', MA Thesis, Khartoum University.

Soumaliot, G. (1966) Statement to the Commission of Enquiry on Congolese Revolution Assets, in Report by Salah Shebeika, Ministry of the Interior, Khartoum.

Yak, J. (1967) Minister of Irrigation, Report to Prime Minister on his visit to the South, February 1967.

3

The Changing Nature
of the Refugee Influxes
1970-1980

The policy towards refugees described in the last chapter was based on the principles of sovereignty and territorial integrity and consequently the condemnation of external intervention in the internal affairs of individual countries. Such a policy was severely tested after the changes in regimes in Sudan in May 1969 and in Ethiopia in September 1974. As before, the presence of opposition groups continued to threaten the security of each regime and created tension between the two countries. In the period from 1976 to 1978, the two regimes abandoned the norms established by the OAU. Instead, they relied on alliances with other states, military buildup, and public support for exiled opposition groups. As a result, Ethiopia witnessed an escalation in fighting between the regime and opposition groups. Military operations expanded to cover larger areas and larger sections of the population were affected. Consequently, the rate of exodus of refugees to Sudan was far greater than anything known before.

This chapter discusses these changes in the relationship between the regimes in Sudan and Ethiopia and the resulting change in the refugee phenomenon. Particular emphasis is placed on the climax of the conflict from 1976 to 1979 as the cause of the rising refugee influx. Discussing the influxes themselves, I shall also emphasise the growth of spontaneous settlement and the phenomenon of urban refugees, in distinction from the commonly-known rural characteristics of refugees in other parts of Africa.

The Change of Regime in Sudan and Implications for Refugee Policy 1969-1976

In Sudan the coup led by Gaafar el-Nimeiry in May 1969 brought to power the radical elements, particularly the SCP, who were previously excluded by the traditional ruling parties. The political programme of the new regime aimed not only to negotiate a peaceful settlement to the southern Sudan question, but also to weaken the traditional power base of the Umma and DUP. An uprising by the Ansar, the armed wing of the Umma, was violently crushed in March 1970. Al-Imam al-Hadi al-Mahdi, the spiritual leader of the Ansar, was killed on his way to Ethiopia, but a small contingent continued and joined leaders of the DUP and the Muslim Brothers in exile. It was the first time since independence that opposition groups from northern Sudan were driven into exile. The Ansar exodus was not simply a flight from persecution with the ultimate aim of reaching safe sanctuaries. It was considered as part of the religious duty of the *jihad*, whereby people retreat in order to reorganise and come back to fight. In exile the northern Sudanese opposition groups organised themselves under the banner of the National Front. As the regime had by then publicly declared its socialist orientation and allied itself with the socialist countries, primarily the USSR, the National Front also found support from Saudi Arabia. It took the National Front six years to prepare to strike back.

In the meantime, splits in the regime had led to the short-lived coup of 19 July 1971 which was associated with the Sudanese Communist Party. But Nimeiry was saved by a countercoup three days later and he then conducted a systematic campaign of persecution against the SCP. In order to eliminate all opposition, Nimeiry continued to rely on the security organisations established originally with the help of Soviet and East German allies in 1970. His regime strengthened its position by the successful negotiation of the Addis Ababa Agreement of March 1972, which offered Southern Sudan regional autonomy. That made it possible for Sudanese refugees abroad to return home. Consequently, the regime enjoyed a period of stability in which a new constitution was drawn up to provide legitimacy for a new presidential system governing the country through a single party, the Sudanese Socialist Union. It also broke with the USSR after the events of July 1971 and soon embraced the West.

As far as the relationship with Ethiopia was concerned, two views existed within the Sudanese Government in the period 1969 to 1976. Before July 1971 there was the view that the ELF should be treated as a liberation movement, while the Ethiopian regime was seen as reactionary and oppressive. This view was particularly espoused by Major Farouq Hamdalla, a member of the Revolutionary Council and Minister of the Interior until July 1971. The special Office for the Liberation Movements he established helped covertly to develop contacts with the ELF leadership. He also tried to bridge the gap that developed between the fighters inside Eritrea and the political leaders who publicised the cause in exile; and introduced the ELF to sympathetic Arab regimes and sought ways to provide facilities for shipment of arms through Sudan (interview with Khalifa Karar, Deputy Chief of Public Security 1970-1978, 15 May 1987, Khartoum).

Hamdalla's policies were suppressed after the coups of July 1971 which led to his execution. The regime adopted a new policy that aimed to secure the support of Emperor Haile Selassie for the peace negotiations on the Southern Sudan question. The role played by Haile Selassie in facilitating the Addis Ababa peace agreement of 1972 between the Sudanese Government and the Southern Sudan Liberation Movement also contributed to friendly relations between Sudan and Ethiopia (Khalid 1985: 540). Shortly after the Addis Ababa agreement, the two regimes agreed to settle the border conflict as well as promoting co-operation in areas of common interest, such as use of natural resources, communication and cultural exchanges (ibid.).

The friendly relationship between Sudan and Ethiopia was maintained even after Haile Selassie was deposed in 1974. The new regime in Ethiopia recognised the need for a political settlement to the Eritrean question. One of the leaders of the ruling Dergue (Committee), Aman Andom, who was Eritrean himself, submitted a programme to end the state of emergency in Eritrea and establish an amnesty for the exiled Eritreans. This led to optimism that the end of the Eritrean conflict was in sight and the repatriation of Eritrean refugees would then be possible. Sudan offered to help the process of negotiations. In late 1974, a committee was established to prepare for the negotiations, including the necessary step of unifying the Eritrean fronts. This failed as a result of conflict within the Ethiopian regime in which Aman Andom was killed. Attempts to secure a peaceful settlement in Eritrea were abandoned. Instead, the military offensives in Eritrea were resumed, intensifying in late 1974 and during 1975 (Lobban 1976: 343).

As hopes for peace in Eritrea were abandoned, representatives of the two Eritrean fronts sought ways to overcome their own differences with public support from the regime in Khartoum. A series of meetings in Khartoum in September 1975 resulted in a plan to achieve unity but it was unsuccessful and subsequent events led to further factionalism. From 1969, the refugee policy of building reset-tlement villages for Eritrean refugees continued, despite the technical difficulties of the resettlement programme supervised by COR and UNHCR. More progress was achieved in including refugee conven-tions in Sudanese national law. The 1974 Constitution contained a special article (Article 44) on the right to seek and enjoy asylum.

Also, in February 1974 the government became a signatory to the UN Convention Relating to the Status of Refugees, the 1967 Proto-col and the OAU Convention Governing Specific Aspects of the Refugee Problem in Africa of 1969. In May 1974, the Regulation of Asylum Act was signed by the President as the national law to deal specifically with the refugee phenomenon in Sudan (DRS 1974b).

The Role of the Security Organisations

One significant development in this period was the intervention in refugee policy of two security organisations established by Nimeiry's regime. Public Security and National Security were intelligence organisations created to ensure the security of the regime both inside and outside Sudan. As the presence of the Eritrean fronts and the refugees had security implications both inside Sudan and between Sudan and Ethiopia, the two organisations quickly became involved. The responsibility for dealing with the Eritrean fronts rested with Public Security as it was originally conceived by Hamdalla in 1970. The security organisations became particularly significant in the period after 1976 when the regime in Sudan adopted a more offen-sive policy towards Ethiopia. Consequently, it became difficult not only to draw the line between refugees and political activists but also to define the areas of competence of the two organisations as to what was internal and external security.

Escalation of Conflict in Sudan and Ethiopia and the Break with OAU Norms

After five years of training in Ethiopia and Libya, the Sudanese National Front fighters infiltrated into Khartoum and launched their attack to overthrow Nimeiry on 2 July 1976. The National Front con-tingent, estimated at 2,000 fighters, managed to seize strategic areas in Khartoum and Omdurman; the capital was thrown into chaos and it took the armed forces loyal to Nimeiry two days to regain control (Sylvester 1977: 76-79). The National Front attack revealed the vul-nerability of the Nimeiry regime; but it also revealed the weakness of the designs of the National Front as it did not gather mass support and quickly collapsed. In the aftermath of the operation, both sides, Nimeiry and the National Front, sought support from external allies. The remnants of the National Front retreated back to reorganise in their training camps in Ethiopia, and the Nimeiry regime sought military backing from Egypt by signing the Joint Defence Pact of 15 July 1976. The defence pact, which was to last for 25 years, gave Sudan and Egypt mutual military support to repel aggression against either of the two countries (Ahmed 1983: Annexe I).

After July 1976 there were unproductive diplomatic contacts between Sudan and Ethiopia. Ethiopia wanted to use the National Front's presence on its territory as a negotiating card against Nimeiry's support for the anti-Dergue groups in Sudan. Nimeiry, on the other hand, wanted to dismantle the National Front camps in Ethiopia while at the same time intensifying support for anti-Dergue groups in Sudan. In late December 1976 Nimeiry began to express hostility towards the Ethiopian leaders. He accused the Ethiopian regime and other Communist regimes of plotting to overthrow his government in Sudan (*SUNA Daily Newsletter* 1976). In January 1977 Nimeiry threatened that if Ethiopia continued plotting, he would retaliate. In addition to Sudan's own military capabilities Nimeiry warned that: 'the presence of 100,000 Eritrean and 40,000 Abyssinian refugees in Sudan is not a secret. Such a number is capable of causing endless trouble for the ruling military regime in Ethiopia' (*SUNA Daily Newsletter* 2 January 1977: 13).

Nimeiry invited the international media to visit the borders of Sudan in order to report to the world on the crimes committed by the Dergue against the Ethiopian people; and the People's National Assembly issued a public statement on 5 January 1977 urging the Sudanese masses to support Nimeiry's plans against the Dergue (ibid.: 14).

Nimeiry's hostility towards the Ethiopian leadership was further exacerbated by the intimacy that developed between the Ethiopian regime and the Soviet Union. The agreement signed between Ethiopia and the Soviet Union in December 1976, whereby the latter provided arms to Ethiopia, occurred when Nimeiry had been cementing links with the West. In February 1977, the ideological polarisation of the two regimes went a step further after the ascent of Mengistu Haile Mariam to become the Chairman of the Dergue. While it appeared that the US had lost its longstanding position in Ethiopia, the Soviet Union's actions in March and April 1977 were aimed at developing a Marxist-Leninist federation in the Horn of Africa, embracing Ethiopia and Somalia. When the attempts to include Somalia and the Eritrean rebels in such a federation failed with the Somali attack on Ethiopia and the continuation of the war in Eritrea, the Soviet Union settled for its new links with Ethiopia (Legum and Lee 1977: 5). In a televised speech, Nimeiry then attacked the Soviet Union, contending that its intensive arming of its supporters in Africa was part of a strategy to invade independent and free African countries under the camouflage of socialism and progress (26 June 1977; cited in Wai 1979: 310).

For Nimeiry, the ideological factor in the conflict with Ethiopia overshadowed the conflict with the Sudanese National Front. The commitment of the Ethiopian regime to Marxism-Leninism and the support offered by the Soviet Union actually blurred the principal differences between Nimeiry and his Sudanese opponents, who were also staunchly anti-communist and pro-Western. Al-Sadiq al-Mahdi, who met Nimeiry to negotiate reconciliation in July 1977, argued: '... the situation in Ethiopia has developed in such a way that we find ourselves in the odd position of aligning with the Soviet Union whether we want it or not. From a patriotic point of view, that cannot be acceptable' (Abdel Wahab 1987).

In June 1977, Nimeiry abandoned any pretence that his regime was still socialist and in November 1977 the US ban on arms sales to Sudan was lifted. In his efforts to circumvent the Soviet presence and to strengthen the anti-Soviet constellation, Nimeiry paid visits to Somalia and North Yemen. The anti-Soviet constellation calculated that the withdrawal of the US from Ethiopia and the arrival of the Soviet Union were inevitably going to threaten the security of the Red Sea, the Gulf, and the states that depend on these waterways both economically and strategically. At the Taez Conference on Red Sea security, which was attended by Sudan, Somalia and North Yemen, Nimeiry stated the position of these states:

> The future of the Red Sea depends on a clear vision of its coastal states which must aim at preserving its neutrality by making it a sea of peace rather than one of conflict. This goal relies, of course, on placing national interests before ideological loyalties, particularly when some circles portray these interests as backward and reactionary. (Cited in Al-Bazzazz 1985: 54)

However, of all the manifestations of hostility against the Ethiopian regime, the stepping up of the Eritrean resistance paid the most dividends. Helped by the support of significant numbers of the Eritrean population who deserted or fled the army reprisals after 1975, the Eritrean fronts reorganised themselves for a protracted struggle. Other resistance groups also mushroomed from central Ethiopia. Although Nimeiry's attempts to unify the Eritrean factions failed, the three fronts: ELF/RC, ELF-PLF and EPLF, achieved a sharp increase in their military capability. The combined force of three fronts was estimated to have 37,000 fighters by early 1977 (more than half the size of the Sudanese army); the ELF had the largest force of 22,000, the EPLF had 12,000 and the ELF-PLF had 3,000 fighters (Farer 1979: 48). Between January 1977 and August 1978, they captured the whole of Eritrea with the exception of Assab, Barentu, and Adi Qaieh. Half of the port of Massawa was captured and the capital, Asmara, came under siege (EPLF 1987). The victory of the Eritreans seemed irreversible. In June 1978 Ahmed Nasir, the ELF leader, visited Moscow to discuss plans for a negotiated settlement with Ethiopia and the EPLF publicly agreed to negotiate with the Ethiopian regime. Both insisted on the right of the Eritreans to self-determination.

In Sudan the successes of the Eritrean fronts were met with great enthusiasm. A mood of optimism prevailed and it was believed that the return of exiled Eritreans to their homes was inevitable. The security authorities tolerated the presence of refugees who fled the fighting to stay in areas which were normally sensitive but strategically important to the Eritrean fronts. In 1977 Nimeiry promised unequivocal support for the Eritreans. He even rejected al-Sadiq al-Mahdi's demand to dissociate from involvement in internal conflicts that negatively influenced Sudanese external relations, particularly with Ethiopia. As the Eritrean town of Keren was captured by the EPLF on 8 July 1977, the same day that the two Sudanese leaders met, Nimeiry predicted that more successes for the Eritreans would follow. He believed that not only in Eritrea, but in all other parts of Ethiopia, the people would rise against the Ethiopian regime (*Al-Siyasa* 1 July 1978: 7).

Among the other Ethiopian groups which opposed the regime in Ethiopia, Nimeiry's aggressive policy had a particular impact on the Ethiopian Democratic Union (EDU). The EDU was formed mainly by men who had held positions of power during Haile Selassie's regime. It was established in 1975 under the leadership of Ras Mangasha Seyoum, ex-governor of Tigray, General Nega Tagegne, former Commander of the Third Division of the Ethiopian Army and ex-governor of Begemder, and General Iyassu Mangasha, a retired military officer and ex-ambassador. From its inception the EDU had found support from Nimeiry's regime. At first, support for the EDU was seen as a reciprocation for the support offered to the Sudanese National Front by Ethiopia. However, after Sudan's national reconciliation, support continued for the EDU; and Sudan tried to transform the EDU from a political party in exile into a fighting organisation. EDU offices were opened in Khartoum and Gedaref and Public Security facilitated the free passage of assistance coming from friendly countries to the EDU (Ministry of the Interior 1985). By early 1977 the EDU had a fighting contingent of 6,000 men armed with Soviet weapons previously supplied to Nimeiry's regime (Ottaway and Blackburne 1978: 209).

The EDU now conducted successful offensives in which the towns of Homera and Metema were captured; but success was short-lived as the EDU forces were driven back by the Ethiopian army in November 1977. The EDU was also engaged in fighting with the Tigrayan People's Liberation Front (TPLF) founded in 1975. In 1978 the EDU fighters were forced out of Tigray. When they subsequently retreated into the Sudanese areas south of Gedaref, further attempts to use them to destabilise the Ethiopian regime became inconceivable. Subsequently the EDU broke into several factions.

Renunciation of the Aggressive Policy towards Ethiopia

By mid-1978 certain factors came into play that limited the aggressive policy pursued by Nimeiry since late 1976. One major factor was the changing fortunes of the Eritrean and Ethiopian opposition groups. Another was the decision by the Sudanese Government itself, to seek more peaceful relations with Ethiopia.

As the Eritrean fronts persisted in the demand for Eritrean self-determination at the height of their military success, Mengistu fought back. In June 1978 the Ethiopian army, encouraged by its recent defeat of Somalia and helped with reinforcements and new arms, conducted successful campaigns against the Eritreans and drove them out of the main towns in November 1978. The fighting and the withdrawal of the fronts were accompanied by the flight into Sudan of thousands of people from areas which were previously held by the Eritrean fronts (Farer 1979: 48).

The military reverses had a marked effect on Sudan as well as on the Eritrean fronts. As the hope of a total victory over the Ethiopian army was eclipsed, the responses of the Eritrean fronts proved that the EPLF had emerged as the stronger organisation. The EPLF withdrew to establish its own base in the north at Nacfa where it began to consolidate its defences. Its emerging strength derived not only from its military prowess, but also from its political programme based on self-reliance, which it applied in the areas under its control. The ELF, which had previously had superiority, suffered decline and division. Its rivalry with the EPLF turned into internecine war that lasted from 1977 until 1981, when the ELF was effectively defeated by the EPLF.

In early 1982 the ELF withdrew with its fighters into Sudan where differences among its leaders led to further division. The PLF also ended up as a fractured organisation after the secession of a group of pro-Iraqi Baathists in 1979. After 1982 the EPLF was the only organisation with a strong presence inside Eritrea.

These changes in the fortunes of the Eritrean groups affected Sudan: the Eritrean fronts had failed to achieve a victory over the Ethiopian Government, while the dominance of the EPLF with its independent line challenged Nimeiry's patronage of the Eritrean cause. The other political organisations such as the ELF, PLF and EDU, which had been favoured by Sudan, turned into a liability as they ended up in Sudan with their weapons and warring factions. The new situation of the Eritrean and Ethiopian opposition groups coincided with a pressing demand within Nimeiry's regime to change its policy towards Ethiopia. Inside Sudan, the return of the National Front after reconciliation with Nimeiry did not generate substantial concessions from the regime towards its former opponents (Hamid 1983: 326). However, the National Front's demand for de-escalation of the tension with Ethiopia elicited responses from certain groups within the regime itself. Two influential views were advanced by the Sudanese army and the National Security Organisation which, for their different reasons, wanted the aggressive policy towards Ethiopia to be discontinued.

There was a view within the regime that the army had always been reluctant to be dragged into a possible conflict in which it would be thinly spread against the Ethiopian army which was numerically superior: estimated at 244,000 troops compared with 65,000 in the Sudanese army (Ahmed 1983: 32). The tension with Ethiopia had not only turned into a personal confrontation between Nimeiry and Mengistu, but had also involved strengthening the opposition groups. It was, therefore, the army that faced the onerous consequences of the confrontation with Ethiopia. According to this view, the policy of confrontation with Ethiopia might backfire and the disaffected officers might act to destabilise Nimeiry's regime itself (Fadl al-Sid 1984: 99). This view was not merely conjecture. In at least one incident, in February 1979, a senior military officer, who was in charge of the Eastern Command, was recalled to Khartoum and eventually relieved of duty just at the time when the Ethiopian army trespassed 12 km into Sudanese territory.[1] Consequently, it

---

1. My interviews in Gedaref, January 1979, revealed that Major Abu Kadok, of the Eastern Command, expressed discontent with the lethargy of the ELF fighters and was willing to fight the Ethiopians. However, his superiors in Khartoum decided that the issue would be resolved in the talks between Ethiopia and Sudan held in Freetown in February 1979.

was primarily the security problems within Sudan that led to the pressure to abandon the aggressive policy towards Ethiopia.

The link between internal and external security had very significant implications for the rivalry between the two security organisations: National Security and Public Security. Both organisations had been subject to criticism during the reconciliation talks, to the extent that al-Sadiq al-Mahdi had demanded their abolition (*Al-Siyasa* 1 July 1978: 7). The situation was skilfully used by the Chief of National Security, Omar Mohammad al-Tayeb, to secure Nimeiry's approval for his plan to merge the two organisations. In mid-1978, he orchestrated a campaign to discredit Public Security. He accused it of being involved in external security issues and of failing to monitor the activities of subversive elements and the unchecked flow of weapons into the country (*Al Ayam* 30 June 1978). As far as the relationship with Ethiopia was concerned, Public Security was portrayed as the major supporter of the aggressive policy, as it was created in 1970 for this purpose. In August 1978 Public Security was dissolved: in February 1979 the duties of the organisation were transferred to the newly established State Security headed by Omar Mohammad al-Tayeb. This change in the security organisations coincided with the regime's move to seek improved relations with Ethiopia.

Attempts at *Rapprochement* with Ethiopia

The new policy of *rapprochement* with Ethiopia was accompanied by an intent to reassert the role of professional diplomacy. Mirghani Suleiman was appointed Ambassador to Ethiopia as part of the trend to normalise relations. The best opportunity was offered by the fact that in 1978 Nimeiry became the Chairman of the OAU and the OAU Summit was hosted in Khartoum. However, in his address to the summit Nimeiry's attitude towards the Ethiopian Government continued to be critical. In presenting the Eritrean conflict, Nimeiry emphasised that the conflict generated insecurity for Sudan. He explained to a press conference on 23 July 1978 that: 'This problem can only be solved politically; but Ethiopia insists that it is an internal problem and that other countries should not intervene; and this is where we differ from Ethiopia' (*SUNA Daily Newsletter* 24 July 1978).

As Nimeiry argued, the humanitarian problem was manifested in the destruction of villages and towns, killings and lack of security which drove people away from their land and caused starvation and displacement (ibid.). On the other hand, as the conflict had led to foreign intervention which had contributed to the escalation of the war, Sudan would continue to seek ways to resolve it peacefully. Raising the issue in the OAU forum was one way to seek a peaceful solution. The President promised to take it even further to the United Nations if that would lead to a solution acceptable to Ethiopia and to the Eritrean people (ibid.). The OAU summit decided on mediation between Ethiopia and Sudan. A mediation committee was selected under the chairmanship of President Siaka Stevens of Sierra Leone with a mandate to address all issues that were causing animosity between Sudan and Ethiopia (ibid.). Nimeiry welcomed the OAU initiative.

With these moves towards a solution to the differences between Sudan and Ethiopia, the period after the OAU conference witnessed a slow-down in the antagonistic propaganda campaign by both countries. By December 1978, reports from the Sudanese ambassador in Addis Ababa suggested that there were good indications that the summit meeting due to be held at Freetown in February 1979, would be successful (Woldegabriel 1980: 39). Unfortunately, it ended in failure. Mengistu accused Sudan of trying to dismember his country: Nimeiry, on the other hand, argued that Sudan had been dragged into the Ethiopian–Eritrean problem, as 200,000 refugees had fled to Sudan from the conflict. Mengistu insisted that Sudan had no right to intervene in the internal affairs of Ethiopia. Nimeiry argued that because of its consequences, the conflict was no longer an internal issue. The Ethiopian and Sudanese presidents departed without either conceding anything to the other (ibid.: 43-44).

Despite the failure of the Freetown Conference, the Sudanese authorities saw it as a positive event which offered the possibility of further meetings (Fadl al-Sid 1984: 71). This led to a more flexible attitude and a will to seek solutions acceptable to both sides, particularly with the concession by Sudan that a solution for the Eritrean question should be sought within the context of a united Ethiopia (Woldegabriel 1980: 44). This concession indicated a complete about turn by Nimeiry, involving not only a withdrawal of support for the Eritrean struggle but also a withdrawal from his preferred role as a mediator (EPLF 1987: 91).

Contacts between the two countries in the aftermath of the Freetown Summit were pursued through two active ambassadors, Yilma Tadessa in Khartoum and Mirghani Suleiman in Addis Ababa. Towards the end of 1979, as a result of bilateral diplomatic contact the two parties again agreed to hold discussions aimed at improving relations. As a result, Omar Mohammad al Tayeb, Chief of the State Security, conducted a secret visit to Addis Ababa in January 1980. The two governments agreed to discontinue support for opposition groups in their countries; to make efforts to improve relations between them; and to revive all specialised joint committees. More-over, they agreed to arrange for the presidents of the two countries to exchange visits (Fadl al-Sid 1984: 80).

In March 1980 Abdel Majid Hamid Khalil, First Vice President of Sudan, visited Ethiopia and met Mengistu Haile Mariam. It is believed that Abdel Majid discussed the Eritrean question with Mengistu in a closed session. He is reported to have stated that Mengistu showed interest in Sudan's experience of negotiating and ending the civil war in Southern Sudan (Woldegabriel 1980: 28). A high level Ethiopian delegation visited Sudan and attended the meetings of the third Congress of the SSU in May 1980. In the same month, the joint Ministerial Committee met to discuss common issues such as borders, refugees, trade and technical co-operation, and cultural exchanges. The Ministerial Committee meetings gener-ated further meetings of experts from both countries on political, defence, and security issues. In May 1980 Colonel Mengistu paid a visit to Sudan and a return visit by President Nimeiry was made in November 1980. As a result several Protocols were signed and joint projects were agreed upon: a highway linking Gedaref and Gondar, linking Khartoum and Addis Ababa by a microwave communica-tion system, cultural exchange, media co-operation and trade.

The Nature and Magnitude of the Influx from Ethiopia

As we have seen, the 1967-1970 influxes of Eritrean refugees were relatively sudden, and geographically specific, in that they involved refugees from one single area within Eritrea. By contrast, after the change of government in Ethiopia in 1974, the influxes came to be characterised by continuity and by ethnic and demographic diver-sity. The new influxes of refugees dispersed over distant and some-times inaccessible areas; they involved very large numbers of people, from a plethora of political groupings. The optimism raised by the success of the September 1974 coup in Ethiopia, and the hope that the Eritrean question would be solved, was completely over-turned by 1975 when the fighting was resumed in Eritrea; later, new ideological conflicts within Addis Ababa led to the persecution of urban groups, particularly student revolutionaries. Severe measures on the part of the government and the opposition movements led to another large influx of refugees into Sudan after 1975.

From that time, the refugees fleeing to Sudan followed two main routes, to Kassala and Wad el Heleiw border village. For the first

time, the refugees came from both Christian and Muslim communities and comprised people from both rural and urban backgrounds.
In Kassala area, 2,000 refugees arrived in March 1975 as a result of
fighting in Agordat and Tessenei. In the same month, fighting broke
out in Um Hagar resulting in the flight of another 3,000 refugees to
Kassala. These were mainly farmers, nomadic herdsmen and merchants. Most of them were Muslims. Wad el Heleiw (42 kilometres
away from the border) continued to host the 4,000 Eritreans who
had arrived in late 1967. In 1975, the town received refugees from
Um Hagar and from Tigray. They included Ethiopians, Somalis and
other groups of Arab origin. A report by the refugee project manager
in Showak provided a breakdown of the refugee population on 12
February 1975 (see table 3.1).

By mid-1975, the entrance points had begun to widen. While the
main entrance points remained in villages of the middle sector of the
border areas between Gedaref and Kassala (Humadaiet, Wad el
Heleiw, Doka, Wad Kawli), the Commissioner Kassala to Dakhlia
reported the arrival of 648 refugees (Eritreans and Yemenis) in Red
Sea Province (Cable to the Ministry of the Interior No.

Table 3.1 *Estimate of Numbers of Newly-Arrived Refugees, 1975*

Tribe	Population	% of Total Population
Sawerta	6,123	26.4
Beni Amer	4,539	19.6
Maria	2,662	11.5
Belein	2,625	11.3
Baria	189	0.8
Baza	234	1.0
Gaberta[1]	875	3.8
Christians[1]	3,433	14.8
West Africans	2,297	9.9
Yemenis and others of Arab origin[2]	126	0.5
Somalis	101	0.4
Total	23,204	100.0

Source: Project Manager's Report on a visit to Kassala and Wad el Heleiw,
12 December 1975, COR, Showak.

1. These two categories refer to religion, not ethnicity (the Gaberta were
   Ethiopian Muslims). I believe this is indicative of the ambivalence on the
   part of the authorities about how to categorise the new phenomenon of
   flight of Muslims as well as Christians.
2. All the Yemenis were eventually repatriated to North Yemen.

CRM1/35/G.12). The local government authorities, while reporting on different influxes, at the same time tried to collect refugees in one reception centre for newcomers located at Wad el Heleiw, but without much success. By the end of May 1975, the total number of refugees was given as 34,000.

At this juncture discrepancies began to occur between the COR and UNHCR estimates of the number of refugees. Apart from the objective reasons that it was difficult to monitor precisely all entrance points, the linking of refugee numbers to provision of assistance played a significant role in obscuring the real situation. Against the figures given by the local authorities, UNHCR estimated the number at only 10,000 (Sargisson 1975). A compromise position later resulted from a survey which stressed that discrepancies might have resulted from double counting by the authorities, or that refugees themselves overestimated their numbers, or that the number given by the authorities included the refugees who had arrived in 1967 as well as the 1975 arrivals. The number suggested by the survey was 13,000 (Gaymans 1975: 5). Estimates for pre-1975 refugees varied between 15,000 and 18,000.

Whatever the exact number of refugees, by the beginning of 1976 it had become clear that they were placing an intolerable burden on the local authorities in the border villages. Neither COR, nor the voluntary agencies in the field (Sudan Council of Churches, Asme Humanitas, and Eritrean Relief Association) were in a position to deploy their resources to all the different points of the border. Refugees were crossing at many border points away from the reception centre at Wad el Heleiw, and were depending mainly on the assistance offered by the local population.[2] The plight of the refugees and of the official Sudanese hosts came to be revealed only by a mission sponsored by the British NGO, OXFAM, which was carried out in spite of UNHCR's intransigence (Seyoum and Juel-Jensen 1976).[3]

This mission report revealed the serious situation of the Ethiopian refugees in the Sudanese border villages of Wad Kawli and Doka as well as those who had moved to Gedaref and Khartoum. The report

2. Voluntary donations by Sudanese citizens, together with NGO contributions, were estimated as US$30,000 (Beshir 1975: 373). Delays in response to the request for the 1975 group after the government request by the first Vice-President on 29 March 1975 and official approval 35 days later, and delay in actual arrival of food, were described in Chambers 1975: 9-10.

3. The Mission and its report were met with contempt from UNHCR, see e.g., letter UNHCR Representative, Khartoum to HQ Geneva (confidential) dated 17 April 1976, and letter R. Reynes UNHCR Representative Khartoum to J. J. Kardosa, Chief of regional section for East Africa (confidential) dated 6 May 1976 in Betts Papers, Refugee Studies Programme, Oxford.

identified three main categories of refugees. Firstly there were the rural Tigrayans:

> ... before their flight they would seek work during the dry season in Addis Ababa, Asmara or Homera to earn cash to buy a cow and then return to cultivate their own farm during the rainy season. Their work opportunities have gone and they are being harassed by the military. Those interviewed showed that above all they wished to cultivate a small piece of land and grow their food. At present they live in a condemned quarter of the town [Gedaref] which has a reputation of housing prostitutes. (Ibid.: 5)

Women depended on brewing beer and 70 per cent of the men earned a living as casual labourers. Five thousand of the 9,000 refugees who had arrived in Gedaref since February 1975 were non-Eritrean Ethiopians and most of them came from Tigray.

Secondly, another group of newcomers had arrived after the attack by the Ethiopian army on five towns in Begemder. Those who fled the towns were predominantly men. But 'from the surrounding areas all the families including women and children got away bringing in several small tractors, some with damaged tyres and none now with petrol' (ibid.: 7). A total of 2,600 refugees flooded into the little village of Wad Kawli and 'were kindly received by the local people who lent them empty *tukuls* and gave them straw for temporary shelter. The food shortage is acute and the community is facing disaster' (ibid.). Some 300 moved to the village of Doka and 500 to Basunda, but the daily trickle from Ethiopia maintained the number in Wad Kawli at 2,000-2,500, 'practically all Amharic-speaking from Begemder.'

The third group identified by the OXFAM mission consisted of the urban refugees in Khartoum. Their number was estimated at 3,000 to 4,000, mainly aged between seven and thirty years, including 600 to 700 secondary school children and 60 to 100 undergraduates from Haile Selassie First University (Addis Ababa University) and other higher education institutions. This group included young people who had worked in government service and who were identified by the report as being 'soldiers, administrators and health workers'. Five hundred women who came with their husbands were also identified (ibid.: 3-4). The large discrepancy between the OXFAM Report findings and the numbers registered by COR refugee registers in Khartoum in 1975 (1,943 refugees) can be explained by the fact that refugees were generally afraid to report in Khartoum for fear of being punished for their illegal movement to the town. The majority who registered were supplied with official letters either from the rural authorities or Public Security in Khartoum. The small number of Ethiopians registered by COR in 1975 (a total of 56) compared with the number of registered

Eritreans (1,887), can also be explained by the fact that there was a general belief among the refugees that the Sudanese were more sympathetic to the Eritreans for political, historical and cultural reasons. Ethiopian refugees in Khartoum, therefore, felt it more appropriate to register as Eritreans (see Karadawi 1978: 24-28).

Towards the end of 1976, new developments inside Ethiopia pushed much larger groups of refugees into exile. By then the EPRP (Ethiopian Peoples' Revolutionary Party) had begun to suffer from persecution in Addis Ababa (September 1976). The TPLF was born in 1975 in Tigray out of the Tigrayan National Organisation and aimed to fight not only the regime in Addis, but also its political adversaries in Tigray, the Ethiopian Democratic Union and the Ethiopian Peoples' Revolutionary Army (EPRA). In Eritrea, as we have seen, the war escalated in an unprecedented manner; the Eritrean fronts (particularly the EPLF and the ELF) pushed the government forces to withdraw to urban centres, leaving most of the countryside under the control of the fronts. The harassment of civilians in the urban areas pushed thousands to move out to join the fronts or to seek sanctuary in rural villages. They stayed there partly because they expected victory over the government forces to come soon, and partly because the fronts discouraged the movement of refugees into Sudan for fear of losing the backbone of the 'revolution' (Goitum 1979: 24). But adverse factors came to make such a stay impossible. The local economy completely stagnated. Insecurity made any kind of productive activity impossible. Transportation of goods was a problem because of the risks involved and because of shortage of petrol. Black marketeering flourished as goods were smuggled from Sudan, and the cost of living rose. Grain became increasingly scarce. Public services, such as health, education, water, and communications, all came to a standstill. Unemployment, lack of food, and the imminent threat to life led to the major exodus of 1977 and 1978 (ibid.: 25).

The economic crises generated by the seeming success of the resistance movements in Ethiopia and Tigray were compounded by the Ethiopian army's recovery, backed by the USSR. The intensive attacks launched during May and June 1978 produced another large exodus, and no authoritative source was able to ascertain its magnitude. Government sources began to give total numbers for Eritreans in Kassala province as 250,000 in 1978 (ibid.: 26). The Ethiopians in and around Gedaref were estimated to number 70,000. However, in August 1978, reports from the local authorities in the Blue Nile Province referred to the presence of 4,000 in Kurmuk and Geisan and an unknown number who had dispersed into the villages of Blue Nile Province (COR 1978). Various reasons were given for their flight (COR, individual cases. File (1971-1972) No. CR/17/B/2). During and after 1976 the refugees were mostly Oromos who claimed that they were fleeing military conscription, which was causing recruits to end up as cannon fodder in Eritrea and Tigray (COR 1978). In the southern part of the border near Nasir, a total of 4,000 Anuak and Nuer refugees were reported to have arrived (NCAR 1980: Vol. II section 2: 3), claiming that their lands had been confiscated by the Ethiopian Government. In the same year (1979) another influx from south-west Ethiopia crossed the border over Jebel Boma in Jonglei province. These refugees were from the Begol tribe. By April 1980 they numbered 3,000 (see map 3.1).

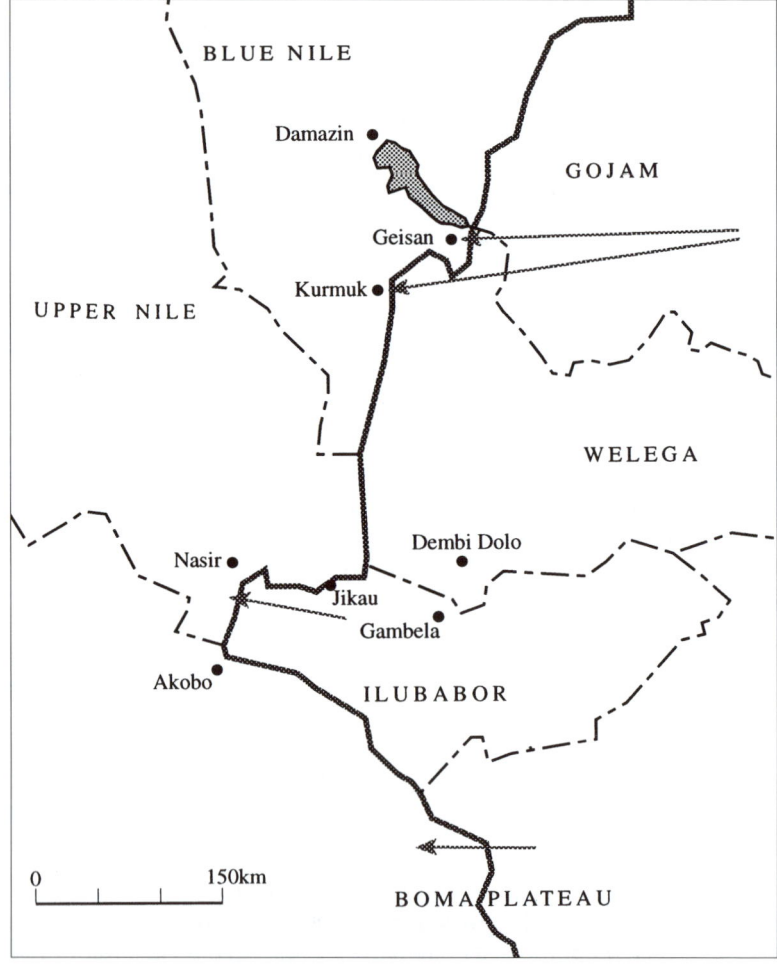

Map 3.1 *Refugee Influx in the Nile Provinces*

By September 1979, the number of refugees from Ethiopia was estimated at 390,000 and by March 1981 they numbered 419,000, based mainly in the Kassala and Red Sea provinces. These figures must be considered as simply indicative and not as exhaustive, because of the sensitivity and confidentiality with which both UNHCR and the security organisations treated the matter. Although the overall magnitude of the influx seems to have resulted from the confrontation between the regime in Ethiopia and resistance movements, other types of secondary, but nonetheless violent, conflict also produced refugees. Internal conflict and factionalism within and between the political organisations, as well as desertion and defection from the government, the army and the civil service brought their own refugees. Aggregate numbers are difficult, but there were peaks in 1977, 1979 and 1982 with the breakdown of the ELF/RC, when deserters moved into Sudan. The TPLF was also reported to have lost some members by desertion. Again, in 1982, as a result of the division within the ELF, members of this front moved into Sudan. Desertion from the Ethiopian army began with small bands of peasants who were forced to join the people's militia in 1916. By 1977, officers as well as soldiers began to arrive. While these categories were looked after by the State Security, it became clear that by 1982 a special group had emerged, consisting of people who needed protection from harassment by the political fronts to which they had previously belonged.

In planning for assistance it was necessary to rely on uncertain estimates, both because of the scale of the influx, and because it occurred over long stretches of the border, as well as for other reasons. It has been suggested by various studies on refugees that numbers are also particularly hard to ascertain because refugees simply move and live among their kith and kin as part of a 'spontaneous' pattern of migration. It will be argued here that although the government policy continued to advocate the transfer and settlement of refugees away from the border, certain factors led to the dominance of spontaneous settlement.

The Phenomenon of 'Spontaneous' Settlement

'Spontaneous' settlement is a term which has generally been used to describe the pattern of settlement whereby refugees reach rural areas in the host country and manage to re-establish survival strategies. Against the government policy of transferring and resettling refugees away from the border, the pattern of spontaneous settlement became dominant in the aftermath of 1975 as an alternative pattern of refugee settlement which was considered preferable to government-planned settlements.

As shown in Chapter 2, in 1967-1968 the government policy towards the refugees was to transfer the new arrivals from the borders, and, where voluntary repatriation was not forthcoming, to assist them to settle through economically viable projects, financed by UNHCR. This formula assumed UNHCR's unquestioning support. Before the influx of 1975, however, the assumption that UNHCR would assist did not prove to be well-founded. The experience of implementing the settlements of Qala en Nahal and Rejaf proved too expensive for UNHCR. The establishment of a settlement for 17,700 refugees stranded in Tokar district after 1970 was subject to delays, resulting from UNHCR's insistence on ensuring the viability of the new site, and on its investigating the possibility of using an operational partner other than COR.

While the new settlement areas were being considered, the 1975 influx began. From then on, the refugee aid network became overwhelmed by a relief operation, to the detriment of longer term settlement planning. Between 1975 and 1979, the rate of assistance fell short of the needs of the continuing influx. It reached an average of $2 million, allowing a per capita allocation of $11.8 per annum, for only 55,000 refugees. The inability or unwillingness of the partners (COR/UNHCR) to cope with the influx from 1975 onwards played a large part in forcing the refugees to seek ways of eking out a living on their own, in different parts of Sudan.

However, the failure of the refugee aid network to devise and implement settlement plans was always exacerbated by the political activists' belief that in assisted settlements, they would be unable to use the refugees as a political constituency. In rural areas the location of border villages allowed easy movement of recruits, and a means of transmitting propaganda to keep alive the hope of a victorious return under the aegis of the various fronts. Constellations of spontaneous rural settlements were preferred by the activists because of their political and strategic, rather than their economic value. Wad el Heleiw, a small village with a population of 2,500 in 1967, grew steadily to 13,000 in 1974, 23,000 in 1976 and 60,000 in 1982. The first arrivals between 1967 and 1977 settled among the Sudanese community working as wage labourers; as a result of the surplus of labour, they often received very low wages.

One basic factor which determined the movement and settlement of refugees from 1975 onwards was the fact that the base areas of the ELF, the EPLF and later the TPLF and EDU were located near the Sudanese border. Transit through these areas was obviously easier than through others controlled by the Ethiopian army. Furthermore, the policies of the fronts themselves were often decisive in shaping the refugee movement into Sudan.

According to Johnson (1979), the EPLF adopted a stronger line than the ELF in discouraging people from crossing the border, on the grounds that the liberation fronts could not win the war if the civilian population continued to leave. Therefore, they attempted to persuade intending refugees to return to their homes whenever possible. As a consequence, a much higher proportion crossed the border from the ELF base area. Furthermore, Kassala, which is closest to the ELF zone, was considerably easier to reach than Port Sudan, which was nearer to the EPLF area. Johnson also claims that the refugees themselves did not want to settle further into Sudan, because of the risk of cutting themselves off to a greater extent from their homeland. In their sojourn in Sudanese border villages:

> … they had access to almost daily bulletins on the military situation and the infrastructures established by the liberation fronts. They could also receive news of relatives living in Eritrea and, if necessary, could make short visits home, thus maintaining their sense of identity as Eritreans. (Johnson 1979: 417-421)

The situation in the villages south of Gedaref, Kassala and Port Sudan was more or less similar, in that thousands of refugees had settled without assistance from COR and UNHCR. In 1976, the inhabitants of Wad Kawli in Doka region expressed concern about the refugees as a political constituency and thus as a security threat. The EDU, which was relatively weak at that time, actually welcomed the transfer of the refugees, particularly from Wad Kawli, for fear of attacks by the Ethiopian army across the border (Seyoum and Juel-Jensen 1976: 8). This threat proved to be real when, in February 1979, the Ethiopian army moved twelve kilometres inside the Sudanese border and annexed Jebel al Lugdi, a move which created considerable tension within the Sudanese army, and prompted the evacuation of the refugees from Wad el Heleiw.

In the rural areas of the Blue Nile Province there was a classic case of spontaneous settlement. The refugees who arrived in 1978 comprised small groups who settled in Khor Yabus and around Kurmuk, Geisan, Agadi and Damazin (see map 3.1). They included a considerable number of Watawit who claimed that they were returning back home to Sudan and that they were not 'refugees' in the strict sense of the word, but the majority were Oromos. This made it possible for the Oromo Relief Association in 1980 and 1981 to establish small-scale projects, with the aim of providing their people with medical care, sanitation and adult education. After 1978, the dispersal of the refugee groups throughout the Blue Nile Region, as well as the reluctance of COR to allow UNHCR to open an office in Damazin and the failure to find finance for its proposed settlement in Agadi, allowed the continuation of spontaneous settlement in these areas.

The Anuak from Gambela had a long history of cross-border migration, moving across the borders whenever the political situation in Ethiopia or Sudan forced them to do so. Those who arrived in Nasir, Akobo and Jikau, were neglected by both the government and UNHCR. The latter believed that the Anuak were integrated with their kin and therefore did not require any assistance. At the same time, the government was facing difficulties in that area. Discontent among the southern units of the Sudanese army stationed in Upper Nile led to rebellion and the rebirth of Anya-Nya II in 1982; consequently, the government saw the Anuak as a security risk. A few Anuak found their way to Khartoum but failed to convince either UNHCR or COR of the difficulties they faced in Upper Nile. They failed to get jobs or education in Khartoum, and the tendency of both COR and UNHCR was to send them back to Upper Nile. In 1984 a group of 45 Anuak who opted to return to Ethiopia were subjected to considerable delays in Khartoum. The State Security suspected that they were agents or active members of the southern Sudanese resistance movement. To allow them to move with UNHCR protection to Addis Ababa, where the opposition to the Sudanese regime was strong and active, would have been politically disastrous (COR, 'Voluntary Repatriation', File No. CR/35/A/4. Exchanges between COR/UNHCR, COR/State Security, 1984).

Another factor which contributed to the proliferation of spontaneous settlement relates to the difficulties refugees faced at the point of entry. Considerable numbers of refugees had to leave the border areas either because of lack of hospitality on the part of the local population (as in the rural areas of the Red Sea province) or because their skills could not be used in rural life, or merely because of their social backgrounds. Some refugees found it hard to remain at the first point of entry, but were also unwilling to accept the blanket solution of moving to agriculture-based rural refugee settlements. These factors may explain why, by 1979, as many as 150,000 spontaneously settled or unassisted refugees lived in the major Sudanese towns rather than in rural areas.

The Urban Refugee Phenomenon

The movement of refugees from points of entry at the border to the main urban centres in Eastern Sudan and in Khartoum is a significant aspect of the refugee phenomenon which reached dramatic proportions by 1979. Since the 1960s, it has been widely assumed that urban refugees represent a distinct category, who differ from rural refugees in their background, pattern of movement, expectations, and needs. Urban refugees were identified as '[a] relatively smaller group of educated refugees who have left their countries with a definite plan to further their education which they cannot do at home' (Aall 1967: 37).

Both the 1967 and 1979 Pan-African refugee conferences identified urban refugees as young people who moved to towns in the host country in search of employment or educational opportunities. This perception led to the belief that urban refugees were individuals (rather than a clearly identifiable group) and bias therefore arose in favour of individual solutions. The Bureau of Placement and Education of African Refugees (BPEAR) of the OAU used such a basis. Some observers identify the pattern of movement of urban refugees as being individualistic and describe it as anticipatory, in contrast to the sudden acute mass movement of rural refugees (Kunz 1973).

Evidence from the Eastern Sudan suggests that while before 1975, the movement of urban refugees fitted this pattern, after 1975 it did not. Those who moved to urban areas did not necessarily move as individuals; moreover, they were not necessarily people from urban backgrounds. In fact, the movement from points of entry to towns within Eastern Sudan, or to Khartoum, was influenced by both 'push' and 'pull' factors. Two main stages in the flight of an urban refugee can theoretically be identified. Firstly, the movement, forced or otherwise, from the home area to a point of safety in Sudan. In legal terms this provides the condition for eligibility to refugee status. Secondly, the movement from the first point of entry to the Sudanese urban area. The latter movement can be classified as rural/urban migration, rather than as a classic refugee flight. Further moves may include departure overseas for study, work or resettlement (Karadawi 1983). After 1975, people of different ages, skills and social background moved into the four cities of the Eastern Region: Port Sudan, Kassala, Gedaref, as well as Khartoum. For a variety of reasons, each town became host to a unique combination of refugees.

Port Sudan

Port Sudan is the only major port in the country and the largest town in the arid province of the Red Sea. The Beni Amer and Habab, Amaraar and Bisharin, live along the international boundaries between Sudan and Ethiopia, but it should not be assumed that harmonious relations existed among them. Their tensions played a significant part in the pattern of settlement of the 16,800 refugees who

arrived in 1970 in Tokar district. The near famine conditions pre-
dominating in the district, the delay in provision of relief aid by
COR/UNHCR from Khartoum, and the failure of local authorities
to keep proper records, encouraged the refugees to move into the
nearby Tokar Delta and Port Sudan to live as squatters in the slums
which grew on the outskirts of the town (ibid.: 6). Between October
1977 and November 1978, the police in Tokar registered 11,000
refugees; in 1979, 6,000 (mostly children) arrived as a result of the
assault of the Ethiopian army on EPLF positions. The route followed
by these refugees from Eritrea into the Red Sea province made it
necessary for them to end their journey in Port Sudan because the
areas away from the town were extremely inhospitable. In fact, by
then, the police reported that there was no way to keep the refugees
in Garora or Tokar. They had to be transported by ERA trucks to
Port Sudan. The influx into Port Sudan included refugees of urban as
well as rural background.

There was a predominance of young people: according to one
survey, 50.7 per cent between the ages of one and nineteen years.
Only 5.2 per cent of the population were between 55 and 64 years.
The same survey showed that there was a higher percentage of
females (52.1 per cent) and a higher number of unmarried refugees
(59.5 per cent) compared with 33.7 per cent married, 4.4 per cent
widowed, 1 to 3 per cent divorced and 0.5 per cent separated. There
was a high ratio of female headed households (39.8 per cent) (ESRC
1982: 39-45). The majority (83 per cent) were Eritreans, both Muslim (73.6 per cent) and Christian (26.4 per cent). The refugees lived
mainly in Deim al-Nur, Salalab, Kuria, and Oleih.

Politically, the refugees in Port Sudan came from the EPLF area
which demanded a high degree of politicisation. Other Eritrean
political fronts such as the PLF had fewer representatives. Before
1982, in the absence of any formal programmes of assistance to
cover all refugees, the EPLF and its mass organisations had been
instrumental in channelling assistance to refugees from voluntary
agencies. Such a state of affairs was incompatible with the normative
policy which the government continued to adhere to in theory.

Kassala

The town of Kassala had its own unique characteristics, which
attracted Eritrean refugees. Its special appeal (apart from its proximity to the border which is 40 kilometres away) was its religious and
historical significance. Kassala is the spiritual capital of the Khatmiya sect which stretches over the Ethio-Sudanese border and has

had a great impact on the political history of both Sudan and Eritrea. The tomb of Sayed al-Hassan al-Mirghani (in Kassala) became the shrine of the Khatmiya, and Sayed Abu Bakr al-Mirghani in Keren had organised and chaired the Eritrean Muslim League party in 1946. Thus, the process by which the Khatmiya constituency was turned into a political party was begun in Eritrea and later repli-cated in Sudan by the formation of the People's Democratic Party by the Sudanese Khatmiya, under the spiritual guardianship of Sayed Ali al-Mirghani.

After Kassala emerged as a strategic and commercial centre in the Turco-Egyptian period, it was briefly annexed to Eritrea by the Ital-ian invasion of 1940-1941. Kassala town also has historic commercial links with the neighbouring lands of Eritrea. The flatness of the land extending from Eritrea into Kassala province allowed the mer-chant/commercial farmer class to engage in border trade; Eritrean coffee, sugar, and other commodities such as spirits, soap and clothes were exchanged for sorghum and sesame abundantly produced in Kassala (Goitum 1980: 128-129). Even with restrictions on such trade imposed by the government, black market commercial exchanges continued, especially the sale of spirits which had officially been banned in Kassala since 1977. Merchants in Kassala forged close links across the border. They were involved in supply of food needs to the ELF, and they also made money buying up Ethiopian cur-rency very cheaply in Sudan and then crossing the border to use the same currency in Ethiopia.

In 1962 Kassala was among the few places where the young ELF opened a branch office. After that time, the whole province of Kassala continued to be an important host for the ELF and Eritreans who came from ELF areas of activity. Its proximity, like Port Sudan and Gedaref, made it a convenient destination for refugees from both rural and urban areas in Eritrea. The refugees from Tessenei area settled in temporary camps on the outskirts of the town. Kassala province became the recipient of the largest refugee population in Sudan.

Like the refugee population in Port Sudan, the majority were young: 81.1 per cent were aged between 25 and 54, and only 12.4 per cent were above 55 years of age (COR 1986: 20). Also, the majority were Eritreans (93.7 per cent) as compared to other Ethiopian nationalities (2.9 per cent Tigrayans and 1.5 per cent Amharas) (ibid.: 28). Also, because of the predominance of the Mus-lim factor (68.5 per cent), 79.7 per cent of the population were mar-ried. The comparatively high rate of widows (9.6 per cent), compared to 3.1 per cent divorced and 7.6 per cent single, was said to be attributable to the war, the famine and the deterioration of

Table 3.2 *Refugees' Dates of Arrival in Kassala Area*

Date of Arrival	Percentage
1959 and before	0.8
1960-1969	8.5
1970-1974	7.1
1975-1979	47.9
1980-1985	35.7

Source: COR.

health conditions (ibid.). According to COR, for the majority of refugees (77.6 per cent), irrespective of sex, wage labour constituted the main source of income, and self-employment accounted only for 6.1 per cent of refugee income (ibid.).

The majority of the refugees arrived in the period from 1975 to 1979 (see table 3.2) during a period of military clashes between the Eritreans and the Ethiopian army and conflict amongst the fronts themselves.

Gedaref

Gedaref is the richest town of the province and the largest producer of sorghum and sesame. As such it has attracted migrants both from inside Sudan and from Ethiopia. The recognition of the town's potential to feed the colonial army in East Africa resulted in the introduction of mechanised rain-fed farming in 1943. That coincided with a high rate of migration from Eritrea (Goitum 1979: 32) and highland Ethiopia. In fact, one of the strategies for dealing with the Ethiopian refugees who came to Sudan after the Italian invasion of Ethiopia was to settle them in Gedaref to work as agricultural labourers (Al-Bashir 1978). After independence, the same method of land use was continued under the management of the Mechanised Farming Corporation, widening the opportunities for agrobased enterprises which need a large contingent of agricultural labour.

As a result of these historical patterns of migration to Gedaref town and its neighbouring area, the refugees who arrived in and after 1975, were dispersed over 21 of Gedaref's 34 residential quarters, particularly in areas previously occupied by other Ethiopians (Mahmoud 1986:23). This fact came to influence the very issue of the eligibility of the 1975 group for refugee status (ibid.: 71). Another characteristic of the refugees in Gedaref was the over-representation of non-Eritreans (Ethiopians). This had a particular impact on the relationships between significant sectors in the town community and the refugee community. The prevalence of non-Eritreans is clear from table 3.3.

Again, as was the case in Port Sudan and Kassala, the refugees were mostly young. The majority were between the ages of 20 to 39 years; 59 per cent were married. The diversity of the refugee community made Gedaref area an arena for the politics of the EDU and TPLF in particular. But of special significance is the fact that this diversity allowed for the emergence of exceptional groups such as the Falasha (Ethiopian Jews), who came to international prominence with their Israeli-organised mass exodus in 1984 and 1985. The Falasha movement began in individual pattern in 1979 and became the subject of COR reports in 1980.

The early refugees who arrived in the town in 1975, came from a variety of backgrounds, and many were agriculturists. At that stage, the belief that rural settlement was potentially a solution for most of them still prevailed (Gaymans 1975: 4). Another group of refugees came to the town in 1977, after the recapture of the Ethiopian town of Homera, which had been taken by the Ethiopian Democratic Union. That brought a large number of Tigrayans whose experience, language and religion were shared with the Eritreans. Some were from urban backgrounds and the alternative of 'semi-urban settlement' was attempted in 1979-80. The complexity of the refugee situation was exacerbated by the continuing trickle from Tigray, which, in the two years after September 1982, became a large influx of drought-affected people (Zemu 1982).

Table 3.3 *Percentage of Ethnic Groups among Refugees in Gedaref*

Ethnic Group	Percentage
Amhara	49
Tigriniya	15
Tigre	13
Tigray	12
Oromo	3
Eritrean	3
Other	5

Source: COR.

Editor's note: The distinction between 'Tigre' and 'Tigray' as ethnic groups is a confusing one. 'Eritreans', too, is not an ethnic designation but refers to 'people from Eritrea' of whatever ethnicity. One may perhaps assume that 'Tigray' here means 'people from Tigray' (of whatever ethnicity), while 'Tigre' means 'people of the Tigre ethnic group, but not from Tigray'.

Khartoum

The capital city, Khartoum, shared the characteristics of all the capital cities in the developing world. It was the place for all the facilities that the young, ambitious refugees hoped to find. In particular, it seemed to offer the opportunity to resume studies, or to leave Sudan for other countries.

Like the other towns of north-eastern Sudan, Khartoum had long known some migration from Ethiopia of unskilled labourers (Goitum 1979: 32). The most memorable influx of refugees were those who came as a result of the Italian invasion and occupation of Ethiopia in the period between 1935 and 1941. These eventually returned home after the defeat of the Italians and restoration of the Emperor Haile Selassie, but individuals continued to arrive at times. Documents of the Ministry of the Interior referred to a group of Ethiopians in Khartoum who tried in 1959 to organise an opposition group against the Imperial Government, with the goal of establishing a 'democratic republican regime in Ethiopia'. The activities of these exiles were constantly detected and suppressed by Ethiopian agents. By the mid-1960s, especially after the October Revolution of 1964, the Ethiopian Embassy was very active in Khartoum, and the Ambassador began publicly to threaten the Sudanese authorities.

By 1971, a trickle of Ethiopian students had gathered in Khartoum. Approximately 100 students of different ethnic origins had come from Addis Ababa, allegedly as a result of the repression of the militant student movement which began to challenge the government in 1965. These were mainly secondary school students, but there were also a few university students. At first the students were looked after and closely monitored by Public Security in Khartoum which offered accommodation at the Police Recruits School at Omdurman. Due to the expense and the need to meet the educational requirements of the refugees, Public Security had to transfer responsibility to the Commissioner for Refugees who, accordingly, established a desk for 'individual cases'. The students, by approval of the Minister of the Interior, were individually offered legal refugee status. While contacts with the Ministry of Education were made for their placement in Sudanese schools, the Ministry of the Treasury approved the release every week of £S100 to pay for their accommodation in third-class hotels and other living expenses.

While this group were considered to be refugees by the government, UNHCR doubted their motives for leaving their homeland. They were labelled 'education seekers' (Karadawi 1983: 11). This difference of opinion arose from the serious shortcomings of the legal definition of refugees. Although the definitions contained in the UNHCR Statute and the 1951 UN Convention Relating to the Status of Refugees were the same, the two documents charged different bodies with applying the definition. Under the 1951 Convention, the host government is the authority which decides who should be accorded refugee status. However, according to the Statute, UNHCR has the final say as to who should be considered a refugee and therefore have the right to international protection under its mandate. As Holborn stated in her study on UNHCR:

> ... recognition as a refugee by the UNHCR will not by itself either secure the admission of a refugee to a country or confer a legal status, and determination of eligibility by one country does not necessarily confer refugee status upon the individual in other countries. (Quoted in de Voe 1980: 91)

In 1971 Sudan offered official recognition to these refugees and UNHCR did not. After 1975 the situation of the urban refugees in Khartoum became more complicated. UNHCR would not recognise refugees in Khartoum until COR provided identity papers as evidence of permission from the government. COR could not provide papers for every refugee who arrived in Khartoum because of overwhelming pressure from other government authorities to restrict the free movement of refugees to Khartoum. The refugees in Khartoum were continually pushed to find their own way without administrative or material assistance.

Although it is difficult to trace patterns in the movements of individuals or small groups of refugees, it is clear from COR records that by 1975 the flow was taking a different shape. It must be noted, however, that these records covered only a small proportion of the real number who needed its administrative assistance. Then the cash assistance provided before by the government was stopped and the individual refugees coming in 1975 had to fend for themselves. The numbers presented in tables 3.4 and 3.5 are only to indicate the size of the post-1975 group, compared with the pre-1975 individual movement of refugees. Between 1975 and 1978, COR registered refugees as either 'workers' or 'students'. Within these categories there was a great diversity of skills and levels of education. In fact, it was possible for a refugee to move between the two groups as the opportunity arose. A student would accept a paid job until he settled in a school, or a worker would take the opportunity to join an educational establishment. Table 3.5 shows that 96.5 per cent came in the period between 1975 and 1978. The increasing number of refugees in 1978 indicates that, in spite of the decision to evict

Table 3.4 *Numbers of Refugees Registered in Khartoum, 1975-1978[1]*

Year	Workers	Students	Eritreans	Ethiopians	Total
1975	923	1,020	1,887	56	1,943
1976	3,708	2,281	5,760	229	5,989
1977	5,158	2,712	7,610	260	7,870
1978	4,041	2,245	5,977	309	6,286
Total	13,830	8,258	21,234	854	22,088

Source: Office of the Commissioner for Refugees, different files on individual cases 1975-78.

1. The records were arbitrarily ended in May/June 1978 when the decision was taken to evict the refugees from Khartoum on the occasion of the OAU summit meeting. A new system of registration under a committee was introduced to cover those already in Khartoum.

refugees in June of that year, the authorities were unable to prevent the influxes from other areas of Eastern Sudan. After that time, attempts to evict the refugees from the city were frequently made, though without much success.

The refugee group in Khartoum was predominantly from the urban areas in Ethiopia and Eritrea (98.1 per cent of the Eritreans were from Asmara, Massawa, Dekemhare, Mendifera, Keren, Agordat and Tessenei (Goitum 1980: 36)). Most were young opportunity seekers, who abhorred the prospect of going back to the rural areas of Sudan. On the contrary, they often tried to find means of leaving Sudan. In 1979 a survey conducted in Khartoum revealed that the majority (75 per cent) expressed their wish to leave the country (ibid.: 40).

Between 1977 and 1982, 37,000 Convention Travel Documents (refugee passports) were issued by COR (COR Individual Cases

Table 3.5 *Date of Entry to Sudan among the Refugee Population in Khartoum, 1974-1978*

Year	Percentage of Total
1974	3.5
1975	5.9
1976	18.9
1977	28.8
1978	42.9
Total	100.0

Source: Goitum 1980.

Unit 1982). Eighty-five per cent of the passports were issued for refugees to travel to Arab countries to find work (Saudi Arabia, the Gulf States, Libya) or places to study (principally Iraq, Syria, Egypt and Libya, exclusively for Eritreans). The other 15 per cent, mainly Ethiopians or Christian Eritreans, travelled to European countries, mostly for education, or for reunion with their families. In addition, large numbers of refugees queued to be accepted for resettlement in second countries of asylum, which was made possible by the introduction of the American resettlement programme in 1981 and the Canadian resettlement programme in 1982.

Conclusion

It is evident from this overall view that the refugee problem of 1975 onwards was much more complex than it had been between 1965 and 1970. It was not possible to contain the refugee problem by settling the newcomers in far-flung, uninhabited rural areas. The refugee movement across the eastern border grew to a point where it was beyond the control of any local, regional or central authority. The right of offering legal status to refugees, which was a recognised right of the state, turned into a meaningless bureaucratic routine.

It is clear that the change in the nature of the problems that generated refugees in Ethiopia had a direct effect on their patterns of movement into Sudan, and within it. The refugees began to adopt a strategy of 'spontaneous resettlement', as vast numbers of them trekked into the main towns of north-eastern Sudan. As a result, the concept of the refugees as a 'threat' was about to take on a new dimension, in that their presence in towns and 'refugee-affected areas' was considered by the people in those towns and by the local authorities as an obstacle to normal life. This xenophobic perception of the refugees at the local level can be compared with the national perception of refugees as a threat to national and interstate stability, as seen in the previous chapter. This is the reason why the very towns which had a special attraction for the refugees after 1975, came to adopt a particularly hostile attitude towards them. Khartoum first made the decision to evict refugees in June 1978, Kassala in the same year, and Gedaref in 1979. Other discriminatory resolutions against the refugees were taken in 1979. We will argue that this feeling of threat, imaginary or real, was exacerbated by the responses and attitudes to the situation inside Sudan itself. Refugees had come to be viewed as a source of problems for Sudan at the domestic level.

References

Aall, C. (1967) 'Refugee Problems in Southern Africa' in Hamrell, S. (ed.) *Refugee Problems in Africa*, Uppsala: SIAS.

Abdel Wahab, M. A. W. (1987) 'The National Reconciliation', *Al Siyasa*, Khartoum, 1 July.

Ahmed, I. A. (1983) 'Conflict in the Horn of Africa and its Implications for the Sudanese National Security' (monograph), The National Defence College, Khartoum.

Al-Bashir, A. R. (1978) 'Problems of Settlement of Immigrants and Refugees in Sudanese Society', D.Phil. Thesis, St. Antony's College, University of Oxford.

Al-Bazzazz, H. (1985) 'The Red Sea and the Arabian Gulf' in Farid, A.M. (ed.) *The Red Sea*, Croom Helm and Arab Research Centre, London.

Chambers, R. (1975) 'Rural Refugees in Africa: Observations on UNHCR Policies and Practices', HCR/140/18/75, Geneva, July 1975.

COR (1978) Report of a Mission to the Blue Nile Province, August 1978.

—— (1986) *Socio-Economic Survey on the Spontaneously Settled Refugees in Kassala*, Khartoum.

Democratic Republic of Sudan (DRS) (1974) *The 1974 Constitution.*

—— (1974b) Act No. 45, *The Sudan Government Gazette No. 1162 – Legislation Supplement.*

De Voe, M. (1980) 'Farming Refugees as Clients', *International Migration Review* 15: 91.

EPLF (1987) Political Report and the Programme for the National Democratic Revolution, Second Congress 19 March 1987 (Arabic).

ESRC (1982) Socio-Economic Survey of Spontaneously Settled Refugees in Port Sudan, Research Report No. 13, Khartoum, February.

Fadl al-Sid, O. A. (1984) 'The Eritrean Question and its Effects on the Sudan' (Arabic), National Defence College, Khartoum.

Farer, T. (1979) *War Clouds on the Horn of Africa: A Crisis of Detente* (revised edn.; 1st edn. 1976), New York: Carnegie Endowment.

Gaymans, H. (1975) 'Report of a Socio-Economic Survey Among Refugees in Wad el Heleiw', Khartoum: UNHCR/COR.

Goitum, E. (1979) 'Prospects and Retrospects of the Recent Mass Mobility of the Eritrean Refugees to the Three Towns 1974-1978', unpublished dissertation, University of Khartoum, Department of Geography.

–– (1980) 'Adaptation and Integration: the Case of the Eritrean Refugees in the Three Towns 1974-1979', dissertation, Khartoum University, January 1980.

Hamid, M. B. (1983) 'Confrontation and Reconciliation within an African Context: The Case of Sudan', *Third World Quarterly* 5(2).

Johnson, T. (1979) 'Eritrean Refugees in the Sudan', *Disasters* 3(4): 417-21.

Karadawi, A. (1978) 'A Note on Urban Refugees in the Sudan: 1975-1978', COR, Khartoum.

–– (1983) 'Urban Refugees', paper submitted to a symposium on 'Causes and Consequences of Refugee Migrations in the Developing World', Hecla Island, Manitoba, August 1983.

Khalid, M. (1985) *Al Sudan wa Al Nafaq al Muzlim*, London, Malta: Aedani Ltd.

Khalifa, S. A. (1969) *Arna Fi Eritrea* (Arabic) Khartoum.

Kunz, E. F. (1973) 'The Refugee in Flight: Kinetic Models and Forms of Displacement', *International Migration Review* 7(2): 125-146.

Legum, C. and Lee, B. (1977) *Conflict in the Horn of Africa*, London: Rex Collins.

Lobban, R. (1976) 'The Eritrean War, Issues and Implications', *Canadian Journal of African Studies* 10: 343.

Mahmoud, U. A. (1986) 'Self-settled Refugees in Gedaref', UNHCR Report, Khartoum.

Ministry of the Interior (1985) 'The Ethiopian Organisations in the Sudan', Memorandum, External Security Division, Khartoum.

NCAR (1980) Documentation for the 1980 Conference: Background and Project Summaries, Vol.II, Khartoum.

Ottaway, M. and Blackburne, D. (1978) *Ethiopia: An Empire in Revolution*, New York.

Sargison, P. (1975) Mission Report, 17 May.

Seyoum, M. and Juel-Jensen, B. (1976) 'Investigation of the Problems of Ethiopian Refugees in the Sudan', OXFAM, April.

SUNA (Sudan News Agency) *Daily Newsletter* (1976) 'Nimeiry's Public Speech in Gedaref 26.12.1976', Khartoum, 27 December.

–– (1977) 'President's Address on Independence Day' (Arabic), 2 January.

Sylvester, A. (1977) *Sudan under Nimeiry*, London: Bodley Head.

Wai, D.M. (1979) 'The Sudan: Domestic Politics and Foreign Relations under Nimeiry', *African Affairs* 78: 310.

Woldegabriel, B. (1980) 'Survey of Sudanese-Ethiopian Relations, especially since the Freetown Conference, Feb.1979', B.A. Dissertation, African and Asian Studies Institute, University of Khartoum.

Zemu, A. (1982) Letter to the author, December.

4

Competing Interests within the Sudanese Bureaucracy and Their Consequences for Refugee Policy

The change of policy to one which aimed at improving relations with Ethiopia left the Sudanese regime with the dilemma of how to deal with the refugee problem. It was evident at the time that neither the Eritrean nor other Ethiopian opposition groups were capable of achieving a decisive victory against the Ethiopian regime. Additionally, there was no way that Sudan could force Ethiopia to create a political atmosphere that would enable the refugees to return to their homes. Since it was not possible to force the contending parties to share responsibility, the refugees became a matter of internal policy for Sudan alone.

As in 1966-1967, the Sudanese authorities realised that they had to adopt measures to contain the problem. However, after 1978 the problem became more acute. Facing the disorganised spread of refugees over different regions, the authorities held conflicting views on how to deal with them and this led to competing policies and the fragmentation of authority among the various government agents. Two factors relating to the structure of the Sudanese Government proved significant for refugee policy: firstly, the marginal position of COR within the central government, particularly its position in the Ministry of the Interior and its relations with the security organisations; and secondly, the administrative decentralisation measures and their impact on refugee policy.

This fragmentation of authority worked to the detriment of the refugees. It will be seen that, in acting to minimise the threat to internal order, Sudan pursued measures to remove refugees from towns and border areas; but the humanitarian policy failed to reconcile the needs of the refugees and the needs of the government.

Marginalisation of the Office of the Commissioner for Refugees

As described in Chapter 2, after 1967 COR was established as part of the Ministry of the Interior in Khartoum. It was established on the basis that the refugee issue was of national concern, and that the central government should therefore oversee refugee policy. Refugee issues were seen to be most closely related to the work of the central Ministry of the Interior, which largely dealt with matters of internal security. This arrangement helped to resolve the conflict which emerged between the Ministry of Local Government (as represented by the Provincial Commissioners) and the Ministry of the Interior.

However, COR fell prey to another type of conflict within the Ministry of the Interior itself which was related to the way the ministry was structured after independence. As a continuation of the office of the colonial Civil Secretary, the ministry continued to be dominated by civilian administrators. It was run by a permanent Under-Secretary who was responsible, in particular, for overseeing the police and prison forces. Another section located within the ministry, also run by civilians, was under the Deputy Under-Secretary. This latter section, called General Affairs, included subsections for Southern Sudan, the Press, Pilgrimage, and Christian missionary activities, as well as COR. The structure was criticised by the police force who saw the Ministry of the Interior primarily as a security organisation. From 1966 onwards, they made systematic efforts to change the system, arguing that the Ministry of the Interior and all its subsections (including COR) should be run by career policemen.

Immediately after the coup of 1969, the police expressed their support for the new regime, and, in a memorandum addressed to Faroug Hamdalla, the Minister of the Interior, they stressed the necessity of restructuring the ministry as a security organisation. The memorandum was signed by all the senior police officers and mainly consisted of an attack against the civilian senior staff of the ministry, particularly against the Under-Secretary. They argued that many of the civilian functions of the Under-Secretary could be transferred to other ministries, such as the Ministry for Local Government and the Ministry for Southern Affairs. The remaining functions of the Ministry of the Interior were purely of a security nature:

> ... the argument that the Ministry functions differently from the police cannot be supported by logic or reality; because the departments of refugees, the international borders, and missionary affairs are part and parcel of the security work and cannot be separated from it. ('Memoran-

dum by police officers to Minister of Interior', Ministry of the Interior File 48/A/1, June 1969)

It is clear that police officers simply wanted the removal of the civilian administration: 'It is high time for the post of the Under-Secretary to go to the Police Director so that all responsibilities of the Ministry can be run without an intermediary' (Circular by the Minister, MOI File M/48/A/1, 27 October 1970).

Faroug Hamdalla did not respond immediately to the demands of the police officers, mainly because he needed time to implement his own version of radical change within the ministry, including the restructuring of the police force. Nonetheless, the police continued to campaign for what they termed the 'policisation'[1] of the Ministry of the Interior, and the Director of Police himself was eventually promoted to work directly with the minister. After his promotion, he argued that his responsibilities overlapped with the role of the Under-Secretary and that this was causing confusion, not only within the Ministry of the Interior, but also in other ministries (Siddig 1970). Eventually the dismantling of the civilian administration was implemented by transferring some of the departments to other ministries as suggested by the police, and the Under-Secretary and his staff were forced to resign. COR and the Archives Department were the only civilian sections allowed to remain within the Ministry of the Interior.

At the same time, the crisis in November 1970, involving a collision between Faroug Hamdalla and Nimeiry, led to further changes in the Ministry of the Interior. Faroug Hamdalla and two members of the ten man Revolutionary Council were accused of leaking the deliberations of the council to the SCP. (The three were later executed by Nimeiry in the aftermath of the aborted coup of 19 July 1971.) In February 1971, as a result of a duel between the pro-communist group and Nimeiry, Faroug Hamdalla was deposed. With his departure, the minister's office established by him also had to go. The ousting of the Under-Secretary and the closure of the office provided a good opportunity for the police to make their final move to gain control of the Ministry of the Interior.

Abul Gasim Mohammad Ibrahim, who succeeded Faroug Hamdalla as Minister, approved the plan to reorganise the Ministry of the Interior as suggested by the police. In April 1971 an official circular declared that the Ministry of the Interior would be divided into five departments, namely the Police, Public Security, Prisons, Finance,

1. The term 'Bawlasa' (policisation) was used by Ali Mohammad Siddig, the Police Director, in 1970 (see Memorandum to the Minister, Police HQ, Ministry of the Interior, 1 February 1970).

and the Central Archives (MOI circular no. MOI/48/A/1). COR was not mentioned. Each of the five departments would be headed by a director. The five directors in turn would be responsible to a Director General. A senior police officer, Ziada Satti, was appointed to this post, and the 'policisation' process then began in earnest. As for COR, which remained as the only civilian-run office, attempts were made to bring it under the control of the police as well. However, these attempts were first slowed down and then abandoned.

Firstly, the resistance of the civilian staff of COR to the idea of joining the police was strengthened by the international links it had acquired through daily cooperation with UNHCR. The relationship which had developed between COR and the UNHCR Branch Office in Khartoum, established in 1968, was so close that COR saw its mandate as similar to that of UNHCR. The exposure of the Sudanese staff to the international forums in Africa, where the Commissioner for Refugees acted as the OAU/BPEAR National Correspondent, and Europe, where Sudan used to sit as an observer in the UNHCR meetings, had offered new experiences that had made them see the management of the refugee problem in a broader context, and had led them to argue against the perception of the refugees as merely a security threat. The successful establishment of the Qala en Nahal refugee settlement in Eastern Sudan offered a practical example of a humane solution to the refugee problem. In addition, the energetic role played by COR in preparing the plan for the repatriation of Sudanese refugees both before and after the 1972 Addis Ababa Agreement, also boosted its image as a humanitarian organisation with strong international links. This was one of the rare occasions when UNHCR was entrusted by the UN as a whole with the role of preparing a relief and rehabilitation plan for refugees after they had returned to their own home (UNGA/Res.2958 (XXVII) 12 December 1972; see also Betts 1974). The intensive involvement of UNHCR in co-ordinating international assistance for the Southern Sudanese had necessitated the involvement of its national counterpart, COR.[2] Thus the image of COR as a non-security oriented organisation had been reinforced.

Secondly, although the perception of the refugees as a threat to internal security had not disappeared, the role of the police in refugee affairs had gradually been weakened by the establishment of Public Security as an autonomous security organisation. Before 1971, the police could argue strongly that refugee work was basically secu-

2. The response to UNHCR's appeal of July 1972 raised $19,684,404. By the end of 1973 1,190,230 persons had returned from exile and the bush and were helped by the Resettlement Commissioner.

rity work and as such it was part and parcel of their responsibility. However, after the successful attempts to resolve the Southern Sudanese question, the bulk of the security work which had related mainly to Sudanese refugees abroad, was no longer needed. Public Security was established by the regime that came to power in 1969 as a way of creating a politically reliable secret police force. With the establishment of Public Security, which had a professional interest in the security aspect of the refugee phenomenon, the police force's interest in refugees became irrelevant.

As a result of these developments, COR was protected from the hegemonic moves of the police.[3] However, it was left as a somewhat marginalised office staffed by three administrators and six clerical staff, occupying three office rooms in the main building of the Ministry of the Interior in Khartoum. The relief operation for the Southern Sudanese ended COR's involvement with the Southern Sudanese, who then came under the auspices of the Provisional High Executive Council for the Southern Region. By the end of 1973, COR was left to manage only two refugee settlements, at Qala en Nahal (Eritreans) and at Rejaf (Congolese). Both were administered by staff seconded from other government departments.

As a small office within a Ministry of the Interior run by the police, who did not share its enthusiasm for a humanitarian agenda for the treatment of refugees, COR remained in an anomalous position. Institutional growth, as well as promotion opportunities for the staff, became ever more unlikely. The office received no additional financial inputs during 1973 and 1974. The only solution for COR was to tighten its mandate and to consolidate its link with UNHCR. In order to clarify its mandate, it succeeded in making the government sign the 1951 Convention Relating to the Status of Refugees, the 1967 Protocol and the OAU Convention Governing Specific Aspects of the Refugee Problem in Africa in 1974. It also succeeded in pushing for the promulgation of the 1974 Regulation of Asylum Act. However, by 1974 its relationship with UNHCR was beginning to deteriorate. Qala en Nahal refugee settlement proved to be too costly for UNHCR and doubts were also raised about the competence of COR in implementing the Rejaf settlement project.[4] At the

3. Several attempts were made to transfer the office to local government, Foreign Affairs ministries and even to the Council of Ministers without success, except for a brief period from May 1979 to June 1980 when the office was put under the authority of the Cabinet Minister for the Council of Ministers' Affairs.

4. The first Project Manager for the Congolese refugee settlement was relieved of his job for mismanagement in February 1972. Further problems arose when the Sudanese Bari returned home and strongly objected to having the Congolese settle in their traditional homeland.

same time, attempts to have staff seconded from local government and to raise money to implement the third settlement in Maharragat were not immediately successful. The 16,700 refugees who had arrived in Tokar District in March 1970 had begun to disperse to seek a living in the Tokar Delta and Port Sudan without assistance (see Chapter 5). The apparent decline in the rate of the refugee influx between 1971 and 1974 contributed to the stagnation of COR. As a result, when the new influx began in 1995, COR was not capable of responding and was unable to implement the 1974 Asylum Act.

Consequences of the Anomalous Status of the Office of the Commissioner for Refugees

The anomalous status of COR was reflected in its administrative isolation: its political alienation and the fact that it was a central government department. It did not have its own staff to perform the duties stipulated in the Regulation of Asylum Act of 1974 (DRS 1974). As large influxes began to occur and recur between 1975 and 1978, COR was not able to implement Article 3(2) which stated that: 'The minister should appoint a suitable person to perform the functions of the Commissioner in the provinces.' It had instead to depend on its unregulated relationship with the local government authorities.

The articles on 'Registration of Refugees' and 'Asylum Application Procedures' also had to be ignored in the absence of a competent and trained staff to implement them. Article 4 stipulated that each Assistant Commissioner should keep a register of applicants for asylum and a list of the names of all the refugees who entered the area 'where he worked'. Having no staff in the provinces and being unable to force the local authorities to implement these procedures, the Commissioner had to accept unsubstantiated reports on mass influxes. The application of the detailed legal procedures was particularly difficult when the influxes between 1975 and 1978 came from so many points along the Sudanese border. The demands on COR were colossal. As a result, a major problem arose as to the legal status of the refugees according to the Regulation of Asylum Act. Instead of using the cumbersome procedures recommended in Articles 4 and 6, COR resorted to the method followed before 1974, whereby refugee status was offered *en masse*. However, the difference was that before 1974, it was the Council of Ministers which took the decision, whereas in and after 1974 this power was given to the Minister of Interior, together with the power to delegate it.

Over the years, and with the escalation of conflict in Ethiopia, it became a normal procedure that everyone who arrived from

Ethiopia was considered a refugee. However liberal this might seem, it did, in fact, create several complications for the Sudanese Government, for the refugees and for foreign aid organisations. This liberal application of the Asylum Act was not accompanied by a similar effort to inform the local authorities about the subsequent rights and duties of refugees. In fact, the failure of COR to disseminate the law to the provincial authorities created a paradoxical gap between the legal definition of the 1974 Act and the local authorities' own perceptions of the refugees. This gap had a detrimental effect on the status of non-Eritrean refugees who came from other parts of Ethiopia in 1976.

The misapplication of definitions is illustrated very clearly by the confusion which arose over the status of non-Eritrean refugees in Gedaref area, resulting in tensions between the Commissioner, UNHCR and the local administrators. In May 1976 there was already controversy between the Commissioner and UNHCR as to whether there were new influxes from Ethiopia south of Gedaref, and whether these persons were refugees or not. In order to persuade UNHCR to provide assistance, the Commissioner for Refugees argued that the newcomers *were* refugees. UNHCR had its doubts and sent a mission from Geneva to investigate. It visited Khartoum and observed the administrative limitations of COR. On its visit to Eastern Sudan, the mission talked to local authorities and explored the situation of the refugees in general. Meeting the Executive Officer at Doka, the latter offered what sounded like a denial of flight. The mission report stated that:

> Many of the *Abyssinians* especially in Doka seem to have been in Sudan for long periods and to be more or less successfully spontaneously integrated into the villages and the labour market in Kassala Province. At one point the Executive Officer in Doka stated that there are 300 Abyssinians there but later said there were no refugees. The *Arabic word refugee* includes economic immigrants as well as refugees and this may be a contributory factor in determining the eligibility of the Abyssinians as HCR mandate refugees. (Beyer 1976: 14)

The UNHCR official was so preoccupied with the attempt to disprove the Ethiopian eligibility for refugee status, and to override the wishes of the Commissioner for Refugees, that he gave undue emphasis to a statement by a local government officer who clearly was not aware of the legal definition. It is not only in Arabic that the word 'refugee' (*laji'in*) can include other categories of migrants. The UNHCR representative would have understood why the local administrator denied that the 'Abyssinians' were refugees had he known the contextual difference in meaning between 'Abyssinians' and 'refugees'. The term 'Abyssinians' (*Habash*) is generically taken to identify people of Ethiopia. However, in the particular context of the political situation of 1976, it was used in Sudan in a narrower sense to differentiate between the people coming from Ethiopia proper and the Eritreans. In Sudan in general, and in the Eastern Region in particular, where people were acquainted with the political conflict in Eritrea and the resulting refugee influxes, there was a tendency to consider the refugees as basically Eritreans. As the public was less well informed about the growing conflict in highland Ethiopia, the label 'Abyssinian' was used to indicate that persons coming from there were not the typical refugees in Sudan. The lack of knowledge by local administrators in border areas of the stipulations of the Asylum Act (1974) continued to produce confusion, which in turn influenced major decisions on the refugee problem. This lack of knowledge was revealed very clearly after the administrative decentralisation in the period after 1978. Different decisions were taken by Kassala Province authorities against the refugees in 1979, and the Executive Council produced a resolution excluding refugee children from post-primary education. In 1985 the Executive Officer at Wad el Heleiw, who, like many officials, believed that 'refugees' were necessarily those who came because of the famine in Ethiopia, denied the right to be considered refugees to 429 persons because they did not seem to suffer from starvation and some were driving their own cars (Interview with K. Tag al-Sir, August 1987).

Even when the Commissioner for Refugees succeeded in convincing the Ministry of Local Government to transfer administrators to work on secondment, he failed to provide them with clear guidelines for refugee work. In the case of the three members of staff who were seconded in 1974-1975, their relationship to the Commissioner in Khartoum was unclear, as was their relationship to UNHCR. Furthermore, they did not know what their position was in relation to the provincial authorities. The latter relationship was particularly important because, according to the Local Government Act of 1971, the Provincial Commissioner was both the most senior administrator and the head of the single party (SSU) in his province. The centralised responsibility of the Commissioner for Refugees cut across, and contradicted the powers of the Provincial Commissioner. The Commissioner for Refugees and UNHCR Resident Representative, both stationed in Khartoum, continued to conduct tours to the Eastern Region in order to persuade the provincial authorities to pursue a particular course of action towards the refugees. However, neither of the two had the political weight to influence decision-making.

COR did not enjoy any political representation in the SSU, nor had the office tried to gain such representation. Having no clear guidance from their superior in Khartoum, the COR staff in the provinces became subject to pressures from the Provincial Commissioner.

In 1975, the Kassala Provincial Commissioner, Mohammad Abdel Gadir, displeased with the slow action of COR, challenged its authority and ordered the refugees to be forcibly transferred from Wad Kawli and Wad el Heleiw to Showak. He used his authority to apply the 1973 Presidential Decree to resettle refugees and requested that the newly appointed representative of COR, in Showak, should implement the decision. On 28 April 1975 an agreement was signed with the World Food Programme establishing Project Emergency 1029. The attempt at forcible transfer failed for various reasons, among them the resistance shown by the refugees themselves; the resistance by local people in Showak, Um Shajara and Gedaref, who had claims over the land; and the objections from UNHCR due to the unsuitability of the site. In spite of this, the move taken by the Provincial Commissioner indicated a growing trend among provincial authorities to intervene in refugee affairs.

By 1977, the representatives of COR had begun to develop their provincial administration in Showak. A series of agreements with the World Food Programme concerning the provision of relief food aid enabled COR's Project Manager in Showak, and the Assistant Commissioner in Gedaref, to provide food for 24,000 newcomers in reception centres in Wad el Heleiw. The COR staff were also engaged in the implementation of new settlements at Um Gargour, Um Gulja, Um Rakouba, and Khashm al Girba where the number of refugees was estimated at 17,500 (Project Management Documents, Showak, 1976). The administrators also gained more knowledge and information about the role of UNHCR and its programming methods, thanks to the presence of a UNHCR member of staff, Michel Barton, who came to the Gedaref UNHCR Sub-Office in 1977 (Interview with GPM, Showak). Nevertheless, because of the size of the influx during 1977 and 1978 and the slow response of UNHCR, the assistance programme was unable to respond adequately to the needs of the new refugees.

The Relationship between the Commissioner for Refugees and the Security Organisations

The growing tension between Sudan and Ethiopia in the period from 1976 to 1978 and the strengthened role of the security agencies threatened the principles previously accepted for the treatment of refugees. These principles were based on a belief that the offer of asylum was a peaceful act, and that refugees should be prohibited from conducting subversive activities against their country of origin. The host country was required to disarm the refugees and to relocate them away from border areas.

While these principles continued to offer guidelines for the work of COR, the security organisations proceeded with their own strategy which was not entirely coherent. On the one hand, they did not show enthusiasm for the policy of resettling refugees away from the border, because they believed that the refugees' presence offered a political constituency for the political fronts with which they had close links (see Chapter 3). On the other hand, they were aware of the adverse effects of the continuing influx and the unchecked movement of refugees from points of entry to both rural and urban areas. The security organisations, therefore, adopted contradictory positions: they sought close links with the Eritrean political organisations, but, conversely, also sought to restrain their political activities. These conflicting positions within the security organisations reflected the old conflict between Public Security and National Security which had not been fully resolved after the amalgamation of the two security organisations in 1979.

Being aware of the different agenda of COR, National Security attempted to impose an agenda of their own. They knew that the influx of refugees did not consist simply of persons who had fled to seek safety. There was a great degree of heterogeneity within the refugee population along cultural and political lines. It was anticipated that such heterogeneity would produce conflict within the areas where the refugees settled. In 1977, National Security asked the Commissioner for Refugees either to allow a representative from the organisation to work within the Commissioner's Office in Showak, or to have one of its staff trained by National Security (interview with GPM, Showak, August 1987). This option was abandoned in favour of an alternative which was to establish security offices throughout the provincial localities in Eastern Sudan, with main sub-offices in Gedaref, Kassala and Port Sudan, all of which were directly responsible to the headquarters of Public Security and National Security in Khartoum. Sub-offices were also established in Wad Medani and Damazin in the Central Region.

In Khartoum, Public Security appointed a Liaison Officer in 1972 to deal with the individual refugees who arrived there. Public Security received the refugees first and they were then referred to COR, which was expected to provide identification papers and also opportunities for education, employment or travel abroad. By 1977 this arrangement was undermined by the scale of the influx. Some refugees began to report directly to COR, and some were passed on by Public Security. The official presence of the Eritrean and Ethiopian political fronts in Khartoum and in provincial centres encouraged the arrival of large numbers of refugees, helped by the intervention of Public Security. Public Security, on receiving lists of supporters from the different fronts, forwarded these lists to COR asking mainly for assistance in helping the special categories of refugees who needed to travel abroad.

COR actively began to register refugees who reported to its office in Khartoum. At the same time, it began to devise means of dealing with the individual problems of refugees. The heavy bureaucratic nature of the job – filling registration forms, identifying courses of action, introducing refugees to other government departments and keeping dossiers for each case – created its own pressures on the office. The Refugee Counselling Service, which was established by agreement between COR, UNHCR, SCC, Sudan Aid, and IUF in 1976, ended up as a small office run by the UNHCR Branch Office and concerned mainly with the provision of cash handouts for individual refugees who happened to know about it.

By mid-1978, the increasing numbers of refugees in Khartoum, and the abandonment of the Sudanese regime's offensive policy towards Ethiopia, resulted in a complete change of heart. In Khartoum, a campaign against the presence of refugees was mounted in June 1978. As part of that campaign, COR was blamed for not being able to control the movement and for encouraging the presence of refugees in Khartoum.

Decentralisation Policy Measures

The devolution of decision-making to the provinces launched by the 1971 People's Local Government Act was reactivated in 1977 with the abolition of the Ministry of Local Government (see Norris 1983 for an evaluation of the People's Local Government experiment). In 1979, seven central ministries were abolished and some of their functions were transferred to the provincial authorities. These were the Ministries of the Interior, Education, Religious Affairs, Youth and Sports, Cooperation, Social Affairs, Commerce and Supply (Presidential Decrees 50-55, February 1979, Presidential Decree File 1974-1981, SUNA).

Although the abolition of the central ministries suggested a drastic move towards decentralisation, Presidential Decrees 50-55 in fact succeeded in devolving some of their functions and relocating others to different central authorities. At the Ministry of the Interior, the Police Force was divided between the provincial authorities and the centre. Presidential Decree 475 of 3 September 1979 transferred the administration of police forces to provincial executive councils (ibid.: 112). The centre maintained the Investigation Department (attached briefly to the Attorney General) and the Passport and Immigration Department (attached to the Council of Ministers). At the same time the Police Force, Prisons and Fire Brigades maintained their autonomous hierarchies with separate headquarters in Khartoum.[5]

The same presidential decrees ignored COR completely and its fate was decided only two months later when a follow up ministerial committee recommended that it should be attached to the General Secretariat of the Council of Ministers.

In July 1980 the Constitution was amended to accommodate the division of the country into regions: Northern, Darfur, Kordofan, Central, Eastern, and Southern; with special status for Khartoum as the national capital. The 1980 Regional Government Act came into effect in the same year, and five governors were appointed by the President prior to the elections of the regional assemblies. By 1981 Sudan was fully administered by regional governments. The 1980 Regional Act outlined the functions of the Regional Government as follows:

1. the development and utilisation of regional financial resources;
2. the fostering of development and supervision of local government councils;
3. the supervision and control of the police services;
4. the fostering of social and regional religious institutions;
5. the regulation of commerce, supply, cooperation and regional industry;
6. the utilisation of water resources;
7. the development of regional communications and transportation;
8. the supervision of public service personnel in the region;
9. the development and control of land use. (Regional Government Act section 8 in Al-Assam 1983: 114)

Section six of the Regional Act, on the other hand, listed functions which the regional governments were *not* allowed to perform. Among those functions were National Defence and Security, Foreign

---

5. Police Headquarters, Prisons and Fire Brigades, and the Commissioner for Refugees were again made departments of the Ministry of Internal Affairs in 1980.

Affairs and Nationality, Immigration and Passports. The fact that the regions were assigned a wide range of responsibilities with little finance to carry them out indicates that the regionalisation measures were politically motivated. The President continued to dominate, and although he increased the number of power centres he continued to act as the single arbiter. The regions, therefore, having no capacity to raise financial and manpower resources to run the services, became dependent on central grants in aid (Fadlalla, n.d.). Even this latter source was not organised in a way that took into consideration the variation between regions. The allocations were mainly done through bargaining. That is, a region prepared its own budget but it ultimately negotiated with the Central Ministry of the Treasury to determine the budgetary allocations.

Consequences of Decentralisation on Refugee Policy

The decentralisation process and its consequences came to have a drastic impact on national refugee policy and on the local authority attitudes towards the refugees. The decentralisation decisions ignored the refugees as a factor in centre-region relations. The fact that COR was not mentioned in the February 1979 Presidential Decrees Nos. 50-55 is significant. The omission was not due to negligence or forgetfulness, but was related more to the political climate before and after 1979. Omer Mohammad al Tayeb, then Chief of National Security, tried to extend his control over the Ministry of the Interior, especially over Public Security, and preferably over COR as well. For him, refugees involved security issues and it was only logical that policies relating to the refugees should be under the control of the security organisation. In addition, he hoped to control the resources that could be generated for refugee assistance from foreign sources (interview with Khalifa Kara, 5 April 1987).

Immediately after the abolition of the Ministry of the Interior was announced, the Chief of National Security proposed that COR should be attached to the newly-formed State Security. This again met with absolute resistance from the staff of COR. The COR staff prepared a memorandum for the Ministerial Committee organised to follow up the implementation of presidential decrees, outlining the reasons against the annexation of COR to State Security (COR Memorandum to the Council of Ministers March 1979, signed by Omar Mohamed Ismail, Acting Commissioner for Refugees). Once again, the main objection was that COR worked with *non-political humanitarian agencies*, and depended on them for assistance for refugees. In fact, the Commissioner for Refugees was already working on a plan to convince foreign donors to support a campaign to give assistance to all refugees in Sudan. The memorandum argued that donors of humanitarian assistance would not favour working with State Security.

These arguments seem to have found credibility with some of the members of the Ministerial Committee and COR was again saved from being attached to a security organisation. Instead it was temporarily attached to the office of the Cabinet Minister at the General Secretariat of the Council of Ministers in May 1979. When COR eventually moved to become part of the newly formed Ministry of Internal Affairs in early 1980, it remained part of central government. However, its position was just as marginal because, as a subdepartment of a central ministry, its claim to represent a national policy towards refugees was seriously challenged, and then overruled, by the powers conferred on the local regional authority.

According to the 1980 Act, the regions had the right to control natural resources and to provide services tailored, presumably, to Sudanese nationals only. COR and its partner aid organisations had no power to decide on the allocation of certain resources within those regions to refugees, despite the fact that the Regulation of Asylum Act and International Conventions urged them to do so. The only practical way to earn concessions for the refugees was through bargaining with the regional authorities. The scene was thus set for the local regional authorities to consider refugees as a threat to local order and as a socio-economic burden. These authorities proceeded to implement a series of measures against the presence of the refugees in particular areas, invoking the legal prerogative offered by the People's Local Government Act (1971 amended 1981) and the Regional Government Act 1980.

Bureaucratic Politics and Stigmatisation of the Refugees

After 1978, both the local government authorities (provincial and later regional) and the central security organisations engaged in a series of measures to evict refugees from both towns and border areas. The assumption was that the refugees constituted a threat to internal public order (as well as to relations between Ethiopia and Sudan). Once the concept of the refugee threat evolved, the decision to end it was made at different levels of government. At the central level it was sometimes taken with reference to presidential decrees, or decisions by the

National Defence Council or the State Security Organisations. At the provincial level, it varied between decisions taken by the provincial Executive Council, the Provincial Security Committee or simply by area councils. In all cases the decisions referred to the areas in the Eastern Region called the 'refugee camps' (refugee settlements where some refugees had been resettled by COR with assistance from UNHCR). The decisions to evict refugees from towns were based on the assumption that refugees constituted an additional pressure on these towns. In border areas, the presence of refugees often resulted in the Ethiopian army attacking Sudanese territory. The collapse of the fronts also brought into Sudan warring factions which clashed with each other.

Another feature of the measures taken to evict the refugees was that while the different local authorities were able to invoke the laws, they proved incapable of executing these decisions. Execution of the decisions was normally left to COR. The latter, despite its marginal position, improvised ways to adjust, if not impede, these decisions at the cost of facing severe pressures from other government organisations in Khartoum and Central and Eastern Regions.

The Official Responses to the Presence of Refugees in Khartoum

Dissatisfaction with the presence of refugees in Khartoum was shown as early as 1976. Eritreans were initially suspected of playing a major role in an aborted coup in July (Palmer 1976). The government accused them of being conduits for the Iraqi Baathist regime. Consequently, the Eritrean refugees in Khartoum suffered from assaults and beatings by members of the public. It was only after intervention by the Commissioner for Refugees that Vice President Mohammad al Baghir Ahmed announced that the refugees had not been involved and that the public should desist from such assaults (Interview with Omer Mohamed Ismail, then acting Commissioner for Refugees, September 1987).

However, in 1977, hostility towards the refugees became even more evident as the municipal authorities in Khartoum began to face growing frustration among the population resulting from the rising cost of living and the scarcity of essential commodities and public services. In December, the Khartoum municipality police reported to the General Director of the Police:

> We have been watching, with great alarm, the continuing refugee influx in Khartoum. Your Excellency will undoubtedly agree that such an un-organized movement will contribute to an increase in the rate of crime. (Provincial Commissioner for Police to Director of Police, 17 December 1977)

The municipal police related the refugee influx to increased crime because of the high rate of unemployment and the tendency among refugees to engage in prostitution (ibid.). The Khartoum Police Commissioner proceeded to suggest measures that should be implemented to restrict the movement of refugees:

> We write this in the hope that your Excellency will contact the competent authority and propose to the Minister of the Interior that he should use powers accorded to him by Article 10(2) of the Regulation of Asylum Act, to restrict the refugee movement from the camps. This will enable us to take the necessary measures to stop this harmful movement which is becoming a threat to our moral values and public decency. (Ibid.)

The letter clearly represented an attempt by the Khartoum Police to deal with channels other than COR. To address the Director of Police and to request him to contact the Minister of Interior implied that the refugee movement to Khartoum should be controlled by the police. The restrictive article 10(2) of the Asylum Act reads:

> No refugee shall exercise any political activity during his presence in the Sudan, and he shall not depart from any place specified for him. The penalty for contravening this sub-section shall be imprisonment for not more than one year. (Attorney General's English text)

The police intended to apply these restrictions retrospectively. The Commissioner for Refugees continued to argue that the influx to towns contained elements of urban, young, and educated Ethiopians who could not simply be confined to rural settlements. In joint meetings organised by the Commissioner for Refugees with the police and Public Security, the Commissioner demanded substantiation of the role of refugees in increasing the incidence of crime. The police failed to provide evidence, and the accusations against the refugees were rejected (Deputy Commissioner Ibrahim al Jamal, correspondence with Khartoum Police, December 1977). Reluctantly the police slowed their lobbying campaign and the influx continued unrestricted.

First Attempt to Restrict the Refugee Presence in Khartoum

However, over the first half of 1978 the police joined hands with Public Security and began to seek political support, particularly from the Peoples' Assembly and the President himself. An opportunity to evict the refugees was offered by the occasion of the OAU Summit Meeting of 1978 which was hosted in Khartoum. In early June 1978

Public Security produced a unilateral ultimatum which came as a shock for the refugees and for COR. The letter, which was signed by the Head of Public Security (who was also the Minister of the Interior) read, 'Due to the occasion of the African Summit Conference in Khartoum, it has been decided that all *African Refugees* shall be asked to leave the town' (Chief of Public Security to Commissioner for Refugees in CRM1/36/3/3, 6 June 1978).

The strongly worded decision to evict the refugees from Khartoum appeared, ironically, qualified: refugees were requested to move by their own volition; and they were to be reassured that the decision was not taken in bad faith against them (ibid.).

Although the decision was to send the refugees out of Khartoum, it was not clear where they should go. A question on what the Minister of the Interior intended to do with the refugees was discussed in the Assembly on 20 June 1978.

The minister also ordered the establishment of a three-man committee (chaired by the Commissioner for Refugees with representatives of Public Security and the police as members) to plan for the evacuation of refugees and to seek support from the Eritrean and Ethiopian organisations to persuade the refugees to leave. It was clear then that the implementation of the decision would degenerate into a police operation using force against the refugees. None of the government organisations, including COR, had any kind of organised communication with the refugees in Khartoum, and it was impossible to negotiate or explain their forced eviction. The reference to the Eritrean fronts assumed, erroneously, that they had control over refugees in the town and that they could be made to help with the evacuation.[6] If the fronts had been in a position to persuade the refugees to leave Khartoum, it was unlikely that they would have done so; for it was in the interest of the fronts for the refugees to stay in Khartoum during the conference to make their voices heard.

The Commissioner for Refugees tried desperately to minimise the negative consequences of the decision, not only to protect the refugees, but also to protect the image of the government itself and its reputation for pursuing a liberal policy of asylum. He believed that if there was any threat to the conference by the refugees, it could be dealt with by other means.

The Police and Security began their operation to collect refugees for evacuation on 20 June 1978. The way the police treated the refugees raised bitter feelings even among some of the officials them-

6. In an interview on 22 February 1987, Ahmed Nasir, Khartoum Head of the ELF, admitted that they were willing to help. The EPLF, however, was not. For the EPLF attitude see Dureux (1979).

selves. The 700 refugees who were arrested were dumped in Khartoum East police station without food or water and without any clear idea of what would happen to them. At midday on 20 June, the police officer at Khartoum East police station expressed his frustration and asked the Committee either to procure food and water or else to allow him to release the detainees. The Commissioner contacted the Minister, who ordered commercial buses to be made immediately available. The panic caused by the operation extended even to the Sudanese who were acquainted with the refugees, whether as employers or as friends. Contacts were made all day in an attempt to make exceptions and to release refugees. A division of opinion occurred within the committee, and the chairman (Ibrahim al-Jamal, Deputy Commissioner for Refugees) reported that the Minister's decision was just an administrative order. It did not, by itself, constitute a law authorising the police to detain the refugees (Memorandum to Commissioner for Refugees 20 July 1978). On the next day, 21 June, the Commissioner for Refugees wrote a memorandum to his superior, the Minister of the Interior. He strongly objected to the way the refugees were being treated. The Commissioner for Refugees did not attempt to hide his feelings, particularly because the starting day of the operation coincided with the annual commemoration of African Refugee Day.[7] His memorandum protested that:

> To say the least, the police operation yesterday was ugly, inhuman and self-defeating. If it is necessary that all refugees are to leave the town, we believe that this should be done in the most disciplined, humane, and wise way in order to minimise the suffering of the people concerned. (CRM1/36/B, 21 June 1978)

The Commissioner denounced the indiscriminate assault on women and children and on those who, having finalised their travel procedures, were waiting to leave the country. He appealed to the minister to issue a public statement to emphasise that this was an emergency decision and that the refugees would certainly be allowed to return to Khartoum later. He also requested that employers, landlords and school authorities should be persuaded to preserve the rights of the refugees during their leave of absence. Furthermore, he demanded that the refugees should be allowed sufficient time to prepare themselves and their families before they moved (ibid.).

7. The African Refugee Day was recommended by the OAU. Member countries are requested to publicise the plight of African refugees and to apply the principles of humanitarian conventions for them. In Sudan the Minister of the Interior used to give a speech on the occasion, and COR arranges debates and discussions on radio, press and television.

The Minister bluntly rejected the proposals and refused to allow any refugee to be exempted from the decision. His written rejection was recorded in the text of the Memorandum itself. He admitted to the Commissioner for Refugees that he was under extreme pressure from President Nimeiry and from the People's Assembly which had called on him to report on the implementation of the decision on 20 June, 1978.[8]

However, the three-man committee was paralysed by the size of the operation and by the lack of resources to implement the decision. It had no funds and therefore no way of hiring the transport at a time of severe petrol shortages. The Sudanese railway authorities failed to make trains available, and the Commissioner for Refugees, who was supposed to receive the refugees, had no facilities for shelter or food in the refugee settlements. He could only offer 100 tents, and sorghum which was available in Damazin but needed to be transported to the settlements. At the same time the three-man committee's offices were jammed with employers, school authorities, Sudanese and expatriate friends who came to argue against the decision, and to get those refugees related to them exempted.

Two days later the police operation had to stop. On 24 June 1978, the committee reported to the Minister of the Interior that the decision to send the refugees out of the town required a bigger operation than the committee could afford (Chairman of the Committee to COR, Letter No. CR/36/B/1/A, 24 June 1978, COR, Khartoum). It was proposed that members of the committee should be released by their respective departments to perform their duties full time. It was also suggested that the Army Chief of Staff should be persuaded to allocate military vehicles for transport. In addition, the committee demanded that the Provincial Commissioner of Khartoum Province should be asked to allocate special quotas of petrol to the commercial vehicles involved.

While the committee was making these arrangements, the refugees tried different ways to hide from the police. Some left their homes to live with Sudanese and expatriate acquaintances. The majority disguised themselves in Sudanese dress hoping that the police would not recognise them. The operation subsided between 24 June and the first week of July. It was resumed from 3 to 5 July when transport was available, but only a few refugees ended up in refugee settlements. Those who were sent out of Khartoum made their way to other towns like Wad Medani, Hasaheisa, and Gedaref or eventually came back to Khartoum.

8. Personal communication by Omer Mohamed Ismail, Acting Commissioner for Refugees, who presented the memorandum to the Minister.

After the end of the OAU Conference in July, the decision to evict the refugees from the town should have died a natural death. However, the experience of implementing the decision reflected the difference in the positions of the security, police and local government authorities, on the one hand, and the Commissioner for Refugees on the other. In the aftermath of the OAU summit, there was another collision between the two sides. The police, security and the local authorities engaged in a wider campaign of vilification of the refugees. The Commissioner for Refugees began to realise that the 6 June decision was only the beginning of a systematic campaign against the presence of the refugees in the town. He had to improvise ways to help at least certain categories of refugees who, he believed, should legitimately stay in the town. His office also realised the shortcomings of its own working methods, which had failed to guarantee the status of refugees through the distribution of legal documents. Although it was difficult for the office to provide every refugee in the country with a certificate of identification, it attempted to develop a system which would ensure that at least the status of refugees who came to Khartoum would be recognised – thus engaging in a battle with other authorities who categorically denied the right of refugees to stay in the town. The regularisation of the status of refugees in Khartoum called for the issuing of Identification Cards[9] which carried legal weight. In order to clarify who should receive these cards in the town, the Commissioner defined broad categories of refugees whose stay in the town should be considered lawful. These categories included:

1. professional refugees with high qualifications and skills such as medical doctors, academics, engineers etc.;
2. skilled workers who were engaged in gainful employment as approved by the Labour Department and the employers;
3. students who had the opportunity to attend or were attending secondary and post-secondary schools;
4. members of families whose breadwinners were gainfully employed in Khartoum;
5. refugees who were being assisted by UNHCR. These were defined as medical cases, refugees expecting to be resettled in other countries and refugees who were attending the Refugee Counselling Services;
6. refugees who had good chances to travel abroad for work, education, or family reunion; and

---

9. The Commissioner had the legal basis for this action in Article 13 of the Asylum Act and Article 27 of the UN Convention 1951.

7.   newcomers who had provided acceptable reasons for coming to
     Khartoum. (COR 1980)

Although these exceptions were apparently endorsed (UNHCR
1979), the police authorities in Khartoum maintained their campaign
against the refugee presence in the city. In a letter to the Commissioner for Refugees the Police Director referred again to the negative
impact of the refugees on Khartoum, and argued that this was causing
agitation among the members of the SSU. He reaffirmed the determination of the executive and political authorities in Khartoum to put an
end to 'this impending danger'. He asked for close co-ordination with
the Commissioner to ensure that no refugee came to the city without
police permission. Otherwise the letter warned 'we will be compelled
to use our right to save our Province from the danger caused by the
refugees' (Police Commissioner KP/POI/CONF/32/B1, 1 July 1978,
copy to Public Security, Provincial Commissioner Khartoum, Police
General Director, Executive Director's Office, Ministry of Interior).

The attempt to send the refugees away from Khartoum surfaced
again in May/June 1979. This time the State Security and the police
contacted the Commissioner for Refugees to ascertain what facilities
existed for the reception of the evicted refugees. The Commissioner
again expressed his dissatisfaction with the decisions that had been
taken without consultation with his office. In a long memorandum to
his minister, he tried to explain the phenomenon of urban refugees,
the failure of arbitrary decisions to prohibit the movement to Khartoum, and the need to design more realistic strategies to deal with
refugees (COR Memorandum 36/B.3.M[2], 25 June 1979).
He traced the refugee problem in Khartoum back to the events
in Ethiopia in 1975 when the Ethiopian towns were very unstable. He
explained that young people found it impossible to stay there because
of political problems and because they had simply lost opportunities
for employment or education. They had come to Khartoum in search
of jobs, schooling, or the opportunity to go abroad. The Commissioner then challenged the assumption that the refugees were the
cause of the crises faced by the people in Khartoum:

> Even if we assume that the refugees are the cause of all these crises, would
> their relocation in other parts of Sudan not do harm to those areas ... and if
> their eviction becomes necessary for security reasons, do the authorities not
> care for parts of this country which are equally dear as Khartoum? (Ibid.: 4)

The memorandum went on to attack the tendency to see the
refugees as people who should be kept in camps and who should
only work in agriculture. He expressed his fears about what would

happen if this perception of the refugees became the official view of the security organisations. Special reference was made to the views of Omer al-Tayeb, the Chief of State Security, who believed that 'refugees should be put in camps' (Interview in *Sudanow*, a monthly publication of the Ministry of Information, May 1979). The Commissioner criticised the usage of the term 'camps' for its unpleasant association with prison-like situations. He emphasised that refugee policy should aim to resettle refugees in villages where they could establish themselves as decent human beings. He argued:

> It is a fact that rural refugees do work in farming. There are already 15 refugee villages where residents either work on their own plots or earn wages for work in other agricultural activities. However, our policy towards refugees who are not acquainted with farming is to allow them to use and promote their skills in non-agricultural activities. (COR Memorandum 36/B.3.M(2): 5)

The Commissioner argued that Security's perception completely ignored the efforts being made by his office in cooperation with international bodies to remedy the problem (ibid.: 6). Any further attempts to evict the refugees would jeopardise the proposals for the 1980 Assistance Programme submitted to UNHCR, which included the establishment of refugee quarters in Port Sudan and Gedaref, and were costed at £S950,000. As far as Khartoum was concerned, the Commissioner was waiting to draw up his proposals in the light of a survey of refugees in the town, being conducted by Taj al-Anbia A. El Dawi of the Social Anthropology Department, Khartoum University. The Commissioner concluded:

> We do not want to see our country becoming like Thailand where the refugees are forcibly returned to where they came from or contained in closed camps. I am afraid we may end up in the same position if we do not restrain the new feeling against refugees.

Since the refugee problem was likely to continue for a long time, the only solution, as the Commissioner saw it, was to persuade the masses to work towards peaceful coexistence with the refugees.

The Approval of the President to Evict Refugees

Although State Security and the provincial authorities were unable to bring the refugees under their control, they did manage to close ranks with other authorities who were opposed to the presence of refugees in Khartoum. They also managed to gain a degree of popular support by involving the SSU in the province. Such an alliance only needed political authorisation from the highest authority: the President. Ironically, when the opportunity arose in August 1979, Nimeiry not only criticised the refugee presence in Khartoum but also attacked the SSU and its ancillary organisations. In his address to the joint meeting of the SSU Central Committee and the Cabinet in 1979, Nimeiry launched a severe attack against the SSU on the grounds that it had failed during the ten years of its lifetime to enforce its political supremacy over national life. Listing the areas in which it had failed, he questioned the SSU's ability to deal with:

> ... the problem of the refugees from East and West and its dangerous social, economic and security dimensions and its consequences for Sudan in general and on our national capital in particular, and ways of confronting it at least with a view to mitigating its risks.[10]

Nimeiry reiterated the need to confront the dangers of the refugee problem in his address to the Council of Ministers on 22 August 1979. This time he ordered the evacuation of refugees from Khartoum as well as from other Sudanese towns. The panic that was caused in the SSU pushed the authorities to implement the President's order with feverish diligence.

The President's intervention was significant, not only because he had chosen to become involved in the decision himself, but also because he clearly saw the refugee presence in the towns as an issue requiring political action by the SSU. His order also coincided with the process of decentralisation, whereby the Regulation of Asylum Act became irrelevant because of the abolition of the post of the Minister of the Interior who would otherwise have been responsible for implementing it. The decentralisation process had given power to the local authorities which were politically closer to the regime and which were likely to adopt the same perspective as the President.

Immediately after the presidential directive to the Council of Ministers, the Cabinet Minister for the Council of Ministers conveyed the directive to the Commissioner for Refugees who had become his subordinate (Cabinet Minister to Commissioner for Refugees No. 36/B/A/1, September 1979, signed by Abu Bakr

---

10. Nimeiry's speech, 7 August 1979, broadcast and televised. The other example he gave to show the failure of SSU was the events following the Tanzanian intervention in Uganda. Here, the invasion of a neighbouring country caused security threats to all countries in the area, and created a socio-economic burden on Sudan, in the form of the Ugandan refugees who fled after Idi Amin's overthrow.

Osman). The Commissioner was informed of the decision to evict immigrants as well as refugees. Refugees should be returned to the refugee settlement areas. This decision had been taken, the letter explained, in order to lessen the burdens resulting from overcrowding and the increasing crime rate. Pending the evacuation of the refugees, the Commissioner for Refugees was requested to execute particular procedures. These were emumerated as follows:

1. To facilitate travel procedures for refugees who were willing to leave Khartoum for other parts of the Sudan;
2. To facilitate travel procedures for refugees who wished to leave the Sudan;
3. To direct the staff of COR in the provinces to prohibit the movement of refugees to Khartoum;
4. To reorganise the refugee registration and issuance of identity cards to those staying in Khartoum.

Although President Nimeiry had referred to other towns, there was a clear understanding that Khartoum should take priority.

COR's Response to the Decision to Evict Refugees from Khartoum

The President's intervention signalled a very serious warning. As the Commissioner for Refugees saw it, a nationwide campaign would not only jeopardise the lives of the refugees, but would also injure the reputation of Sudan by making the refugees a scapegoat for its social and economic problems. Bearing these long-term implications in mind, the Commissioner nevertheless continued to work on a plan to implement the decision to restrict the refugees' presence in Khartoum in coordination with other government authorities. Through his link with the Council of Ministers, he asked the central ministries to provide various facilities in order to help the transfer of the refugees.

The Technical Committee appointed for executing the decision, chaired by Brigadier Ibrahim Abdalla of State Security, was to be provided with funds and logistical support to transport, accommodate, and feed the refugees. Refugees were not to be indiscriminately deported. The Technical Committee was to conduct a process of registration, screening individual cases and producing identity cards for refugees. On 3 September, the Commissioner presented his plan outlining ways to implement the decision in the short and long term (COR Memorandum to Minister, CR.36/B/1/A). The plan was submitted after meetings with the COR subordinates in a joint meeting with the Technical Committee on 5 and 6 September.

The Commissioner estimated there were then 20,000 to 25,000 refugees in Khartoum. According to the short term plan, 9,000 refugees were to be relocated in rural settlements. The target group included the unemployed and persons who had no real opportunities in the town; careful screening by a subcommittee including representatives of COR and the Labour Department would be carried out in the transit centre at Soba, a suburb of Khartoum. Students, professionals, skilled workers, and those who were leaving Sudan were to be allowed to stay in Khartoum. The plan also called for allowing the affected refugees to have ample time to prepare before they were sent to rural settlements. The proposed reception areas are listed in table 4.1. The Commissioner had already managed to obtain 1,200 tents and had asked the Ministry of Transport to transfer food from Port Sudan to Gedaref. WFP agreed to allocate food rations and promised to consider giving a diversified food basket of tea and sugar in addition to pulses, dried milk and cereals. UNHCR was asked to assist by providing food in transit and by financing the issuing of identity cards (Commissioner for Refugees 36/B/1/A/ 3 September 1979). A total of £S124,000 was requested.

The Commissioner's plan also outlined the security measures that would be necessary to guarantee the effectiveness of the operation, and recommended that the operation 'must be done in a most careful and appropriate way to maintain the good reputation of Sudan'. He expected the first phase of the plan to be completed by 30 October.

In the second phase, a further 9,000 refugees would be resettled inside Khartoum (2,000), in Fau (2,000), in Abu Rakham (3,000) and in Um Rakouba (2,000). (See map 4.1 for the final picture of refugee

Table 4.1 *Projections by COR for Relocation of Refugees Evicted from Khartoum*

Site	No. of Refugees
Um Gulja	1000
Fau	1000
Khashm al Girba	1000
El Sheikh Es Sammani	2000
New Halfa (Kilo 26)	2000
Abul Naja	2000
Total	9000

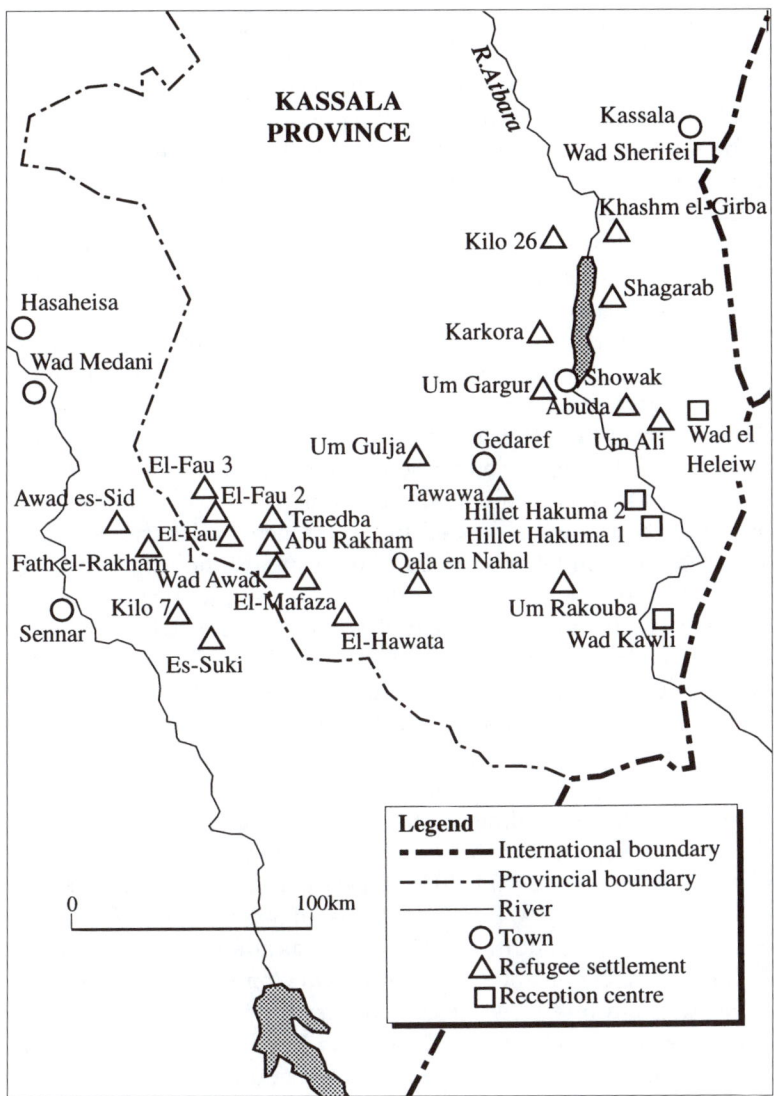

Map 4.1 *Refugee Settlement in Eastern Sudan*

settlement in the region.) The 2,000 who would be resettled in Khartoum could be employed in a poultry and vegetable production project located in a suburb south of Khartoum. About 5,000 would stay in Khartoum legitimately. This group would consist mainly of professionals, skilled workers, students and their dependents. The commissioner's plan called for the secondment of local government officers to augment his staff and to act as project managers in new refugee villages. He particularly emphasised the need for a trained administrative cadre to implement the plan (ibid.).

However, despite the fact that the preparations in 1979 appeared to be much more organised than in June 1978, bureaucratic delays threatened the smooth implementation of the plan. The Technical Committee failed to get immediate approval for funds from the Ministry of Treasury to reconstruct their offices in Soba and begin work. The approval, which was issued on 27 September 1979, provided only £S10,000 of the requested amount of £S50,000 (Ministry of Treasury letter No. THE/114/4/18). There were also delays in the arrangement of transport, despite the intervention of the head of State Security (Chief Security letter No. SS/MR/1/B/3/2) and a directive from the Minister of Transport. Because of the delays the transfer of the refugees could not start until the beginning of November 1979. On 4 November, the Commissioner for Refugees pro duced a declaration addressed to the refugees in Khartoum which was broadcast on television and Omdurman Radio. The statement called on those residing in Khartoum to meet the Technical Committee for registration in the period 4-15 November 1979. They were asked to collect registration forms from COR in Khartoum or from police stations in different parts of the city, and to attach with the registration form any identification documents they had acquired to help with the screening procedures. The statement warned that refugees who did not register in the specified period might be subject to punishment according to the 1974 Regulation of Asylum Act (CR/COM.Ref./36/B/1/A 4 November 1979).

By 14 November 1979 7,000 refugees had reported to the Technical Committee. UNHCR provided a list of 803 refugees as their special cases, in addition to 18 Ugandans and Zaireans (UNHCR/KRT/M/2303). The Technical Committee was only able to register and interview 2,105, and after the screening, 1,791 were exempted. Only 314 were asked to leave Khartoum. In other words, 85 per cent of the registered refugees were allowed to stay according to the criteria set by the Commissioner for Refugees. In order to interview 125 cases per day, the Committee needed approximately two more months to interview the whole group. This was longer than the two weeks anticipated in the plan (CR/36/B/1/A, 3 September 1979).

The commissioner reported the slow pace of the work and appealed for the release of local government officers to assist (COR to Minister No. CR/36/B/1/A, 18 November 1979). He requested further: that the Committee should be provided with four vehicles to facilitate their daily contacts with the government departments involved; that Kassala Province's quota of rationed commodities, particularly sugar, be increased; and that the police force guarding against refugee infiltration back to the capital should be provided by Khartoum, as the Kassala authorities could not provide this from their own resources. These last demands on behalf of Kassala Province anticipated the apprehension of the Kassala authorities who were being made to shoulder the burden of the refugees.

The Security and municipal authorities in Khartoum were not impressed by the report. For them, the original decision had been to evacuate refugees from Khartoum, and the Commissioner was exempting far too many people. The work of the Technical Committee was criticised and the Security and municipal authorities believed that if they accepted COR methods the refugees would never leave the city. Towards the end of December they decided to take matters into their own hands. In a circular issued to police directors in Khartoum, Khartoum North and Omdurman, the Khartoum Commissioner of Police informed them that the response to the decision to send refugees to refugee camps had been ineffective. It had become necessary to launch a new initiative which was outlined as follows:

1. Police operations would be conducted in refugee residential areas after appropriate information had been provided by State Security;
2. The State Security representative would meet with each Area Police Director in order to exchange information. State Security would provide one informant to accompany the police force in each area. These preparations would be made 24 hours before conducting the operations;
3. After consultation with the representative of State Security, a particular deadline would be fixed for the beginning of the police raids;
4. The Police Directors would make available a certain number of police officers with a certain number of vehicles in addition to a truck to carry the refugees' luggage;
5. The first operations would begin on 7 January 1980;
6. It was hoped that the police force would help with information gathered on the location of refugees. (Khartoum Police Commissioner to Police Director letter KPP/67/B/2, 31 December 1979)

The police operations, conducted in the first week of January, did affect some of the refugees in Khartoum, but efforts to deport them were still impeded by lack of resources. On 13 January 1980, another

200 refugees were sent to Khashm al Girba, although some of them were allowed to leave the reception area after they had produced Ethiopian passports (personal observation by the author). The operations were also influenced by the declaration of 1980 as the Year of Refugees in Sudan, the year in which the International Conference on Refugees in Sudan was to be held.

The Technical Committee established in 1979 and presided over by the General Director of Police (appointed by the National Defence Council, August 1979) continued to meet and evaluate the refugee situation in Khartoum until mid-1981. From then on the eviction of the refugees from Khartoum became part of a grand design to evict immigrants of all kinds, by invoking measures to create order and discipline in the city.

The eighth meeting of the Technical Committee for the evacuation of immigrants from Khartoum, held on 30 September 1981, sought to add to its responsibilities the application of orders aimed at price controls, organisation of traffic and elimination of squatter settlements (Letter to Chairman of the Supreme Committees from Vice President and Chief of State Security, 30 September 1981). At this meeting Chadian and Nigerian immigrants were referred to, but not the Ethiopians and Eritreans in particular. The Commissioner, again, made the point that exceptions were to be made for refugees lawfully staying in the city. He informed the committee that the identity card project had been approved by the Minister of Internal Affairs and that all refugees who had previously been registered would receive identity cards ('Meeting of the Supreme Committee, 30 September 1981' Agenda 4 October 1981). The committee agreed to establish a special committee representing the Commissioner for Refugees, the Central Investigation Department (Police) and State Security to revise the procedure for issuing identity cards.

On 9 December 1981, the Commissioner instructed the Identity Card Committee on the type of person to whom identity cards should be given. In addition to the categories defined before, the Commissioner added a new category of refugees, consisting of those who were assisted by the refugee-related humanitarian organisations: Relief Society of Tigray (REST), the Eritrean Red Crescent Society, and the Eritrean Relief Association (ERA) (COR to Chairman of ID Committee No. CR/36/A/2, 9 December 1981).

The Identity Card Committee submitted its report in mid-January 1982, in which it showed the distribution of identity cards to refugees, as shown in tables 4.2 and 4.3. As the Committee had to stop its work on 28 November 1981 on the order of the Technical Committee, the continuing demand for identification cards was dealt

Table 4.2 *Distribution of Identity Cards to Refugees in Khartoum by Category*

Category	No. of Identity Cards Produced
Professionals	378
Workers	2,348
Students	775
Housewives	504
Dependants	98
Baby Minders	721
Total:	4,824

Source: COR/CR/3/A/2/Confid., 1981.

with by COR. Despite the failure of the authorities to expel refugees from Khartoum, the general hostility to them among the police continued to surface thereafter.

The Attempts of the Provincial Authorities in Gezira Province to Evict Refugees

The Gezira provincial authorities began their contacts with COR in May 1979, requesting funds for the evacuation of refugees from Wad Medani and Hasaheisa towns. The Gezira authorities intended to expel the political factions of the EDU as well as the TPLF contingents whose conflict in Hasaheisa and Managil was considered a threat to public order. The Ethiopians were also blamed for their engagement in prostitution (Gezira Province Delegation meeting with COR, 15 May 1979). In June 1979 the Gezira Provincial Com-

Table 4.3 *Distribution of Identity Cards to Refugees in Khartoum by Nationality*

Eritreans	3,650
Ethiopians	880
Ugandans	35
Zaireans	259
Total	4,824

Source: Report of the ID Committee on the period 21 November 1981 to 7 January 1982, MIA/COR/36/A/2/Confid., 16 January 1982.

mittee took action by recommending that the National Security Council should prohibit the political activity of the TPLF and EDU (Meeting of the Gezira Province Security Committee, 27 June 1979).

A month after the presidential directive, the Gezira authorities again requested that COR should help with sending the refugees to refugee camps (Gezira Police to Commissioner for Refugees No. 57/SA/21/Conf., 16 December 1979). The Commissioner again tried to silence them by reaffirming that their case would be considered by the Supreme Committee which would certainly make recommendations on the refugee situation in different areas (COR to Police [Gezira] No. CR/36/B/1/1, 27 December 1979). He was aware that the Ethiopian community in Gezira predated the refugee influx which began in 1975. He did not favour the idea of moving them to Kassala as he already faced pressure from Kassala Province authorities to move refugees out of towns.

Provincial Authorities in Eastern Sudan and Responses to the Presence of Refugees

The enthusiastic response shown by the local people towards the Eritreans in 1967 had, over time, changed dramatically. In 1979 the process of decentralisation coincided with a declining enthusiasm for the refugees and their cause. This was caused by the changing composition of the influx, its size, geographic spread, and political diversity. These factors were compounded by the internal problems created by the deterioration in the Sudanese economy. By 1979, refugees in the Eastern Region were perceived both as a security threat and as a socio-economic burden. The Eastern Region had to face the stark consequences of the escalation of conflict inside Ethiopia and the aggressive policy then pursued by the regime in the Sudan.

The discussion about evicting the refugees from towns in 1978/1979 occurred at the same time as an influx from Ethiopia caused by the collapse of Eritrean and Ethiopian opposition groups. By the end of 1978 there were at least four authorities which, from their different perspectives, were attempting to deal with the refugee problem in Eastern Sudan. First were the representatives of COR in Showak and Gedaref who were trying to co-ordinate and implement a planned relief programme to transfer refugees to approved sites, and to run refugee settlements. Secondly, the Sudanese army was worried that the concentration of refugees in border villages would encourage the Ethiopian army to launch attacks inside Sudanese territory, and therefore wanted the refugees moved away from the border. Thirdly, the provincial and local government authorities were faced with budgetary constraints, pressures on public services, and the shortages of basic facilities for the Sudanese population. Fourthly, the State Security authorities were concerned about the presence of the political fronts and their factions, who encouraged infighting and the infiltration of weapons into the Sudan.

The security threat caused by the presence of refugees in border areas was recognised by the OAU. Consequently, as noted earlier, the OAU Convention called for the resettlement of refugees away from frontiers (Article 2[b]). In Eastern Sudan, the presence of refugees in border areas was tolerated during the policy of confrontation with Ethiopia. After the abandonment of that policy, the presence of refugees was resented by the Sudanese authorities themselves. From December 1978 the police expressed their worries about the presence of refugees in the border villages (Gedaref Police, GAP/P/Confid./32/B/1, 6 December 1978). However, in January 1979, the authorities faced a more serious problem that led to extreme tension. The Ethiopian army pursuing the EDU forces launched attacks around Jebel al-Lugdi about 12 km inside the Sudanese border. The EDU contingent was transferred by the Sudanese army to al-Darabi to await relief assistance from COR (State Security to COM.Ref. No. 3/14/1/2/230, 10 January 1979). This incident led to fears that Wad el Heleiw, with its growing number of refugees, including representatives of the fronts (ELF, PLF, EDU), would be the next target for the Ethiopian army. The attacks on the Sudanese border indicated that the Ethiopian Government was gaining the upper hand militarily. They also had a significant impact on relations between Ethiopia and Sudan.

Tension developed in the border village of Wad el Heleiw and was further complicated by the attitude of the refugees themselves who withstood the efforts of the local authorities to transfer them. Throughout the previous years, attempts to relocate the refugees in permanent refugee settlements in Qala en Nahal, Suki and Maharragat had been delayed because of a series of new influxes which had caused plans to be changed (Al-Bashir 1978: 368). In 1979 it was ultimately the security situation that prompted the authorities to transfer the refugees. The authorities were concerned, not only about the attacks by the Ethiopian army across the border, but also about the consequences of the confrontational policy of the Nimeiry regime, which had allowed the opposition fronts to consolidate their positions and to operate freely in the border areas. Throughout 1978 reports were exchanged between the local government authorities, the Security Organisations and COR on the situation in Wad el

Heleiw (interview with H. M. Osman, GPM, Showak, 20 January 1979). The general theme of those reports was that:

1. In Wad el Heleiw there were Ethiopian and Eritrean refugees from diverse ethnic and religious groups who were divided between the rival political fronts (ELF, EPLF, PLF, EDU).
2. All these fronts had established their separate offices and each had its own members. This created a tense atmosphere among the refugees and between them and the Sudanese authorities.
3. The fronts received external aid in cash and in kind (food and drugs) which increased their power over their supporters.
4. Public services – eight schools, one mosque, two churches – had been established and run without legal licence from the Sudanese authorities.
5. Large quantities of arms had infiltrated into Wad el Heleiw. The weak, understaffed police station was not capable of stopping this infiltration.

The resistance of the refugees in the face of attempts to transfer them from Wad el Heleiw was exacerbated by the mutual suspicion between the provincial authorities and the fronts.

As a response to the presence of the fronts, the Provincial Security Committee (chaired by the Provincial Commissioner) resolved that:

1. The police force in Wad el Heleiw should be increased and an officer of higher rank should be appointed.
2. The police should conduct raids to search for and confiscate arms.
3. An army contingent should be stationed in Wad el Heleiw to ensure the maintenance of law and order.
4. The representative of the Commissioner for Refugees and members of the Provincial Security Commission should engage in dialogue with the refugee leaders in Wad el Heleiw to persuade the refugees to move to either Qala en Nahal or Suki. (Kassala Province Security Meeting, Gedaref, 20 December 1978)

In response to the one month notice given by the authorities, only nine families expressed their wish to move. When they were again asked to prepare to move and were told that preparations had already been made for their reception (Declaration by GPM Showak, 10 January 1979), they did not show any sign of enthusiasm. In fact, they submitted a petition in which they expressed their view that they had been given permission to stay permanently in Wad el Heleiw; this permission, they argued, had been granted by the Vice-

President in 1976 and by the United Nations (Petition addressed to Wad el Heleiw Executive Officer, copies to the Omda and Police Superintendent [Wad el Heleiw] 15 January 1979). They also argued that they were well established in Wad el Heleiw and that the decision to transfer them had come as a surprise. The refugee representatives warned the Wad el Heleiw Executive Officer that if the COR General Project Manager (GPM) implemented the transfer of refugees he would be responsible for the consequences.

When the COR GPM arrived on 15 January, he explained that the decision to transfer the refugees was a government decision and he insisted that the refugees would have to move to the proposed new sites. The police in Wad el Heleiw were in favour of filing cases against the ringleaders who had allegedly threatened to assassinate the GPM. As this allegation proved to be unfounded, the police were content with sending the petition to the Security Commission in Kassala. Consequently, the Security Commission ordered an increase in the police force in Wad el Heleiw to 100 and decided to meet there on 22 January 1979.

Upon their return to Gedaref, the Security Commission reported to the Provincial Commissioner at Kassala. On 24 January, the refugees wrote another petition in which they repeated their claim that Wad el Heleiw had been offered to them by the Vice President and the United Nations. They argued that the decision to deport them to Qala en Nahal and Suki had been taken by the COR GPM. They demanded the withdrawal of the police force which 'terrorised' their children. The refugees made it clear that they would not accept the decision to transfer them and said that they would not recognise any authority other than that of the Commissioner for Refugees and the Representative of UNHCR ('Petition by the refugees in Wad el Heleiw' addressed to GPM [Showak], copy to the Provincial Commissioner, A/C Police, 24 January 1979).

The Provincial Commissioner, Hayder Hussein, visited Wad el Heleiw on 25 January, and in informal talks with the refugee leaders he was again told that the refugees demanded the presence of UNHCR. The Commissioner was upset by the attitude of the refugees, and considered it as a serious challenge to law and order. He declared that he would not allow the refugees to act like a state within the Sudanese state. He and his local government subordinates agreed to engage in a series of measures to remove refugees from border areas, as well as from Kassala and Gedaref towns. Unlike the Commissioner of Khartoum Province, the Provincial Commissioner in Kassala helped positively by allocating settlement sites for the refugees in Abu Rakham, Um Ali and Kilo 26.

In the particular case of Wad el Heleiw, it was impossible to implement the decision to transfer the refugees immediately because the COR staff were unable to organise the evacuation and also because State Security intervened to delay the action. At a meeting of the Security Commission the Provincial Commissioner was surprised by a cable from National Security in Khartoum overruling the Commissioner's decision to transfer the refugees. In a few brief words the cable ordered that the transfer be stopped. Security's action appeared to have been influenced by the fronts (EDU, ELF, EPLF) which continued to have close links with it. At that same meeting an envoy of the Minister of the Interior, who had been sent from Khartoum, conveyed the message that refugees should be transferred, using persuasion rather than coercion. The lack of a co-ordinated plan for dealing with the border refugees is obvious. The incidents at Wad el Heleiw eventually led to the transfer of some of the refugees to the wage-earning settlements in Suki.

Even when the relationship between Sudan and Ethiopia showed signs of improvement in 1979 and 1980, the drive to transfer the refugees away from the border continued. In May 1980 the senior administrator in al-Fashaga ordered the evacuation of all the Ethiopians from al-Fashaga area. As it was a contested area in the border conflict between Sudan and Ethiopia, he argued against the presence of Ethiopians there, irrespective of their legal status. In his view, if the presence of the Ethiopian nationals was tolerated this would offer the Ethiopian Government a negotiating card to justify its claims over the area (Commissioner for Eastern Borders to Commissioner for Refugees, letter no. CEBA/8/A/1, 31 May 1980).

In the Red Sea Province, the police authorities helped the refugees who came via Garora and Marafit to move directly to Port Sudan. The 11,000 refugees who arrived during 1980 were registered at Tokar and then moved by trucks to Port Sudan because there was nothing that the local authorities could offer them in the arid border lands of the Red Sea province. Port Sudan became the major recipient of refugees arriving in the Red Sea Province (Data collected from Police Records, Port Sudan in October 1980).

The most serious problems developed in the border sector southeast of Gedaref. Firstly, armed groups were present among the refugees as a result of the breakup of the EDU. From this *shifta* (bandit) activities arose along the Sudanese-Ethiopian border.[11] Secondly, there was the continuing influx from Ethiopia resulting from the

11. For a sociological and historical account of the *shifta* phenomenon, see Crummy (1986). *Shifta* is derived from the Amharic verb *shaffata* to mean a bandit or rebel (ibid.: 133).

Ethiopian army campaigns in Begemder, Wollo and Tigray, which increased the number of refugees and encouraged their dispersal in the Sudanese border villages of Homera, Hamadaiet, Zehana, Sefawa, Hilat Hakouma, al Hashaba, Duka, Um Rakouba and Wad el Heleiw. Thirdly, the Sudanese army had to launch systematic campaigns to contain the fighting among the armed groups and to confiscate weapons. In doing so the army found it difficult to distinguish between those carrying arms and the ordinary unarmed refugees. All these factors explain the continuing attempts by the authorities to remove the refugees from the border areas.

The *shifta* activities in Eastern Sudan were perhaps the major factor which shaped the authorities' views of the threat posed by the refugees. The traditional armed banditry, which had its roots in Ethiopia, had been drastically changed by the conflicts and acquisition of modern weapons. In the past, the *shifta* bands had moved only by night. They also placed a high value on their ammunition. According to one source 'they used to shoot only at a definite target. They could not afford to waste bullets' (Interview with Ismail Ibrahim, Assistant Commissioner for Refugees in Gedaref, 1987). By 1981 the *shifta* had easy access to machine guns and to ammunition. They had also acquired a larger territory for their activity both in the Sudanese border lands and across the Ethiopian border. Equipped with modern weapons and moving in small bands over a wider area, the *shifta* came to enjoy an advantage over the Sudanese police and army. On several occasions the Sudanese authorities sought assistance against the *shifta* from the TPLF. In 1984, a famous *shifta* leader was captured by the TPLF in the Armachu mountains and handed over to the authorities in Gedaref (ibid.). The *shiftenat* offers an interesting example of a protest movement which was not confined by the boundaries of one country. Crummy argues that *shiftenat* is a form of 'protest which assumes some common social and political order linking protesters and those to whom the protesters appeal. Protesters tend to direct their energy to the redressing of grievances arising from within that order' (1986: 10). It may be argued then that the phenomenon of the *shiftenat* introduced in Eastern Sudan is novel in that this form of protest was directed against Sudanese targets in Sudan rather than against the established order in Ethiopia.

By early 1981 the *shifta* had begun to act in daylight. In late March a band attacked the bus from Kassala to Wad el Heleiw. The passengers were ordered to disembark and their property was looted. A week later a commercial truck was again attacked. A policeman was shot dead and the lorry driver was seriously wounded (Assistant COR, Gedaref, Memorandum to COR, Khartoum, ACR/35/C/1,

24 June 1981). As a result, a police force was sent from Kassala to hunt the *shifta*. On 1 April 1981, the police were caught in a trap and the officer leading the force and three policemen were killed. In the village of Zehana, in the same month, the army organised patrols along the border areas. Two soldiers were shot dead by the *shifta*.

As the Sudanese army stepped up its operations, the garrison in Gedaref began to oppose the presence of the Ethiopian refugees in the villages of al-Hashaba (4,000 refugees) and in Hilat Hakouma/Sefawa. The military authorities accused the refugees of giving sanctuary to the *shifta* (ibid.). They requested the Commissioner for Refugees to transfer the refugees from these villages. COR could not respond quickly and eventually the army could not wait any longer and adopted its own measures to fight the *shifta*. On 22 May, a military contingent was sent from Um Barakit to search for and confiscate weapons hidden in Sefawa village. The village, particularly the quarter occupied by the refugees, was besieged and some of the refugees were beaten. The Assistant Commissioner for Refugees in Gedaref reported these beatings to the military commandant at Khashm al Girba. The officers and soldiers involved were disciplined. The Resident Representative of UNHCR sent his own protest to the Commissioner for Refugees stating that:

> It has come to my knowledge that the ongoing military operations along the Ethio-Sudanese border in Gedaref area have had some very unfortunate consequences on the security of refugees living in the area and the physical integrity of asylum seekers.[12] On the 22nd May 1981 a village called Sefawa was occupied by the army forces and I have been told by reliable sources that some of its refugee inhabitants were beaten up – to the extent that the refugee villagers now request to be moved from the area. (Robert Muller [UNHCR Res. Rep.] to COR, No. 81/KRT/C/84 [Conf.], 7 June 1981)

With the recurrence of the *shifta* operations, the army faced the dilemma that it had to perform a policing role without being able to distinguish who was a refugee and who was not. Even their operations to subdue the EDU armed groups, which had been successful in 1980, were frustrated in 1981. The refugees who were transferred from the border villages in 1980, and those who arrived later from Ethiopia, were moved away from the areas where the army was operating (Ismail Ibrahim, Memorandum to COR, ACR/35/C/1, 24 June 1981). In 1980 refugees were transferred to Um Rakouba settlement.

---

12. A reference to three refugees detained by the army after the killing of three soldiers by the *shifta* in Zehana, 40 km from the border.

Another threat was introduced in 1981 when the army began to face the sabotage apparently organised by Ethiopian government agents (GPM to COR 36/A/4-52/1/1, 13 January 1983). In November 1981 State Security provided information that the Ethiopian Government was involved in 'subversive' activities, in order to make life difficult for the refugees in the region so that they would have no alternative but to return to Ethiopia. Security argued that this was part of a broader plan; Ethiopia was claiming that the Ethiopian refugees were returning from neighbouring countries in order to justify its demand for material support from the international community. Security provided as proof of Ethiopian involvement, information gathered from refugees who had gone back to Homera. The refugees had been told that guarantees for their security on their return would be offered only if they went back to destroy refugee camps inside Sudan as they had done in Homera (ACRG to COR, ACR/35/C/1, Confid., 26 November 1981).[13] The view that unrest was caused by Ethiopian intervention began to preoccupy the army and the Security. Even when incidents which had no link with the Ethiopian authorities occurred, the first reaction was to suspect Ethiopian Government involvement. For example, the bloody fighting which occurred in Um Gulja refugee settlement in late July 1982 was at first thought to be organised by the Ethiopian authorities. In fact, the fight was between the EDU and TPLF members: an EDU contingent attacked TPLF supporters, killing eleven people and leaving eight wounded (El Sir al Mek to COR, Report 1 August 1982). However, the fact that the perpetrators escaped and were later captured in Hilat Hakouma on their way to Ethiopia was taken as a clue that those who committed the massacre had originally been sent by the Ethiopian authorities (ibid.). This suspicion was sustained as the refugees themselves, particularly the TPLF, insisted that the Ethiopian authorities were sending infiltrators whose role was to:

> Destabilise the situation in the refugee settlements and force the refugees to return to Ethiopia on the grounds of lack of safety in the Sudan, which would strengthen the Ethiopian allegations about voluntary repatriation. (COR, 'Memorandum on Visit to Gedaref', 36/A/4, 13 January 1983)

The refugees also explained that the Ethiopian Government's 'subversive' operations were intended to make the Sudanese Government regret the decision to offer unrestricted admission to refugees (ibid.). The refugees began to provide the Security in Gedaref with names of suspected Ethiopian agents. The refugees

13. Information provided by eleven refugees in Um Gulja Refugee Settlement.

believed that the introduction of identification documents for all refugees, inside and outside refugee settlements, would be a helpful way of identifying refugees who wished to lead a peaceful life (ibid.). COR was able to provide only 33,203 such documents, rather than the 100,000 that were needed for the refugees in settlements (GPM to COR, 36/A/4, 13 January 1983).

Although it is difficult to see how identification cards would have exposed the covert operations of the Ethiopian Government, the army continued to demand that refugees should be provided with documents. Provision of identity cards continued to be a problem because of the inability of the authorities to monitor the refugees at entrance points, where they could be registered at reception centres. Lack of funds was also a major reason. It was only in 1984 that $400,000 was allocated but this did not help the issuance of identification cards. In late December the officer in charge at Doka was ordered to investigate the identity of refugees living in the Doka Area on the grounds that:

> Any refugee who does not carry an identity card should be treated as an infiltrator who constitutes a threat to the security of the country. [Against such persons] you may take all the necessary measures to guarantee the maintenance of public security. (Ibid.)

This ultimatum was based on information that armed groups were expected to come from Ethiopia into Gedaref (Doka) area. The COR GPM intervened to persuade the army authorities not to engage in indiscriminate operations against the refugees in the hope that, as more identity cards were ordered from Khartoum, refugees entitled to identity cards would be saved harassment. Meanwhile, the transfer of the refugees to newly established villages continued at an extremely slow pace.

The security situation in the border areas in 1982 was further complicated by the arrival of the ELF factions in the previous year. After their arrival in Karakon, the ELF fighters were looked after by the State Security and the army. Their presence created a problem for the Sudanese authorities. The ELF, supported by the State Security and the army, considered themselves as a fighting group which would not submit to conventional treatment as refugees. Although their weapons and ammunition were confiscated by the Sudanese, the ELF fighters were promised that the weapons would be given back once the internal conflict between their leaders had been resolved. During 1982 they did not require the material assistance normally offered by UNHCR, in co-ordination with COR, as they were able to fend for themselves thanks to assistance from Saudi Arabia and the Red Cross and Red Crescent Societies (GPM Memorandum 36/A/4/Confid. 23 March 1983).

The Commissioner for Refugees, in any case, calculated that UNHCR would not provide assistance for a fighting group as such. Therefore he took the view that his office could only become involved if the ELF fighters accepted the new reality of refugee status and prepared themselves for a long stay in the Sudan. As this decision would ultimately be a political one, COR blocked the attempts by UNHCR to visit and to assess the situation of the people in Karakon (COR Memorandum 36/A/1/Confid. 20 December 1981). The attitude of COR probably seemed paradoxical to UNHCR. In fact, Karakon was considered a closed military area between late 1981 and June 1982, even for the Commissioner for Refugees himself (ibid.). It was clear that State Security wanted to keep the ELF intact by imposing a formula for unity between the different factions. In order to do this, they would not allow outsiders to come in and frustrate their efforts by treating the fighters as 'refugees'.

However, State Security's attempts to keep Karakon as a closed area, and to achieve a reunification of the ELF, were hampered by the deepening conflicts between the ELF factions. The ousting and detention of Ahmed Nasir, the ELF leader, and the emergence of irreconcilable factions under Habte, Abdalla Idris, and Girgis respectively, also led to the emergence of a new group which did not belong to any of the other factions. In December 1982 Security had to loosen its tight grip over Karakon since by this time the new group of former ELF members had become *de facto* refugees.

Nevertheless, COR maintained its non-involvement in the absence of a political decision towards this particular group. The deadlock was only broken in March 1983 when State Security contacted COR to establish whether there was a possibility of treating 2,000 former ELF members – mainly young men, women and children – as refugees (Meeting between Omar Mohamad al-Tayeb, Vice President and Chief of State Security with COR, GPM, 20 March 1983 in 36/A/4/Confid. 23 March 1983). However, in the event only forty-five families wanted to move out as refugees, and only then did COR show its willingness to relocate the 'refugees' in the refugee settlement of Mafaza. Another group, estimated at 1,000, of those who held military and political functions in the ELF, were considered as a special group 'security risk' for fear of reprisals by other factions. A few of them were helped by the Resettlement Programme to leave Sudan for the US and Canada (Interview with Ahmed Osman, previously of the Eritrean Red Cross (Red Crescent), 1984).

Attitude of the Authorities towards Refugees in Kassala and Gedaref Towns

Just at the time when decisions were taken in Khartoum to relocate the refugees away from the town, similar decisions were being taken by the provincial authorities who were particularly concerned about the presence of refugees in Kassala and Gedaref. In their attempts to relocate the refugees in rural settlements, the provincial authorities had to make alternative locations available and to approve the allocation of land for the new settlements. For the material costs involved in preparing the new settlements, the provincial authorities relied heavily on the representatives of COR in Showak and Gedaref. This co-operation led to the building of new refugee settlements during and after 1979, mainly for refugees from border areas and for newcomers. As for the evacuation of refugees from towns, the pressure from different directions (Khartoum, Gedaref, Kassala, Gezira) was met by the COR GPM in Showak and by the Assistant Commissioner for Refugees in Gedaref with delaying tactics as they manoeuvred between the different political groups. For example, throughout 1979, the GPM tried to resist pressures by Kassala town authorities by claiming that he was authorised to receive refugees from Khartoum only. As a result, expulsions from Kassala had to be slowed down.

The transfer of refugees from Kassala town began in August 1978 when a group of 4,000 new arrivals was moved to a permanent settlement at Khashm al Girba. After the incidents at Wad el Heleiw in January 1979, and the decision to evacuate refugees from towns in Kassala Province, priority continued to be given to the resettlement of refugees to rural areas. In May 1979, the Commissioner for Refugees was requested to implement the decision to transfer 500 members of the EDU from New Halfa. The Kassala Province Security Commission headed by the Provincial Commissioner resolved that the 500 Ethiopians should be transferred to the refugee settlements in Gedaref (Mohamed Mahjoub Hassaballa to COR, KP/Police/Confid./32/B/1/5, 17 May 1979). The refugees were sent to Um Gulja settlement in Gedaref (see CR/36/B/Confid. COR to GPM Showak, 6 August 1979). In late October 1979, the Security Commission decided to reopen the reception centre in Wad Sherifei which had received refugees in 1975 (Kassala Province Security Committee, Meeting No. 15, 28 October 1979). As this decision would require the availability of services such as shelter, water, food and health, the Provincial Commissioner requested the GPM in Showak to prepare the reception centre (GPM, Showak to Provincial

Commissioner No. CRSH/35/A/1, 4 November 1979). The GPM in Showak replied that since the reception centre had been opened in 1975 with relief assistance from UNHCR, funds were no longer available. He asked for a more detailed proposal to be submitted to UNHCR with a request for more assistance.

In reaction to the GPM's apparent reluctance to co-operate, the Provincial Commissioner ordered the immediate evacuation of 2,000 refugees from Kassala town to refugee 'camps'. He then authorised the Administrative Assistant Commissioner in Kassala to execute the plan within one month. Kassala authorities began to transfer refugees to Khashm al Girba in late November, and by 5 December, 1,182 refugees had been transferred. However, the GPM in Showak did not have reception facilities, particularly tents. The operation in Kassala signalled a crisis, particularly as the refugees evacuated from Khartoum were due to arrive on 13 December. The GPM in Showak reacted by informing Kassala provincial authorities that he had no funds and that he was authorised by the Commissioner for Refugees only to receive the refugees coming from Khartoum. He also gave directives to the Project Manager in Khashm al Girba *not* to receive any refugees sent from Kassala.

As a result of the tension that developed between the GPM in Showak and the provincial authorities in Kassala, the refugees were faced with being unwanted in both places. This difficult situation resulted in interventions by UNHCR and COR in Khartoum. UNHCR sent its Protection Officer from Khartoum to report on the refugee situation in Kassala.[14] Neither UNHCR nor COR's delegates objected to the relocation of the refugees outside Kassala town. However, UNHCR expressed criticisms about the way the refugees were being treated by the police authorities in Kassala. The UNHCR report related that:

> The movement of the refugees from Kassala has started on Monday November 26th, 1979. On that date 312 refugees, all male, were rounded up indiscriminately in the streets and in the market and immediately transferred to a temporary settlement in Khashm al Girba.

UNHCR expressed concern particularly because the political fronts had promised to provide lists of refugees who would go voluntarily

14. Since 1978, UNHCR began to bring in Protection Officers who mainly reported on legal problems facing the refugees. As the UNHCR policy towards providing assistance to refugees in towns was ambivalent, they tended to report on the problems as violations of *legal* rights of refugees. They did not analyse *why* these problems arose in the first place.

to the settlements. Had this promise been kept, a police operation would have been unnecessary (Dureux 1979).

Unlike in Khartoum, there was readiness, even among some of the refugees and the fronts, particularly the ELF, to assist with the transfer to rural areas. The ELF prepared a list of 3,000 families, a number which exceeded the provincial government's expectations. The refugees who were supposed to be moved according to the ELF estimate fell into three categories:

1. persons of rural background who had moved to Kassala from border areas simply because they did not know where to go. For this group, town life had proved to be costly because of low incomes and the high cost of living;
2. families of fighters in the battlefield inside Eritrea;
3. families whose breadwinners were children working in low paid jobs in the town, or those whose male guardians worked in remote places or abroad.

The relocation of refugees in 1979 was only partially successful in that only two new settlements were established, at Khashm al Girba and Kilo 26, a village on the border of New Halfa Scheme with 3,000 refugees.

The authorities at Kassala became concerned about the impact of the refugees on the public services. In September 1979, the People's Executive Council for Kassala Province produced a resolution aimed at minimising pressure on educational facilities. It expressed concern about the growing numbers of refugee children in post-primary schools (8 per cent) and advised the Assistant Commissioner for Education that, 'No student should be admitted to the Junior Secondary Level unless a Sudanese Nationality Certificate is presented by his/her parent' (Kassala Province Executive Council Res. 514, 23 September 1979. Directive from Secretary to Assistant Commissioner for Health No. KP/Exec./16/D/11/2/11, 1 October 1979).

This decision meant that the refugees were to be excluded from opportunities to receive schooling in Kassala beyond the primary level. The issue was one of limited resources. Therefore the Commissioner for Refugees intervened with the provincial authorities, arguing that the problem could be solved more effectively by creating educational opportunities than by excluding the refugees. He promised that more schools would be included in the proposal submitted to UNHCR for funding in 1980. Donors would show sympathy only if the Sudanese indicated a willingness to allow refugees to benefit from opportunities within the Sudanese educational system

(COR to Kassala Provincial Commissioner, CR/17/C/1/5, 10 January 1980). To this end, the Commissioner for Refugees requested that the prohibition on refugee education should be lifted. In reply, the Kassala authorities argued that they were not in fact against refugee education, they simply could not afford to offer opportunities for refugees indefinitely. Nevertheless, as a response to the promises of the Commissioner, the Council postponed its decision to restrict the admission of refugee children (Kassala Provincial Commissioner to COR, KP/Exec./16/D/3/14, 28 August 1980, referring to Executive Council Res. 540, 25 March 1980).

Measures to restrict movement to Kassala, and efforts by the police and immigration authorities to apply them, continued throughout 1980. In November 1980 the Provincial Executive Council again produced a local order aimed at regularising refugee movement in the provincial towns (Local Order No. 75 [1980] 'Regularisation of Refugee Movement within the Towns of Kassala Province'. No. KP/Exec./16/C/2/3 23 November 1980). The local order applied severe restrictions on refugees residing in the towns of Kassala, Khashm al Girba, New Halfa, Aroma, Showak and Gedaref. It imposed a curfew against refugees going out between 6 p.m. and 6 a.m. without permission from State Security (ibid.). Any refugee who broke this law was given a prison sentence and/or fined (Assistant Commissioner for Refugees, Gedaref to COR, Ref. ACR/35/C/1/Confid. 16 December 1981).

The implications of the law proved to be harsher than the refugees had anticipated, whether they obeyed it and stayed at home or moved and faced punishment. In the three months between November 1980 and January 1981, 5,000 cases were reported to the People's Courts in Gedaref alone. On average 50 to 60 cases were tried per day. The sentences ranged from fines of £S5, to prison sentences of one or two weeks. Reacting furiously, the Assistant Commissioner for Refugees in Gedaref pleaded with the Commissioner for Refugees: 'The fact that such large numbers have broken the law, indicates that the problem lies with the law itself rather than with those who break it' (ibid.).

The Commissioner and his staff expressed their fears about the spreading antagonism against the refugees and the danger of letting the local authorities design their own policy. This would not only affect plans to gain external assistance, but could also lead to the victimisation of the refugees without solving the problems faced by the Sudanese (ibid.). However, as COR plans did not produce results, and as the influx continued through 1981, the antagonism was exacerbated by further decisions at the national level.

On 10 December 1981, the National Security Council decided that the refugees in Kassala should be relocated outside Kassala town in new camps provided with the necessary shelter, food, water and health services (National Security Council to Commissioner for Refugees SC/1/B/2/3/549/Confid., also MOI/35/B/1, 17 December 1981). The Commissioner was requested to make a progress report to the Council at its forthcoming session. Exactly a year later, General Omar Mohammad al Tayeb chaired a meeting to discuss the problems caused by the refugees. It was attended by the governors of Eastern and Central Regions, the Minister of the Interior, Provincial Commissioners, State Security and Police. The Vice President and Chief of State Security again invited discussion of 'the serious security problems caused by the presence of the refugees residing in border areas as well as in the towns' (Minutes of a meeting at the Council of Ministers premises, No. 36/A/4, 23 October 1982). Again the meeting resolved that the ideal solution was to regroup the refugees in particular areas in the Eastern and Central Regions. The meeting also recommended that the provincial authorities should make the necessary preparations for the refugees to be transferred to the new sites to be established by COR (ibid.).

Gedaref Town

The decisions to evict the refugees from Sudanese towns had a particularly serious effect on those who lived in Gedaref. The town shared the popular views about the refugees; in fact by 1979, Gedaref had witnessed violent conflict between refugees and several sections of the local population. As mentioned in Chapter 3, Gedaref and its area councils were the major recipients of refugees from highland Ethiopia. They were mainly concentrated in particular quarters of the town: Deim al Nur, Riwina, and Taradona. The local authorities employed to the full the stereotype of the refugees as Ethiopian 'Habashi', and as non-Muslims, who tended to engage in prostitution and in alcohol brewing (Mahmoud 1986: 57-67).

Action taken in Khartoum and Kassala set a precedent for similar measures to be taken in Gedaref. Immediately after the Provincial Commissioner's directive in Wad el Heleiw in January 1979, the local Security Committee in Gedaref ordered the evacuation of the Ethiopian quarters in the town and the transfer of the refugees to the village of Um Gulja (12 km from Gedaref) (Assistant Commissioner Gedaref to Commissioner for Refugees Khartoum, Memorandum 5 July 1979). The Assistant Commissioner succeeded in persuading the Gedaref Security Committee to delay the evacuation until the committee representing the Commissioner of Refugees, the local councils, and the SSU local units, had investigated the matter. The idea was that, since an immediate transfer of the refugees was beyond the capabilities of the Assistant Commissioner of Refugees' office in Gedaref, it was more advisable to incorporate the plan to establish the village of Um Gulja and Tawawa in the suburb of Gedaref, into the annual programme of assistance by UNHCR for 1980 to 1981. While this was being considered, dramatic events broke out in late October 1979.

On 28 October 1979, a single incident involving a fight between a Sudanese and an Ethiopian in the residential quarter of al-Rabaa led to a fight between the two communities. As a result, 500 huts occupied by the Ethiopians were burnt down, other property destroyed and several people were killed or wounded.[15] The army was called in and the refugees were moved to Gedaref football stadium before being transferred to the refugee settlement in Um Gulja. This incident and the subsequent feeling generated by it prompted the local authorities to take measures which were believed to be necessary for maintaining public order. Immediately after the events, the People's Executive Council in Kassala enacted a by-law, which imposed a curfew on the refugees. This pattern of reaction continued as similar incidents occurred in the ensuing years: in a fight which broke out on 30 April 1981, a refugee killed three people. Popular violence broke out. The refugees were again attacked. The police intervened and kept them in police custody and later transferred them to Tawawa. To relieve tension new refugee settlements were established in Eastern Sudan. Um Gulja, which was originally a village with 1,000 residents of West African origin, became the suburban settlement for Ethiopian refugees. Similarly, Jebel Tawawa became a refugee settlement. In both villages the refugees who were previously in Gedaref, were enabled to have their own residential quarters with the approval of the local authorities, and services financed by external assistance.

Conclusion

From the above account it appears that, contrary to the conventional assumption, the problem for refugees was not one of gaining admission to the country of asylum. The most important principles in

---

15. The refugees gave the number of those killed as 50, and 250 wounded, see letter to Amnesty International 21 November 1979, where Mahmoud (1986: 87) gives the figure as 'more than 100'.

international refugee law, allowing refugees to enter freely and without the threat of forced repatriation, were upheld by the authorities in the Sudan. Refugees were freely allowed into the country over the years and were not expelled to their country of origin. In fact, even when it was suggested that the Ethiopians should be repatriated, with or without their consent, the Sudanese authorities, under several regimes, adamantly refused to cooperate.

The main problem was the socio-political condition of the host country. A very clear distinction should therefore be made between the problems experienced by the refugees as victims of natural and man-made disasters, and the problems that refugees themselves cause. From the above account it is apparent that the Sudanese authorities tended to see the refugees as a cause of problems for Sudan. To them, the hosts were in fact the victims. Clearly, the attitudes and subsequent decisions, particularly in towns, indicate that the Sudanese were, at the very least, *involuntary hosts.* This distinction is crucial.

As the attitudes and decisions of the political authorities and bureaucracy revealed, by 1979 the regime in Sudan did not seem to have either the ability or the willingness to translate rights into practice. It seemed to be more concerned about the economic crisis that had been escalating since 1978. It was concerned about the deterioration of the economic infrastructure and its complete inability to put an end to that deterioration. The political credibility of the regime was in decline, as revealed by the failure of the SSU to mobilise the people, the emergence of competing power centres and the growing discontent and alienation of the impoverished Sudanese. Facing these challenges, the authorities portrayed the refugees as a threat to the security of the country and as an additional burden. The refugees were redefined as an unwanted group, which would become a source of trouble if left unattended, and which should be kept in particular places away from towns and from border areas. While demanding the confinement of the unwanted refugees to particular places (camps in the Eastern Region), the authorities were not willing to commit government funds to prepare places where refugees could re-establish their own means of survival.

The plight of the refugees was compounded by the irony that after 1979, decisions were taken to expel even poorer Sudanese migrants from the big towns. It became usual for the Sudanese authorities, when asked about the evictions of the refugees from towns, to reply that they were not victimising the refugees because the immigrant Sudanese also had to leave the towns (RSP Report 1987). Another feature of the policy of the authorities was that it always left COR to bear the financial costs, and to implement their decisions to move the refugees away from particular areas. This continued to be the case, in spite of the fact that COR is itself a government office.

With the growing hostility towards refugees after 1978, COR was confronted with the irreconcilable position of being both a government office that was obliged to abide by government decisions, and at the same time, an office that was basically established to provide solutions for the refugees themselves. Between mid-1978 and July 1979, COR countered attempts to send the refugees away from towns with measures aimed at allowing some people to be exempted. Efforts were made with some success to regulate the legal status of refugees by issuing identity cards and work permits. But these attempts by COR were not appreciated by other departments. What COR considered a temporary decision in June 1978, was only the beginning of a phase in which the political bureaucracy tried to remove refugees from towns and rural areas. COR was required not only to deal with the repeated decisions to evict the refugees in the short term, but also to devise a long term plan that would help to stop the tendency to stigmatise the refugees.

It was clear that the refugee problem was converging with the problems faced by Sudan itself. For COR, the crisis could not be solved by Sudan alone. A new approach had to be sought through international assistance beyond the relief phase in order to minimise the burden on the government. Consequently, COR began to articulate a new plan to involve international donors. The arguments developed by COR were based on the belief that refugee problems were an international responsibility and that attempts to tackle these problems should take into account the principles of international cooperation and burden sharing.

References

Al-Assam, M. M. (1983) 'Regional Government in the Sudan', *Public Administration and Development* 3: 111-120.

Al-Bashir, A. R. (1978) 'Problems of Settlement of Immigrants and Refugees in Sudanese Society', D.Phil. Thesis, St. Antony's College, University of Oxford.

Betts, T. F. (1974) *Southern Sudan: The Ceasefire and After.* London: The Africa Publications Trust.

Beyer, G. (1976) *Report of a Mission to Sudan* Geneva: UNHCR.

COR (1980) 'Administrative Assistance to Individual Cases, A Guideline', Khartoum.

Crummy, D. (ed.) (1986) *Banditry, Rebellion and Social Protest in Africa.* London: James Currey and Heinemann.

DRS (Democratic Republic of Sudan) (1974) The Regulation of Asylum Act, Act No. 45, signed 21 May 1974.

Dureux, J. F. (1979) 'Note for the File: Report on a visit', UNHCR KRT/M/2440 dated 1-2 December 1979.

Fadlalla, B. O. (n.d.) 'Financing Regionalisation in the Sudan' in De Wet, P. and Ahmed, A. (eds.) *Perspectives on Development in the Sudan.* Khartoum: Development Studies and Research Centre.

Mahmoud, U. A. (1986) 'Self-Settled Refugees in Gedaref', UNHCR Report / University of Khartoum.

Norris, M. W. (1983) 'Local Government and Decentralisation in the Sudan', *Public Administration and Development* 3: 209-223.

Palmer, M. (1976) 'Report to the Board on the Refugee Situation in the Sudan', *ACORD*, p. 3, London, September 1976 in Betts Papers, RSP, Oxford.

Siddig, A. M. (1970) A Comment on the Proposed Reorganisation of the Ministry. Police HQ. Ministry of the Interior, 1 February.

SUNA *Daily Newsletter,* 2 January 1977.

UNHCR (1979) 'Note for the File: Minutes of a Joint Meeting between Commissioner for Refugees and UNHCR Representative', KRT/M/995, 9 September.

5

The Role and Limitations of Assistance to Refugees: UNHCR and COR, 1975-1978

As COR was coming into conflict with other government depart-ments in its attempt to reconcile the need to contain the real or per-ceived threats posed by the refugees, and the need to guarantee the refugees' rights, its position was strengthened by its link with inter-national donors, as represented by UNHCR. As argued in Chapter 4, COR's close association with UNHCR saved it more than once from being attached to the security organisations, or from being abolished altogether. Since the government was concerned not only to contain the security threat but also to minimise the socio-eco-nomic problems posed by the refugees, COR was able to maintain its position by arguing that it at least had a role to play in addressing the latter issue. COR, therefore, occupied a pivotal position as an intermediary between the Sudanese Government and UNHCR. Whilst attempting to guarantee the security of the refugees, in the face of opposing demands from Sudanese authorities, COR was also responsible for providing for their material needs. In the govern-ment's view, the task of alleviating the socio-economic problems caused by the refugees necessarily involved approaches to interna-tional donors: indeed, the government believed that the interna-tional community had an obligation to share the burden.

In the period after 1980, the question whether the international community was under any obligation to respond to the needs of African refugees became the subject of debate. At the national level, however, the seeds of this debate were sown as early as 1975, with the failure of the first rural refugee settlement in Eastern Sudan, and the realisation that neither COR nor UNHCR would be able to meet the financial costs involved. This gave rise to a tension in the relationship between UNHCR and COR which paralleled the tension between COR and other government departments, and further complicated the government's response to the refugees.

This chapter examines the mounting tensions between COR and UNHCR and the context in which these tensions occurred. Although the problems between COR and UNHCR related primarily to the technical difficulties involved in managing the refugee assistance programme, certain other fundamental issues were also at stake.

After 1966, the option preferred by successive Sudanese governments was to provide relief for each new refugee influx and then to settle the refugees in special villages away from the border, with assistance mainly provided by UNHCR. This was thought to be an appropriate political option that minimised the security risk created by the presence of the refugees inside Sudan and the potential tensions between Sudan and Ethiopia. Although an afterthought, the economic rationale of helping the refugees to re-establish their means of survival complemented this political option.

It was taken for granted that UNHCR would provide financial assistance. Although UNHCR's mandate stressed its role in providing international protection (GA Res. 428 [v] Chapter 1, 14 December 1970), it also acted as a major provider of assistance to host countries (GA Res. 1166 [xii], 26 November 1957). Therefore, in the case of Sudan, a kind of partnership emerged between the government and UNHCR. In theory, both UNHCR and COR were created with a view to facilitating assistance and devising solutions to the refugee problem. However, their mentors (the member states of the United Nations and the Sudanese Government respectively) wanted assistance to be provided at minimum cost. COR and UNHCR thus shared the aim of seeking cost-effective solutions to the refugee problem; yet, ironically, it was precisely this similarity in their objectives which drove them apart.

At first, the mentors (and later the donors) of UNHCR intended to assign responsibility primarily to the country which received the refugees. UNHCR assistance was intended to be limited and short-lived; UNHCR was under constant pressure to avoid expensive programmes. COR, in turn, was expected to minimise the cost to the government and the local Sudanese population; it relied almost entirely on external assistance. In the period after 1975, this difference in the perspectives of UNHCR and COR had repercussions for the refugees themselves, as it proved almost impossible to devise programmes which satisfied the criteria of both organisations.

In spite of the political imperative to move the refugees away from the border – and the government's desire to see all refugees in organised settlements – questions arose as to whether this was possible, given the financial constraints. UNHCR began to equivocate and to explore alternative and more cost-effective ways of dealing with the refugee problem. The second part of this chapter will discuss developments in UNHCR policy, and the factors which contributed to an eventual crisis in 1978.

Establishing Refugee Settlements: The Challenge to UNHCR/COR Cooperation

The joint UNHCR/COR programme to resettle the 1967 Eritrean refugees took five years to complete. The delays, relating to the two tasks of building a settlement infrastructure and transferring the refugees to Qala en Nahal, are well-documented elsewhere.[1] Nevertheless, by 1972 both the government and UNHCR were satisfied with the outcome. Twenty thousand, nine hundred and seventy-four refugees were resettled in six villages, which were provided with water, health, education and community development services. Plots of agricultural land were allocated to refugee families for them to produce sorghum for food and sesame for sale. The refugee settlement was considered a success, in that it had both provided the opportunity for refugees to support themselves and helped to transform an undeveloped region into a viable productive area. In 1974, the total contribution of UNHCR and WFP to the cost of establishing the settlement was estimated at $2,437,500.

In principle, this joint programme between UNHCR and COR was successful in that it achieved the political imperative of transferring a particular group of refugees away from the border. However, because of the time and expense involved, it seemed unlikely that the two parties would be able to maintain their success at Qala en Nahal, when dealing with new influxes of refugees. This first experiment illustrated the danger of dealing with one isolated group and ignoring the fact that political problems in the country of origin were likely to produce more refugees.

Moreover, even at this time there were differences in opinion between UNHCR and COR as to what the goals of assistance should

---

1. Qala en Nahal Refugee Settlement, as the government's first such experience, was considered a success story during its initial years 1969-1973; see Holborn 1975: 1336-1347; UNHCR 1972; Al-Bashir 1978: 332-360; Karadawi 1977: 98-113. However, after the settlement was completed and handed over to the unprepared local government authorities in Kassala, several studies appeared criticising COR for its poor planning and local government for poor management, e.g., Huntings Technical Services Ltd., 1976; Betts 1982; Rogge 1985: 92-108.

be. In practical terms, UNHCR considered that its role was to provide minimal assistance over a short period. The ultimate goal was 'local integration', which meant that once the basic infrastructure was completed, UNHCR would hand over responsibility to the host government. 'Integration' meant the process whereby refugees became part and parcel of the local community. The government, on the other hand, did not see the settlement policy as a step towards the granting of full Sudanese citizenship to refugees. For COR, 'integration' necessarily involved linking the services established in the refugee settlement with the local Sudanese infrastructure, in a zonal plan. In fact, UNHCR and COR were using similar language to mean different things. Most importantly, this led to conflict over spending; UNHCR intended to limit its financial contribution, whereas COR wanted to raise more funds for its plan of zonal development.

In 1973, UNHCR decided that the refugees in Qala en Nahal had reached a level of self-sufficiency comparable to the local Sudanese, and that additional assistance from the agency could not be justified. As the implementation and administration of the Qala en Nahal settlement was performed by COR itself, the handover of the settlement by UNHCR to the government meant, in simple terms, that UNHCR was to withdraw its funds. COR itself did not have funds to provide for the running costs of the refugee settlement (estimated at £S115,113 per annum). In fact, COR believed that as the management of the refugee settlement had been reduced to a routine task, the settlement would no longer require COR's special attention. A plan to link the refugee settlements to neighbouring Sudanese development schemes was not received favourably by development agencies such as UNDP, and eventually died a natural death. COR therefore suggested that responsibility for managing Qala en Nahal settlement should be transferred to the provincial authorities of Kassala.

The official transfer of the settlement to Qala en Nahal local council in July 1974 happened unexpectedly, and arose out of a sense of urgency rather than as a result of a well thought out plan. Neither the refugees nor the local council were prepared for it. The withdrawal of both UNHCR and COR amounted to the abandonment of the refugee settlement and from then on, the settlement experienced a gradual decline. Protests by refugees against the decision to levy taxes, and a poor harvest in 1975, made it even more difficult for the new management to meet the running costs of the settlement, including maintaining the water supply system and providing fuel for agricultural operations. The difficulties mounted in 1976, as the refugees faced food shortages and large numbers had to leave the agricultural schemes or move to towns. At one stage, the population of the settlement dropped to 7,500 (Huntings 1976, section 2-3).

This decline of the first refugee settlement after the withdrawal of assistance resulted in an extreme sense of disappointment, and had far-reaching repercussions. In particular, it had a profound effect on the relationship between COR and UNHCR as they began to plan strategies for refugee assistance in the ensuing years.

The Attempt to Establish a Second Refugee Settlement

The experience of Qala en Nahal had a direct impact on the government's plan to establish a second refugee settlement for Eritrean refugees who arrived in Red Sea Province in 1970. Once again, the Sudanese Council of Ministers had urged the transfer of the refugees away from the border. Relief assistance was requested pending the resettlement of the refugees. The plan prepared by COR envisaged the building of five villages to accommodate 22,000 refugees. An area of 926 km^2 was designated at Moharragat, near Showak. Taking into account the nomadic background of the refugees, the new settlement was planned to be based on animal husbandry, and families were to be provided with cows, sheep and poultry. An agreement was drawn up whereby the finance for the project would be provided jointly by the government ($854,200), UNHCR ($750,000) and by WFP, which would provide food assistance valued at $833,000 (Ministry of the Interior 1972).

In considering these plans, UNHCR justifiably demanded verification that the settlement was suitable for economic investment and for human settlement. This required careful and thoughtful planning, and was inevitably a timeconsuming process. In addition, UNHCR attempted to obtain certain guarantees from the government. In particular, reference was made to what was seen as the incontestable right of refugees to own land. UNHCR also inserted a possible role for NGOs, which had been avoided as implementing partners until then. As a result of protracted negotiations, the agreement was not signed until December 1972. One year after it was signed by the Minister of the Interior it was endorsed by the President of the Republic for the first time (Presidential Decree No. 126, 27 November 1973). By this time, the refugees had already spent three years in the Sudan.

To make matters worse, the geophysical explorations conducted in 1973 and 1974 revealed that sources of ground water were unreliable. The search for alternatives continued until 1976 (Huntings Technical Services Ltd. 1976, Ch. 5 para. 5.4). Eventually:

> ... the delay in establishing this fact and the conflicting feasibility reports of the Sudanese and UN experts inside and outside the country on the animal husbandry side ... determined the fate of El Showak as an unsuitable site for the settlement of refugees. (Al-Bashir 1978: 373)

After six years, therefore, the assistance partners had failed to implement any plan to resettle the Tokar refugee group.

This procrastination led the refugees themselves to seek alternative solutions. Different factors converged to push the refugees away from temporary camps established in Tokar and Wad el Heleiw in 1970. The suspension of relief by WFP and its resumption by the government resulted in irregular and insufficient food supplies to the area. The Tokar area generally becomes inaccessible in the period between April and August each year, when the local residents traditionally migrate to hilly areas away from the flooded delta. The area suffers from a shortage of drinking water and vulnerability to drought. The refugees, who were mostly from the Habab and Beni Amer, had to join their Sudanese kith and kin in enduring the harsh environment.

Little is known from the records about how and when the refugees began to disperse. When COR began to investigate the whereabouts of the refugees, it could only find vague information and rough estimates.[2] The Commissioner had to admit that the delay in preparing a settlement site in Showak, and the extremely harsh conditions at the reception centres, had led to 'the dispersal of the refugees over the whole region, where they settled themselves ... contrary to the wish of the government' (ibid.).

Ironically for UNHCR, the dispersal offered a better option in that it exonerated UNHCR from the cost that would have been incurred if the Showak settlement had been established. Therefore, it no longer considered the settlement of the Tokar group as a matter of priority. As one UNHCR report stated:

> Although project 72/LS/SUD-3 had originally been established to provide a permanent settlement solution for over 22,000, no more than 5,000 would now be served, the remainder have drifted off to spontaneous settlement elsewhere. Therefore, to maintain this project as a separate allocation seems unnecessary. (Beyer 1976)

2. A report by the Deputy COR stated that the refugees moved to work as cheap labour for landowners in the Tokar Delta (15,000) or as unskilled labour in Port Sudan, where they lived in Deim al Nur (4,500); a few (2,000) moved to the hilly areas of Adarat and Eiterba.

Having failed to resettle the Tokar group, COR directed its attention to another group of refugees who were beginning to arrive in Kassala Province.

UNHCR Responses to the Post-1975 Influxes

The new influx began at a time when COR and UNHCR were least prepared. A resigned mood of indecision governed not only the progress of UNHCR-assisted settlements, but also the reaction to the new refugee flows. At the time of the new influx, which began in 1975, UNHCR justified its lack of action by drawing attention to its doctrine of 'non-operationalism' (UNHCR Statute Ch. 1 para. 1), whereby the stipulation that UNHCR would assist governments was taken to imply that it should not itself administer the refugee programme directly; the Branch Office in Khartoum claimed that it was not the role or the responsibility of UNHCR to investigate any new refugee influx (Beyer 1976: 4).

Even when the government requested emergency assistance for the refugees who arrived at Wad el Heleiw in March 1975, the UNHCR response was slower than expected. As analysed by a UNHCR consultant, it took UNHCR 35 days to authorise the expenditure of emergency funds, even though the government request for $250,000 was signed by the Minister of the Interior, who was then Vice President of Sudan (Chambers 1975: 9). When the belated authorisation was made

> [it] did not include any food items except salt, the intention being that WFP would provide food items. However, neither WFP nor UNHCR were at the time of authorisation providing funds for pulses, which was why the Resident Representative [UNDP] took the unusual step, without prior consultation with UNDRO, of issuing the Sudanese Government with a cheque for $15,000 for the purchase of urgently needed essential food items. (Ibid.: 10)

During the period between their arrival and receiving emergency supplies, the refugees were fed from donations made by the local people of Gedaref.[3]

The delay in authorising the emergency funds arose because UNHCR in Khartoum did not have the authority to respond to the emergency without prior approval from its headquarters in Geneva.

---

3. 450 sacks of sorghum, 10 sacks of dried vegetables, 10 sacks of onions, and 15 cans of vegetable oil were donated by local people in Gedaref, and 50 sacks of sorghum by the Sudanese in Wad el Heleiw (COR-Showak special file, 1981).

There, decisions within the UNHCR office, and between UNHCR and WFP, concerning the approval of emergency funds were subject to timeconsuming delays. The Geneva office displayed a reluctance to entrust emergency funds to a UNHCR representative immediately after a refugee influx was identified (Chambers 1975: 11).

The reluctance of UNHCR to make decisions can be seen even more clearly in its response to the Ethiopian refugees who arrived in south Gedaref district in 1976. UNHCR in Khartoum wanted to adhere to the policy of non-involvement and to the doctrine of 'non-operationalism'. It was reluctant even to investigate the plight of these refugees, on the grounds that 'the government itself would take a very dim view of such "interference" into its role and responsibilities' (Beyer 1976: 5). Subsequently, it became clear that UNHCR was not merely adhering to its own rules, but was trying to avoid extending assistance to these refugees. Reports by UNHCR tried in different ways to play down their plight. During 1975, UNHCR Headquarters was informed about the presence of newly arrived refugees in Gedaref district and the Branch Office in Khartoum sent a mission to investigate. It reported that:

> ... these were probably not mandate refugees, being economic migrants, many already integrated into the villages and in no need of emergency assistance. The government itself seemed quite casual about the problem. (Ibid.:4)

It is interesting to consider here, the labels which different parties applied to the refugee group to suit respective organisational interests. For example, in an initial stage the country of origin labelled the exodus as one of 'outlaws and rebels'; subsequently, to minimise the threat to both host and country of origin governments, the term 'refugees' became convenient for depoliticising them. In the quotation above, the differentiation between 'economic migrants' and 'refugees' was being applied for the first time in Sudan to disqualify refugees from assistance. UNHCR also sought to explain government pressure for assistance by implying that the government was inventing the presence of refugees for economic and political reasons.

UNHCR's Change of Attitude towards Ethiopian Migrants: The OXFAM-Sponsored Mission

This period of inaction was effectively broken by the arrival of an independent mission commissioned by OXFAM and led by Ras Mangasha Seyoum and Dr Bent Juel-Jensen. Ras Mangasha was internationally recognised as an expert on the situation within Ethiopia; as a prominent Ethiopian, ex-Governor of Tigray, and leader of the EDU, his knowledge of the plight of the refugees could hardly be questioned. He himself had reported the plight of the Ethiopian refugees to UNHCR in Geneva, but had received a negative response. In March 1975, he and other Ethiopian representatives in exile approached OXFAM for help (Seyoum and Juel-Jensen 1976: 1-2). OXFAM needed to investigate the situation. On the way to Sudan, its mission stopped in Geneva and visited UNHCR, where it was told that:

> According to the [UNHCR] Branch Office in Khartoum, the Sudanese authorities had not approached OXFAM for help and the findings of the Branch Office had not shown need for help. (Ibid.: 2)

In Khartoum, COR welcomed the arrival of the mission. UNHCR, on the other hand, was uncooperative. At first it was unwilling to provide information, and when it finally did, it was only after receiving a cable from Geneva urging it to do so. A UNHCR official informed the mission that the Ethiopians in Gedaref were self-settled and that 'no direct assistance [was] needed'. The government's estimates of the numbers of refugees in the area were dismissed by UNHCR as 'serious exaggerations' (ibid. (quotation marks in original)).

After visiting Gedaref, Wad Kawli and Doka, the OXFAM mission reported on the extremely difficult conditions facing the Ethiopian refugees there, as well as in Khartoum. As mentioned in Chapter 3, the report documented the unsatisfactory living conditions experienced by these refugees, and described their health status as 'critical'. The mission recommended, in particular, the establishment of a 24 bed ward for the seriously ill in Gedaref, an ambulance to serve both refugees and Sudanese, blankets, beds, mattresses, and a large supply of drugs (ibid.: 5-6). For refugees in Wad Kawli, it recommended their transfer to a settlement site where they could cultivate land and have access to shelter, medical and educational services (ibid.: 7-8).

These findings and recommendations were discussed at a meeting between COR, UNHCR Branch Office, and the mission team. The OXFAM Mission's report of this meeting states that:

> … it was agreed that the problems were as outlined above, despite the initial reluctance, very strange, on the part of the UNHCR representative to accept facts rather than speculations. (Ibid.: 9)

The OXFAM Mission's final report suggested that the cost of the relief for the 20,000-22,000 refugees would amount to $1 million. The report ended in an appeal to OXFAM:

> We request that OXFAM makes what contribution it can in cash or in kind and suggest that any aid must be channelled through COM. Ref. with full co-operation from HCR, the Sudanese Red Crescent and SCC [the Sudan Council of Churches]. (Ibid.: 10)

The publication of the findings of the OXFAM Mission report had a strong impact. Ras Mangasha Seyoum considered the Ethiopian refugees from Wollo, Tigray and Gojam as his own people (interview, 1979). He also had close links with the government in Sudan, particularly with Public Security (see Chapter 3), and had influential connections abroad, particularly in Britain, where the Ethiopian Refugees' Self-Help Organization (ERSHO) had patrons such as the Archbishop of Canterbury and Sir Anthony Eden. The arrival and activity of the mission thus emphasised the political factors behind the Ethiopian refugee influx to Sudan, and challenged UNHCR's view that the refugees were simply 'economic migrants'. Simultaneously, by drawing attention to the scale and severity of the problem, the report implicitly and explicitly contradicted UNHCR's findings, and exposed the inadequacy of the aid programme. COR was able, on the basis of the mission's findings, to make a formal request for assistance.

UNHCR's reaction to the report's findings was mixed. Its representative in Khartoum dismissed the report as an exaggeration (Reynes 1976a) and denied any connection with the proposals made by the OXFAM mission (Reynes 1976b). His hostility did not seem to be shared by UNHCR Headquarters. A mission visited Sudan in May 1976 and its report cautiously praised the role of the OXFAM mission (Beyer 1976: 4). The excuse improvised by UNHCR Headquarters was that the ambivalence towards the new refugee influx had been caused by government inaction. UNHCR was handicapped by the fact that it had to wait for government requests for assistance. According to the UNHCR mission:

> The Juel-Jensen OXFAM mission seems to have acted as a catalyst, prodding the Sudanese Government into action on the problem of Abyssinian refugees. It cannot, however, be given the credit for discovering the problem. (Ibid.)

The report admitted that 'UNHCR Branch Office had received reports in 1975 of problems with these refugees'. Without referring to the fact that UNHCR had itself investigated the problem in 1975, and concluded that the Ethiopians were not refugees according to UNHCR's mandate, the report went on to blame the government for not providing sufficient information at that time:

Operating in the context of non-operationalism, [UNHCR] immediately requested the Commissioner for Refugees for information about numbers, locations, conditions, needs and settlement plan; but despite several follow up reminders, and until the arrival of the OXFAM mission, had had no response from the government. (Ibid.)

Twisting the argument further, the UNHCR mission argued that although Dr Juel-Jensen was indeed a catalyst, this was:

... a role more easily done from the outside (since he then flew back to London and did not have to continue working with the *Sudanese officials he had offended*) than by the B.O. [Branch Office] which must maintain a good day-to-day working relationship with the government. (Ibid.: 5; emphasis added.)

In fact, neither in the OXFAM mission report nor in the minutes of the meetings with COR was there any evidence that the 'government officials' had been offended. The Commissioner, Dr Abdel Rahman Al-Bashir, was sympathetic to OXFAM while he was in Oxford, while Dr Juel-Jensen praised the Acting Commissioner, Omar Mohammad Ismail, in Khartoum. The report had even recommended the channelling of aid through COR.

In May 1976, UNHCR agreed to respond to the needs of the Ethiopian refugees, whilst simultaneously making it clear that the belated response was due to the lateness of the request submitted by the government (UNHCR Agreement 1976). An emergency relief programme for 8,000 refugees was finally approved, and UNHCR simultaneously agreed to contribute $127,000 from its emergency fund to assist the government in moving refugees to selected sites at Um Rakouba near Doka, and Um Gulja near Gedaref (ibid.).

Questioning the Role of the Government as an Implementing Partner

In reacting to the specific case of the 1975 Ethiopian refugees, UNHCR had been uncertain about its relationship with the government. The dilemma for UNHCR was that, while pursuing its policy of non-operationalism, it had to rely totally on COR, whose administrative structure it described as 'intricate, confused and overlapping with serious fragmentation of authority and responsibility' (ibid.).

In the May 1976 Report, Beyer argued that the available government staff and budget resources were extremely limited and subject to competitive and mutually exclusive political demands. As a result,

'Local government officials are not paid and roads, clinics etc., are not maintained.' He went on to argue that even if the urge for development was desirable, this policy had no chance of success. The reason was that the imbalance between the desires of the government and the limits of the system militated against any major efforts to develop. He concluded:

> In this context, expecting the Sudanese Commissioner for Refugees Office and local government to practice westernised, cost-effective PERT [Project Evaluation and Review Techniques], planned implementation of HCR programmes seems unrealistic. To somehow expect the B.O. to obtain such action from the government is likewise unrealistic and unfair. The problem is, of course, to what extent can and will UNHCR take into full consideration what the B.O. calls the 'local pattern of life', the 'local rhythm of life', in designing and monitoring HCR programmes? (Beyer 1976: 13)

It is doubtful whether the UNHCR staff in Khartoum had a different view from Geneva or that they were capable of offering alternatives for refugee programmes inspired by, or in tune with, the local rhythm of life. The staff who were posted in Khartoum were expatriates who had the same 'western' values, and were detached from the areas of the Sudan where the majority of refugees were settled. In addition, as argued earlier, the policy of 'non-intervention' prevented them from taking measures to investigate and report on each new influx. A more real failing of the relationship between Geneva and Khartoum staff was the latter's ambiguous view of its own role. According to the May 1976 UNHCR mission report:

> The question seems first and foremost to be one of authority and responsibility and the latter must be accompanied by an appropriate level of the former. HCR programmes operated through non-operationalism delegate authority to government but leave the responsibility often with HCR. This is not only unrealistic but also unfair. The B.O. must work every day with COR without authority over it and is therefore reduced to making requests, suggesting reminders and visits. How much responsibility must they bear for conditions wholly within the control of a sovereign nation?

In reality, therefore, it was a question of competitive claims for control. UNHCR provided funding for the programmes but was unable to control their implementation. The frustration experienced by the branch office staff led to further passivity, and this affected both the development of new programmes and the maintenance of existing settlements.

UNHCR's Reassessment of Its Policies and Practice

UNHCR Policy Review 1974-1976

This uncertainty within UNHCR in Khartoum was a reflection of a general debate which had begun at headquarters. In the period between 1974 and 1976, UNHCR hired Robert Chambers, a rural development specialist, to evaluate and advise on its performance in Africa. During this consultancy, he visited Sudan twice in May 1976. Chambers wrote a series of reports in which he called for changes in UNHCR policy and practice (see e.g., Chambers 1975, 1979, 1982, 1986).

Chambers warned against a detached diplomatic approach, which led to the neglect of the issues of rural poverty that threatened both refugees and rural host populations. Rural refugees, who outnumbered urban refugees, were worse off than was often realised. Therefore, he argued:

> ... the natural bias towards urban and diplomatic activities should be corrected by more frequent, longer and more perceptive visits to areas of spontaneous settlement and to organised settlements. (Chambers, in Coats 1978: Annex 11)

Chambers's call for UNHCR to address the issue of rural poverty challenged the UNHCR doctrine of minimal involvement. He also stressed the importance of viewing the refugee problem in the context of rural poverty generally. The organised settlements might be expensive, and might tend to perpetuate dependency, but this did not mean that spontaneously settled refugees were better off or that local populations would indefinitely cope with the refugee burden. UNHCR should become more informed in order to establish the merits of the different patterns of settlement for each refugee group. It was quite likely that UNHCR would need to invest more money in rural refugee assistance programmes.

In the conclusion of his final report, Chambers left UNHCR with a choice: they could either continue their previous practices, 'which would mean that hundreds of thousands of the most deprived people in Africa would remain trapped in a vicious circle of poverty and impotence' or they could change their ways so that 'these same people would be enabled to break out of the vicious circle and achieve acceptable levels of living and security' (ibid.). The latter choice would involve 'a painful reappraisal and reorientation in UNHCR, a change in perception, priorities and direction, and reorganisation'.

In an action programme he recommended that UNHCR should:

1. Persuade governments to allow effective investigation of spontaneously settled rural refugees;
2. Initiate more organised settlements;[4]
3. Intensify and diversify assistance to spontaneously settled
   refugees, focusing on access to land and work;
4. Include the poorer local people in assistance programmes, especially where they were worse off as a result of the presence of
   refugees;
5. Improve the knowledge and understanding of spontaneous settlement by:
   a) pooling the knowledge already gained
   b) sponsoring research
   c) conducting field investigations;
6. Raise more money by explaining to donors the poverty orientation of UNHCR's programme for rural refugees.

Part of Chambers's analysis was clearly based on the Sudanese experience, and his views certainly affected the refugee situation in the
Sudan. His attempt to influence this situation can clearly be seen in
the suggestions relating to the desirability of establishing large scale
projects (Chambers 1975: Recommendation R.7.4), involvement of a
third party as implementing partner (ibid. Recommendation R.5.1),
a more active role for the UNHCR Branch Office (ibid. Recommendation R.11.1-11), and the importance of socio-economic surveys and feasibility studies for different phases of emergency relief
and post relief assistance (ibid. Recommendation R.7.1).

The Appointment of Huntings Technical Services as Consultants to Advise UNHCR Policy

As a result of Chambers's recommendations that more feasibility
studies should be conducted, UNHCR decided to hire a private consultancy group, Huntings Technical Services, to conduct socio-economic surveys and to propose new ways of planning and managing
settlements. There was a view within UNHCR that Huntings might
itself be used as an implementing partner. According to Chambers,
apart from any other consideration, Huntings had a big enough stake
in the Sudan 'to have every reason to want to do a good job on the
feasibility study' (Chambers 1976: 1).

---

4. In his observations on the experience of Sudan and Tanzania, Chambers recommended the establishment of large settlements because they allow economies of
   scale, more freedom for refugees, more non-agricultural employment, and have
   better opportunities for self-help.

Huntings had links with UNHCR as early as January 1976, when it was hired to prepare a report on the general refugee situation in Eastern Sudan (Project 75/LS/SUD-4[SUD]; also Huntings Technical Services 1976: Appendix A). In February 1976, after discussion of the findings with UNHCR staff, it was decided that more definite terms of reference should be provided for another report. After getting the approval of COR for Huntings to do the study, UNHCR developed a clearer set of guidelines. Huntings was asked to proceed with a feasibility study with the aim of improving UNHCR's knowledge of the characteristics of the refugee groups to be resettled (Reynes 1976c). UNHCR indicated that it was willing, in particular, to consider establishing a settlement in Jebel Maharragat (near Showak) in spite of the previous difficulties there. It also expressed willingness to provide assistance to Qala en Nahal settlement even though it had been handed over to the government. The terms of reference not only stressed the need for careful planning of a new settlement, but also called for advice on an effective management structure that could implement and guarantee a smooth handover. Huntings was asked to prepare a master plan with a budget and multi-year projections.

At this stage, UNHCR headquarters sent a cable to Khartoum setting out what they called their own 'major concerns'. They again expressed dissatisfaction with the government implementation of the refugee assistance programme, and hoped that Huntings would advise on measures to get approval for entrusting implementation to a trusted third party. If COR objected to these plans, approval should be sought from the highest government authorities. If this attempt to involve an implementing partner failed, UNHCR should consider the alternative of increasing its own staff in Khartoum and Gedaref (UNHCR Headquarters to Branch Office Khartoum, cable, 16 June 1976).

It was clear that by hiring a private consultancy and describing its terms of reference unilaterally, and by suggesting prescriptions for resettlement policy, UNHCR aimed to recapture the initiative from COR.

The Outcome of the 1976 Feasibility Study

The findings of the Huntings team were submitted in a report two months later. Following Chambers's proposals, Huntings first attempted to establish the goals and principles for refugee settlement. The consultants called attention to the need to understand the problems and contradictions involved in the resettlement of refugees. Firstly, for example, although it was generally recognised that the refugee problem was 'a temporary one', the overstay of refugees made them, in effect, permanent settlers. Secondly, there was a need to relocate the refugees away from the international border, for reasons related to relations with the country of origin and the potential friction between refugees and local inhabitants. Thirdly, the assumption that refugees were of rural, farming backgrounds made it difficult for those with urban skills to adapt to rural settlement. Given the complexity of the situation, it was impossible to deal with the 'refugees as a whole', and to provide 'once and for all solutions' (Huntings 1976: ch.3.1).

The proposals made by Huntings reflected some of the contradictory problems they themselves had identified. For example, the following guidelines were suggested for the establishment of refugee settlements:

> Since most of the refugees will return to their homes as soon as conditions permit, *the settlements will usually be of a fairly temporary nature* and should be designed with this in mind. Thus, for instance, expensive installations which cannot be moved to other sites and which will not be used after the refugees have left should be avoided as far as possible. On the other hand, the facilities *must be capable of lasting a reasonable length of time*, in order to provide a degree of flexibility in case the situation in the refugee homeland does not improve as soon as expected. (Ibid.; emphasis added)

Another problem, also related to the difficulty in predicting the future within Ethiopia, was that it was almost impossible to predict future influxes. Huntings based their estimates of the number of refugees to be resettled on those already in Sudan. However, they argued:

> ... if conditions in Eritrea deteriorate and more refugees cross the border, some could probably be absorbed in the Qala en Nahal and Jebel Maharragat projects proposed here; but if the numbers were at all substantial, a major new settlement will be required. (Ibid.)

The specific proposals put forward by Huntings represented an attempt to merge the interests of UNHCR, the government, and the refugees. To meet UNHCR's criteria, Huntings recommended that settlement plans should be technically sound, economically viable, and cheap to develop. Large settlements were preferred because of the economy of scale and administrative convenience. To meet COR's criteria, Huntings proposed that settlements should be far from the borders. For the refugees, the settlements should allow easy access to employment opportunities, while facilities to enhance self-sufficiency should be designed so as to meet their cultural and social requirements.

In accordance with the terms of reference provided by UNHCR, Huntings proposed that 20,000 refugees from Wad el Heleiw should be resettled in Jebel Maharragat (near Showak) and that an additional 10,000 should be moved to new villages in Qala en Nahal. The viability of Jebel Maharragat was thought to be guaranteed if the 11,000 farmers from Showak and Wad el Heleiw were allocated 10 to 20 *feddans* for rainfed sorghum production. The other refugees would gain incomes from agricultural labour in Khashm al Girba and Rahad agricultural schemes. As far as urban refugees were concerned, the consultants did not recommend the establishment of urban refugee settlements, because the skills of the refugees who had come in 1975 were not particularly needed in Sudanese towns.

When the consultants provided their preliminary draft in May 1976, they made the reservation that the planning and cost estimates should be treated as indicative rather than precise estimates. In Chapter 5.11 of the preliminary report, only capital costs were tabled for Jebel Maharragat. To the dismay of UNHCR, the indicative cost of approximately US$6.5 million for resettling 20,000 refugees, far exceeded the actual cost of settling the same number, under government control, in Qala en Nahal (US$2.4 million). UNHCR made it clear that:

> ... the first estimate for capital costs for Jebel Maharragat is far beyond any expenditure that HCR could realistically realise. What we require is a detailed planned budget for full implementation and running of the projects from 1 July 1976 to 30 June 1978, and to have been submitted by 30 June 1976.[5]

For these reasons, Huntings were obliged to rewrite the preliminary draft, taking into account considerations of cost effectiveness, the need to resettle more refugees including 'urban refugees in Gedaref', the need to establish an alternative management structure, and means of promoting refugee labour in Sudanese agricultural schemes.

A final version of the 'Refugee Resettlement Project in East-Central Sudan: A Pre-Investment Study', was then produced (Huntings 1976: 137). The report attempted to cover all the questions posed by UNHCR. Of special significance was its redefinition of the number of refugees needing to be resettled, the estimated cost, and the management and administrative alternatives. The new estimate for the number of refugees to be settled was 30,800. Huntings offered two alternatives for the resettlement of these refugees. The first, called Master Plan I,

---

5. UNHCR typed draft, undated and unsigned, but according to Betts, 'obviously written by either Chambers or the UNHCR Representative in Khartoum addressed to Huntings'. See Betts papers, RSP, Oxford.

proposed that 7,500 urban refugees would be settled near the town of Gedaref (3,500 at Abul Maja and 4,000 in Khashm al Girba). The remaining 23,300 would be divided between Qala en Nahal settlement (6,600 farming refugees) and Jebel Maharragat (16,700 farming and non-farming refugees). Master Plan II, on the other hand, proposed the resettlement of all refugees away from urban areas. According to this alternative, 6,600 were to be settled in Qala en Nahal and 24,200 at Jebel Maharragat. The estimates of capital costs for alternative I were $4,752.3 million (£S1,897.1 million), and estimates for alternative II were $5,514.0 million (£S2,205.6 million). Master Plan I needed running costs (1976-1978) of £S442,800 and Master Plan II, £S504,500. Although these two alternatives reduced the high figure of $6.5 million in the preliminary report, the costs were still twice as high as the cost of implementing the first settlement at Qala en Nahal.

Suggested Alternatives for the Implementation of UNHCR Assistance Programmes

The Huntings consultants considered different alternatives for the implementation of the refugee resettlement projects. Ironically, Huntings made a very clear case for the importance of the continued role of COR. Although it pinpointed the gaps in the existing system, it called for strengthening the performance of the government agency rather than abandoning it altogether. The consultants argued that a pattern which aimed to hand over responsibility for managing the refugee settlements to local authorities was not commendable. There was little advantage in integrating refugee settlements into the local government administration. They believed that on social and other grounds, the refugee settlements would always be somewhat different from the Sudanese villages and towns and there was little point in administering them on the same basis. In addition:

> [The local authorities] have neither the specialised experience and staff, nor the financial resources required. Another drawback is that, in the event of specific problems requiring help from COR and other central government bodies, contact with these organisations is lengthy and complicated, because of the number of stages through which requests have to go. (Ibid.)

In order to improve the efficiency of project preparation and implementation, one possibility was to involve nongovernmental organisations. However, these organisations should work with the existing government refugee administration. Refugee resettlement would inevitably involve the government:

... the entry of an external organisation into the situation could cause severe misunderstandings and conflict unless the organisation worked very closely with the government agencies involved. If it were to achieve its objectives, it could not operate as an independent body, but would have to be seen as an arm of the government agencies concerned. (Ibid.: 137-138)

The consultants proceeded to offer four specific alternatives (ibid.: 138):

1. COR would continue but would undertake the post-implementation, as well as the preparation and implementation, of the refugee assistance programmes.
2. A special administrative structure would be established, which would have its own budget and would supervise and conduct all work including planning, implementation and operation of refugee settlements. This would be similar to the patterns of management which had been established for the Sudanese development schemes at al-Rahad, Khashm al Girba, and Gezira. This was not seen as a favourable alternative, as this kind of structure would be difficult to abolish at the end of the project.
3. All tasks involved would be entrusted to existing specialised government agencies, while COR would do the co-ordination. For example, the Mechanised Farming Corporation would implement and manage agricultural programmes, the Rural Water Corporation would plan and operate the water sector, etc., as part of their own general programmes. However, this would involve a greater degree of co-ordination than COR could manage.
4. COR would continue to be responsible for refugee resettlement, but with its capability strengthened either by the addition of a permanent project planning and implementation team, or by the hiring of specialised organisations.

The consultants showed a particular preference for the last option, though the idea of COR hiring an outside organisation was not favoured because of the high cost charged by private companies and because there were no NGOs that could undertake the planning and implementation role (ibid.: 140). The advantage of augmenting COR with a specialised team was that this would not disrupt the existing institutional arrangements. The costs would be low, the effectiveness of planning and implementation would be improved, and the COR staff working alongside the team would benefit from their experience (ibid.: 141).

Consequences of the 1976 Feasibility Study

Huntings thus produced proposals which undermined many of the assumptions held by UNHCR, even though UNHCR itself had prepared the terms of reference for the study, and had attempted to pre-empt its conclusions. The Huntings report provided further evidence that an adequate assistance programme would cost more than UNHCR was prepared to spend. Furthermore, quite unexpectedly, it failed to recommend ways of replacing COR as the main implementing partner.

After the final reports were submitted, UNHCR headquarters chose to dismiss the whole exercise. In particular, it criticised the high cost of the Huntings proposals. It contended that it was up to UNHCR to fix a specific fund for its programme in eastern Sudan; Huntings was only expected to provide a costing of alternatives (within the limits of that fixed fund) from which UNHCR could make a choice. This was considered to be sufficient reason for ignoring the report's conclusions and 'a mood of disillusionment about the use of such consultants was established within UNHCR' (Betts 1982: 45). Having rejected the findings of the Huntings team, UNHCR entered another period of inaction. The idea of involving a nongovernmental third party was dropped, and UNHCR once again had to improvise its own alternatives without relying on outside partners.

UNHCR Options for Lowering Costs and Controlling the Management of the Refugee Assistance Programmes (1976-1978)

Following their disappointing experience with the Huntings consultants, UNHCR opted for a combination of measures to control the assistance programme, and to respond to the challenge of new refugee influxes at minimum cost. In particular, it adopted two strategies. Firstly, it attempted to minimise the cost of the refugee programme by avoiding the establishment of permanent rural settlements. Secondly, it developed a closer working relationship with the refugee authorities in Showak, at the expense of its relationship with COR in Khartoum.

Strategies for Refugee Assistance (1976-1978)

After 1976, UNHCR delayed the establishment of new refugee settlements, and concentrated instead on a series of relief operations. UNHCR was clearly reluctant to build any new settlements, because of the costs involved; the conclusions of the Huntings report served as a reminder that new settlements might cost even more than the original settlement at Qala en Nahal. At this stage, however, events within Sudan and within Eritrea provided justification for a 'wait and see' approach. The war within Eritrea intensified, and Sudan launched its offensive policy against Ethiopia between 1977 and 1978. If the Eritrean fronts were successful, there was a possibility that the refugees would return home. If the war dragged on, it was assumed that the refugees who were already in Sudan would fend for themselves by working as agricultural labourers in Kassala Province or in other parts of the country, at no cost to UNHCR. In both cases it seemed better for UNHCR to postpone the establishment of new settlements.

In 1976 and 1977, only 1,200 refugees were resettled, in spite of the increase in numbers moving to the reception centres and towns. It appeared that the refugees were reluctant to move to organised settlements, as long as there was a real possibility that the war would come to an end. However, with the freezing of Sudan's aggressive policy and the failure of the Eritrean fronts in 1978, it became obvious that the resettlement programme would need to be accelerated. By then, thousands of refugees were living outside the UNHCR assisted programme in both rural and urban areas, and were most unlikely to return home.

In February 1978, therefore, UNHCR revived the idea of a master plan to resettle 25,000 refugees in new settlements. As lack of water and arable land limited the choice of sites, it was expected that large numbers of refugees would be moved to areas neighbouring existing Sudanese agricultural schemes, where wage labour opportunities were available (see e.g., Cuénod *et al.* 1983). The previous findings of Huntings on the possibility of resettling refugees in 'wage-earning settlements' became attractive, as this also seemed to be a more cost-effective solution. Thus in 1978:

> Several thousand other refugees were to be moved to wage-earning settlements, mostly in the neighbourhood of Es Suki and Khashm al Girba agricultural schemes, and for these only limited provision of 1.5 holdings was made for vegetable and poultry production, on a family basis, with *minimal infrastructure, and reliant, under the general control of COR*, on the thirty voluntary agencies at the time actively engaged in refugee work for the *equally minimal social services.* (Betts 1982: 63; emphasis added)

It is important here to establish UNHCR preference for wage-earning settlements as an alternative to the more expensive land settlements, because in later years the wage-earning settlements in Suki and Kilo 26 (Khashm al Girba) were severely criticised by UNHCR, for failing to offer real opportunities and acceptable living standards for the refugees. The UNHCR role in initiating them is rarely mentioned.

The Role of the Project Manager in Showak

In 1976, after publication of the Huntings report, UNHCR explored new ways of exerting influence over the implementation of refugee assistance programmes. In particular, it attempted to strengthen both the UNHCR Branch Office and the COR regional office at Showak. In the ensuing years, boosted by extra financial allocations, the COR Regional Office in Showak came to resemble a local implementing partner with control over expenditure on specific projects in eastern Sudan. A clear vertical division began to emerge, between the regional administration in Showak and the central office in Khartoum. In the Eastern Region itself, there was also a clear division between the regional refugee administration and the provincial and regional government authorities; ironically, the surviving link between the local refugee administration and COR in Khartoum helped prevent the local authorities from appropriating funds intended for refugees, or from interfering in other ways. UNHCR used this situation to its own advantage. Since funding was project-specific, UNHCR was able to concentrate on assisting specific numbers of refugees and to monitor each project more strictly.

The 1978 Master Plan aimed to strengthen the administrative capacity of the COR regional office in eastern Sudan, so that it would be better able to cope with the burden of establishing more settlements. UNHCR recommended that the Showak office should be upgraded, and that a General Project Manager should be appointed who would supervise the managers of the different refugee settlements.[6] Following Huntings's recommendations, UNHCR also supported the idea of providing the Showak Office with a technical team, specialising in the fields of agriculture, engineering, construction, accounting, community development and public health.

In the ensuing years, problems arose over the role of the General Project Manager, and his position *vis-à-vis* COR in Khartoum and the regional authorities in Kassala. Hampered by various institutional and resource constraints (i.e., dependence on the political decisions of the government in Khartoum, funds from UNHCR, and concessions from the regional and local authorities), he had to assume a role assigned to him in annual agreements between COR and UNHCR.

6. Hassan Mohammad Osman, a qualified senior administrator in local government, became the General Project Manager. Under his able management, the refugee programme witnessed a great expansion and continuity, particularly during the transitional period which COR suffered in 1980-1981 when conflict with the Minister of the Interior (1980-1984) led to the departure of the long-serving Commissioner, Dr Al-Bashir. The management ability of GPM created discomfort with UNHCR and tension arose between UNHCR Sub-Office and GPM.

As UNHCR did not consider itself to be under any obligation to assist all refugees everywhere (see Coats 1978: 4), the agreements between COR and UNHCR only covered certain groups.

The Manager's role, as he perceived it, was to ensure that UNHCR-funded programmes defined by these agreements were properly implemented, and that the agreed budgets were adhered to. As a sub-office of COR, his role was to liaise between COR and local government authorities, but to concern himself only with those refugees who lived in UNHCR-funded settlements, or who were receiving relief assistance in reception centres. Those who lived in towns and border villages were not his direct responsibility. Thus, for example, he was able to resist attempts by the provincial authorities in Kassala, Gezira, and Khartoum to send refugees in their areas to the assisted settlements.

The dilemma which arose in 1978 disclosed a discrepancy between the role of COR in Khartoum, and the role of the Project Manager as he perceived it. Although COR was responsible for all refugees, the Project Manager was only able to deal with the minority who received assistance.[7] He was not even able to monitor new influxes, or to provide reliable estimates of the numbers involved. The rough estimates provided by the government were always considered exaggerations by UNHCR; yet UNHCR never made any effort either to verify or to disprove the government estimates. For example, it made no serious attempt to provide advice or finance for the provision of identification papers for refugees, despite relentless efforts by COR to win concessions from the government for refugees whose presence in towns could have been legalised if identification papers had been issued.

Conclusion

By the end of 1978, a crisis developed, as the influx of refugees from Ethiopia reached a new peak. Since the development of new settlements had been delayed, and because neither COR nor UNHCR were even monitoring the influxes, the refugees dispersed throughout the region and only a small minority received assistance. Ironically, however, the government chose this moment to abandon its confrontational policy towards Ethiopia, and put more pressure on COR to confine the presence of the refugees to specific areas, as required by the Regulation of Asylum Act (1971). This change of policy was not accompanied by a willingness to allocate more resources

---

7. By the end of 1979, UNHCR reported that 42,000 Ethiopians were established in refugee settlements out of the estimated government total figure of 340,000 Ethiopian refugees (see UNHCR 1980).

to refugee programmes, or to strengthen the administrative capacity of COR.

UNHCR, in the meantime, continued to adhere to its multi-year Master Plan, which was by no means intended to meet the needs of all the refugees. After all, UNHCR considered that it was the government's responsibility and not its own, to provide long term solutions (Coats 1978: 4).

References

Al-Bashir, A. R. (1978) 'Problems of Settlement of Immigrants and Refugees in Sudanese Society', D.Phil. Thesis, St. Antony's College, University of Oxford.

Betts, T. F. (1982) 'Spontaneous Settlement of Rural Refugees in Africa: Research Project 111, Sudan', Euro-Action ACORD.

Beyer, G. A. (1976) 'Report on Mission to Sudan', UNHCR, Geneva.

Chambers, R. (1975) 'Rural Refugees in Africa: Observations on UNHCR Policies and Practice', HCR/140/18/75.

—— (1976) Report to Dr J.J. Kadosa, Chief of Eastern and Southern Africa Section, UNHCR, Geneva, 25 Febuary, ref. 75/LS/SUD-4, 72/LS/SUD-3, 100-SUD-ETH, in Betts papers, RSP, Oxford.

—— (1979) 'Rural Refugees in Africa, What the Eye Does Not See', *Disasters* 4(3): 381-392.

—— (1982) 'Rural Refugees: Past, Present and Future Experience', (unpublished) Khartoum.

—— (1986) 'Hidden Losers: The Impact of Rural Refugee Programmes on Poorer Hosts' *International Migration Review* 20(2): 245-263.

Coats, P. (1978) 'Material Assistance: Some Policy Problems Reviewed in the Light of Robert Chambers' Evaluation Report', HCR, Geneva, January.

Cuénod, J. *et al.* (1983) 'Assistance Review Mission to the Sudan', UNHCR Mission Report, Geneva, January.

DRS (Democratic Republic of Sudan) (1970) Council of Ministers Resolution 1-A-5-4/891-893, 13 September.

—— (1973) 'Presidential Decree on the Project for Resettlement of the Refugees in Showak, 1973', No. 126, 27 November.

Holborn, L. (1975) *Refugees: Problem of our Times*, Scarecrow Press, Methuchen.

Huntings Technical Services Ltd. (1976) 'Refugee Resettlement Project in East-Central Sudan, Pre-Investment Study', Borehamwood, England, a study commissioned by UNHCR/COR.

Karadawi, A. (1977) 'Political Refugees: A Case Study from the Sudan, 1964-1972', M.Phil. Dissertation, Reading University.

Ministry of the Interior (1972) 'Rural Settlement of Refugees from Ethiopia in Showak', agreement between government of the Democratic Republic of the Sudan and UNHCR, Khartoum, 28 December.

Reynes, R. (1976a) R. Reynes to HQ (no number), confidential, subject: Non-Eritrean Ethiopians in the Sudan, 17 April 1976, in Betts Papers, RSP, Oxford.

—— (1976b) R. Reynes (UNHCR Rep. Sudan) to J.J. Kadosa, Chief of the Regional Section for East Africa, HCR, Geneva. Confidential (no number), 6 May 1976.

—— (1976c) Memorandum: 'Huntings Mid-Term Report', 29 May, in Betts papers, RSP, Oxford.

Rogge, J. (1985) *Too Many, Too Long*, Rowan and Allanheld, Totowa.

Seyoum, M. and Juel-Jensen, B. (1976) 'Investigation of the Problems of Ethiopian Refugees in Sudan', OXFAM Mission Report, April.

UNGA (1957) 'International Assistance to Refugees within the Mandate of the UNHCR', Resolution 1166 (XII), 26 November.

—— (1970) 'Status of the office of the United Nations High Commissioner for Refugees', Resolution 428 (V) of 14 December.

UNHCR (1972) 'Waterway to Development', *Refugees* Special Issue.

—— (1976) 'Agreement under the Programme of UNHCR', project symbol, 76/EF/SUD -2, undated, not signed. COR, Khartoum.

—— (1980) Report to the United Nations General Assembly, August 1980.

6

Refugees as an International Responsibility: The Sudanese Initiative of 1980 and Its Consequences

The last two chapters have argued that in their responses to the refugee phenomenon, both government authorities and UNHCR, from their different positions, adopted measures which ultimately contributed to a crisis situation. The government resorted to measures to force refugees out of areas where they had spontaneously settled; UNHCR failed to help the government or the refugees to find more constructive alternatives. It was COR that took the initial step of proposing that the responsibility for refugees should be shared with the international community and that the crisis situation in Sudan could only be remedied by massive international assistance. However, in spite of the strength of the arguments put forward by COR, the specific case of Sudan was overlooked internationally, as other African countries in a similar position simultaneously made their own financial demands on donors.

In response to the situation in which it found itself, COR, with support from the government, formulated an international campaign to raise funds for refugees in the Sudan.

The International Fund-Raising Campaign for Refugees in the Sudan

Internal and external factors contributed to the broadening of COR's campaign, which began as an attempt simply to contain the overwhelming pressure by other government authorities to evict refugees from certain areas.

After June 1978, COR was attached to the General Secretariat of the Council of Ministers and worked under the Cabinet Minister, Abu Bakr Osman. The Minister, a career diplomat, encouraged COR's attempts to influence national policy towards refugees and its criticisms of the assumptions held by international refugee aid organisations. In September 1979, the Commissioner convinced the government that the refugee settlement operations needed sums of money that it could not provide (COR to Cabinet Minister, General Secretariat of the Council of Ministers, No. CR/36/B/1/A/Confid., 11 September 1979). The government was then persuaded to endorse a plan aimed at a combined effort inside Sudan and abroad. The aim was to approach external donors, whilst simultaneously launching an internal campaign to inform the Sudanese people about the conditions in neighbouring countries which were forcing people to become refugees. COR believed that an internal campaign was a necessary symbolic gesture that would enhance positive responses from international donors (COR 1979: 10).

At its annual meeting in 1979, the UNHCR Executive Committee was informed by Sudan's Vice President Abel Alier that 1980 would be the Year of the Refugees in the Sudan, and the Sudanese international campaign was thus officially launched. Meetings to explain the aims of the campaign were held with UNHCR, ICVA and representatives of governments and NGOs in Geneva and London in October and November 1979. The Commissioner for Refugees made a tour of the Scandinavian countries in December to enlist their support.

The international fundraising campaign attempted to achieve two sets of policy objectives. It aimed both to re-establish the government's refugee policy objectives, and to create mechanisms to safeguard against arbitrary government decisions adversely affecting the refugees, thus providing guarantees to bilateral and multilateral donors that their donations would be put to the best possible use. The government policy objectives were outlined as follows:

1. to put an end to spontaneous unassisted settlement of refugees by settling all refugees in planned villages;
2. to provide solutions for urban refugees, particularly students;
3. to pay special attention to vulnerable groups such as refugee women, children and the physically disabled;
4. to launch a programme for the long term integration of refugee projects with local development plans. (Ibid.: 4)

While providing reasonable proposals to meet the demands of other government authorities, these objectives were also intended to meet the normative standards established by the OAU convention. Spontaneous settlement was to be discouraged for three reasons. Firstly, it tended to take place in or near the border areas in contradiction to the OAU Convention. Secondly, the heavy concentration of refugees in particular rural areas led to pressure on the land and upset the local ecological balance. Thirdly, during a period of strain on most sectors of the Sudanese economy, the large refugee movement to urban centres had contributed to shortages in public services and job opportunities (NCAR 1980a: 2-3).

The second set of objectives that COR hoped to achieve from the campaign, was to create a national advisory council for refugees (National Refugee Council), representing the different government authorities. The intention was to have a national umbrella group which would guarantee government commitment to the refugee policy designed by COR. In theory, such a body would help to boost the position of COR within the central government and would offer a better negotiating position with regional authorities which controlled the areas where the refugees lived. The advantage of this council would be to help terminate the uncoordinated and divided positions of the government authorities.

Similarly, it was proposed that a Refugee Fund should be established where all donations would be pooled. This proposal related to the attempt to diversify funding sources and to break Sudan's dependence on the restricted funding of UNHCR. The Refugee Fund would be run by a committee that would include donor and Sudanese Government representatives who would monitor the use of donations. In the initial proposal for the Refugee Fund, COR suggested that it would be managed by a committee composed of UNHCR, COR, the NGOs and the Ministry of Planning (COR to Under Secretary Foreign Affairs, No. CR/20/F/1, 7 September 1980). The Refugee Fund was proposed in anticipation of the donors' queries about safeguards and accountability for the sums they allocated for refugee assistance. Moreover, it was envisaged that the establishment of the fund would allow the flexibility necessary to overcome the restrictions resulting from incompatible priorities of funding agencies. For example, if UNHCR would not provide support for secondary education, the Refugee Fund would offer finance for this priority area.

The international campaign would not have attracted attention, had it not been for certain external factors. Firstly, an attempt to articulate the plight of Sudan as a host country coincided with the continental effort organised by the OAU and manifested in the Pan-African Conference held in Arusha, Tanzania in May 1979. The

Pan-African Conference highlighted a deterioration in the refugee situation in many parts of the continent. Secondly, the number of refugees had increased from one million in 1967 to four million in 1979. Thirdly, the refugee burden was unequally distributed between the forty nine OAU member states. Eighteen carried the burden of providing asylum to 90 per cent of the refugees in Africa.[1] Finally, inequity existed in the distribution of international assistance, whereby African refugees fared worse than refugees in other parts of the globe. The majority of African refugees (60 per cent) were not covered by international assistance (Neldner 1981).

Furthermore, the 1979 campaign in Sudan coincided with controversy over refugee aid, aroused particularly by the response of Western countries to the plight of the Indo-Chinese refugees. At the conference held in Geneva in the same year, and attended by sixty-five nations, the Western countries, especially the United States, accepted total responsibility for the Indo-Chinese refugees. Both settlement in first countries of asylum, and repatriation to countries of origin, were considered to be out of the question by Asian countries. Consequently, 265,000 Indo-Chinese refugees were offered asylum by countries of Europe and North America. A sum of US$200 million was allocated for Indo-Chinese refugees who were held in camps and an 'orderly departure programme' for the Vietnamese was conducted by UNHCR from 1980.

Despite the differences between the situations in Sudan and Southeast Asia, the Sudanese officials behind the campaign tried to reinforce their position by comparing the two. They argued that Sudan, like some of the Southeast Asian countries, was at the hub of a refugee crisis and that the interests of the West were at stake, particularly in countries neighbouring Sudan, such as Zaire, Chad and Ethiopia. Sudan did not wish to incarcerate refugees in camps, nor was it seeking to have the refugees physically resettled in Western countries. Sudan was willing to offer opportunities for refugees to settle inside the country, but it needed help in order to do so. As one document argued:

> It is realised that this initiative is taken at a time when [international] attention is focused on the plight of the boat people... it is also hoped that it will be understood that the absence of drama and disaster among refugees in Sudan has not been achieved without great efforts or sacrifice. Sudan owes much to the United Nations Commissioner for Refugees, the

1. Statement by Peter Onu, Assistant Secretary General of the OAU for Political Affairs, in the Plenary Session, 'Pan-African Conference on Refugees', Arusha, Tanzania, 5-19 May 1979; also in Amate 1986: 470.

WFP and numerous voluntary agencies for the help they have provided, but it is now in a position where it will have to ask for more if the intent to cope with the situation before it gets out of hand, is to be realised. (NCAR 1980a: 2)

This line of argument was considered attractive at a time when the Nimeiry regime had begun to consolidate its links with the West in general and with the United States in particular. In 1979 the United States, West Germany and France became the major arms suppliers for Sudan (Abd Alla 1983: 28-29).

The International Conference on the Situation of the Refugees in Sudan, 1980

As a result of a positive response from some governments and international organisations contacted in late 1979, the government began to organise an international conference in Khartoum. It was expected that by putting its case there, Sudan would convince donors to provide massive support. Vice-President Alier was appointed as Chairman of the National Committee for Aid to Refugees, which would supervise the international campaign. A Technical Committee was also formed involving the Ministries of Health, Education, Culture and Information, Agriculture, Planning, Foreign Affairs, Department of Statistics and Southern Regional Government and the Provinces of the Red Sea and Kassala. Members of the Technical Committee were seconded to work with the Commissioner for Refugees to provide technical advice and prepare project proposals for the conference.

As COR sensed a lack of enthusiasm on the part of UNHCR, it sought help from USAID, the Ford Foundation, and ICVA. Through financial and technical assistance from these agencies, COR augmented its Technical Committee with experts from a consultancy firm, Development Alternative Incorporated, who helped with the preparation of the conference documentation. Other UN agencies, such as the Economic Commission for Africa (ECA) and UNDP, also contributed to the preparations. While the Technical Committee was expected to provide well-prepared project proposals, the involvement of the expatriate experts was considered necessary to make these presentations meet the professional criteria demanded by donor countries and organisations.

In the period between March and June 1980, the campaign was well underway. Subcommittees were organised inside Sudan to publicise the Year of the Refugees in Sudan. However, more emphasis was given to publicising the plan outside Sudan through international media and through intensive efforts to persuade governments and organisations to attend the international conference.

On 5 April, Vice-President Alier wrote to the UN Secretary General with a request for a UN inter-agency mission to assess the magnitude of assistance needed for the refugee relief and settlement programme. The UN Economic and Social Council (ECOSOC) approved the request and it was arranged that the mission would visit Sudan in June 1980 (UNGA 1980a: 1). In the meantime the conference documentation, prepared by the National Committee for Aid to Refugees and the Technical Committee, was compiled in four volumes including the government plan and its financial estimates. The documents included project proposals for the establishment of new refugee settlements in rural areas and related needs in different sectors. The financial needs were estimated to be $230 million over a period of three years (see table 6.1).

Thus, before the conference opened on 20 June 1980, the government had taken every precaution to ensure that its proposals would be well received. The event itself was judged by some as an indication of the success of the pre-conference activities. It was considered:

Table 6.1 *Summary of Project Type and Cost Estimates for the 1980 Plan*

	US$
1. Urgent Humanitarian Assistance	
Settlement Programme (29 Settlements)	122,427,070
Food	18,000,000
Sub-total	140,427,070
2. Urgent Development Assistance to Strengthen Economic and Social Infrastructure	
Education	35,114,476
Health	21,843,290
Agriculture	31,178,000
Feasibility Missions	741,000
Sub-total	88,876,766
Total	229,303,836

Source: Inter-Agency Mission Report, UNGA/A/35/4/410.

the first initiative of its kind undertaken by a third world government with
the realisation that a problem which was extra-ordinary in its magnitude
and complexity needed extra-ordinary solutions. (NCAR 1980b: 1)

In response to government invitations, the conference was attended
by 27 governments, 18 intergovernmental organisations, 58 non-governmental organisations and 25 representatives of the international
media. In his inaugural speech, President Nimeiry made clear that
Sudan could no longer absorb great numbers of refugees without sac-
rificing some of its developmental priorities. Vice-President Alier, the
Chairman of the Conference, explained the interrelation between the
plight of the refugees and that of Sudan in the following terms:

> The Sudanese people had received refugees and extended assistance to
> them in true African tradition. Through joint efforts between the gov-
> ernment and UNHCR, a number of settlement centres had been set up
> for refugees but only a minority of refugees had been absorbed into
> them. The vast majority had settled spontaneously putting a strain on the
> inadequate resources and services available, causing competition over
> jobs and making the refugees' situation more vulnerable since they were
> unable to attain economic viability. The gravity of this problem coin-
> cided with the economic difficulties the country had to face. The gov-
> ernment had therefore decided to phase out spontaneous settlement and
> to search for new imaginative solutions to these problems. (Ibid.: 3)

As a result, the settlement of refugees in specially designed villages
constituted the priority in the 1980 plan. However, as the government stated, its severely limited resources made it difficult to shoulder such a responsibility on its own (ibid.: 4). During the three-day
deliberations, the reactions to the request were generally reserved,
although some pledges were made (see table 6.2).

The argument for assistance beyond relief aid and for linking
refugee aid to development, was enthusiastically received. The message of the UN Secretary General reflected this when he stated that
the previous assistance given by UNHCR had helped countries like
Sudan to meet refugee needs in an emergency situation only, 'but little has been done to improve the fragile socio-economic infrastructure in areas where refugees are located or resettled' (ibid.: 4). The
UN Secretary General argued that additional resources had therefore
to be obtained in the development field from the international community and the UN system and used in a co-ordinated, cost effective
fashion with the aim of helping refugees become self sufficient.

The importance of the concept of additional resources for development related projects in refugee-affected areas came to dominate

Table 6.2 *Pledges for the Refugee Assistance Programme during the 1980 Khartoum Conference*

Donor	Amount	Channel	Nature of Aid Pledged
United Kingdom	£850,000	Bilateral	Tractors, spare parts, workshop and training in agriculture, Qala en Nahal and Showak
The Netherlands	Fr. 2.5m	UNHCR	
Sweden	Kr.5m	Bilateral	Water Services
Islamic Development Bank (Jeddah)	$900,000	Bilateral	Construction of hospital in Southern Sudan and health centre for Ugandan refugees
Islamic Solidarity Bank (Jeddah)	$150,000	Bilateral	For priority programme
EEC	$4.2m	UNHCR	
Italy		WFP	4,000 tons wheat
Belgium	BFr.7m	Bilateral	
Norway	$500,000	UNHCR	Education (3 Schools)
USA	$1m		Water
Libya	$600,000	Bilateral	Food commodities
Pakistan	$25,000	Bilateral	For Ugandans

Source: COR 'The Aftermath of the Refugee Conference', Memorandum 20/F/1, 4 October 1980, Khartoum.

the final resolutions of the conference. The participants commended the initiative taken by the government and considered it as a 'tangible action based on the concept of burden-sharing as enunciated by the Arusha Conference in May 1979, and in accordance with the international conventions relating to refugees' (ibid.: 13).

The conference participants drew attention to the gravity of the socio-economic problems created by the presence of large numbers of refugees. As a result, a resolution urged that:

> ... assistance for the integration of refugees be over and above the assistance programmes, whether multilateral or bilateral, provided by the international community for the development of the Sudan. (Ibid.: Recommendations A, para.12)

Despite the fact that the conference did not bring a large immediate response, it was believed that it marked the beginning of a process in which refugee assistance programmes would increase over time.

The momentum of the June conference was helped by the arrival of the UN inter-agency mission during June and by ECOSOC's resolution in July 1980. The ECOSOC resolution commended the initiatives and endeavours of the government in convening the conference which had drawn the attention of the international community to the plight of the refugees in Sudan and the magnitude and complexity of their situation (ECOSOC Report E/1980/L.53 22 July 1980). As a result, ECOSOC decided to review the situation of refugees in Sudan at its first regular session in 1981 (UNGA 'Report of the Mission to the Sudan', ECOSOC Report A/35/410 16 September 1980).

The report of the inter-agency mission was submitted to the UN General Assembly's 35th session (ibid.: 4). The finding of the inter-agency mission confirmed the government's view that:

> The serious economic constraints together with the government's heavy external debt, make it difficult for the government to provide normal social services to a large number of refugees. The refugee burden in the eastern province is particularly onerous. (Ibid.)

The report of the mission also endorsed the government's national settlement plan and its policy to develop long term programmes which would go beyond humanitarian assistance and relief by encouraging refugees to become self-supporting and productive members of economically viable communities (ibid.: 4 para. 12). However, it ignored the extensive research that had already been conducted, and suggested that a series of sectoral missions should visit Sudan to complete planning, feasibility, and project design work on the government's proposals. The sectoral missions were also required to make adjustments to government proposals to meet the technical requirements of the multilateral donors.

Consequences of the 1980 Fund-Raising Campaign

When the UN Mission Report was approved by the General Assembly in December 1980, the Secretary General was requested to send follow-up missions, in co-operation with UNHCR. UN agency missions continued until 1984 and produced yet more reports on the background of the deteriorating situation in Sudan, so that the 1980 proposals were blurred by changes and reviews of mission reports.

The first follow-up mission, comprising UNHCR, UNHS, and FAO, questioned the technical feasibility of most of the proposed refugee settlements in eastern Sudan. Eleven settlement sites were disqualified on the grounds of inadequate rainfall, poor soil fertility or lack of drinking water. These were Moharragat (seven sites), Goz Rejab (two sites), Adirgawi, and Kilo 20. Two of the proposed settlements (Agadi in Blue Nile Province, and Marafit in Red Sea Province) were simply not mentioned in the report. The Mission approved only three refugee settlement villages: Abuda, Um Ali, and Teneidba, which had been considered for financing within the UNHCR budget of 1981. Even when the sites had been approved, the mission recommended that refugee 'settlements should not be occupied before measures had been taken to provide shelter, temporary health care facilities, safe and adequate water as well as emergency food supplies' (UNHCR/COR 1980: 2).

The ILO Technical Mission

The second Technical Mission, led by ILO and UNHCR, cast doubts on the settlement policy as a whole and its ability to offer the opportunity for refugees to attain self-sufficiency from farming or by earning incomes from seasonal wage labour (UNHCR/ILO 1982: 17). ILO argued that with constraints on agricultural land and depressed wages in the agricultural sector, the refugee settlements would never be economically viable. The main thrust of the ILO report was that solutions to the problem of employment lay beyond the narrow focus of refugee settlements based on agricultural production or seasonal labour. ILO therefore engaged in an extensive study of the Sudanese labour market, including a refugee skills survey and the identification of self-help projects for income generation. Between August 1982 and March 1983, ILO conducted extensive research resulting in a package of proposals for income generation.

A memorandum of understanding was signed between COR and UNHCR on 26 May to launch these proposals. ILO wanted to create a new institutional framework for its projects to make them independent of COR. ILO was critical of what it claimed to be institutional legal constraints within the settlement structure (ILO/UNHCR 1984: xi). An 'organisational structure project' was included as part of the ILO proposals which became the subject for the first tripartite agreement between UNHCR, ILO and the government (ILO/UNHCR/COR 1983). The draft agreement stated that the proposed organisational structure:

> aims to overcome a number of obstacles such as:
> a) the scattered and isolated location of most of the settlements and their poor communication facilities;

b) legal constraints on refugees to obtain work, business and travel permits;
c) lack of managerial training. (Ibid.: Annex A: 3)

The income-generating arrangements envisaged a vertical structure composed of three levels. In the refugee settlements and towns, income-generating activities would be organised through income-generating associations and women's production groups. Fifteen women's production groups and thirty other income-generating associations were to be organised for the fifteen refugee settlements. At the second level the settlements were then to be clustered as groups with each cluster forming a federation. In all there would be ten federations, five for agricultural activities and five for non-agricultural activities.[2] At the top level there would be the supervising team headed by the Technical Adviser.

The staff was to consist of a chief technical adviser (an expatriate), a co-operative adviser, an adviser for women's projects, an accountant, ten managers for the federations, fifteen managers for the income-generating associations, fifteen women social workers, ten storekeepers, five secretaries, ten drivers, five messengers and ten watchmen (ibid.).

While UNHCR and ILO shared the fundamental responsibility for funding and management, the government was given a very limited role: nominally it had 'overall responsibility for the administration of the project' (ibid.: part 1 para. 1), but it could act and advise only in consultation with UNHCR (ibid.: para. 2). In fact, there was no reference to COR, the Labour Department, or the regional authorities, although ILO had expressed enthusiastic support for these institutions in 1981. Nor was there any reference to the Sudanese population in the refugee-affected areas, as originally agreed in the ILO/UNHCR terms of reference.

The proposal to create new alternative structures was seen by COR as part of a plan to exclude the government from direct implementation of the refugee assistance programme.[3] A memorandum submitted to the Commissioner by his subordinates called for revision of the agreement with a view to re-establishing the active role of COR and other government authorities. It called for direct involve-

2. The five clusters were the following: (1) Kassala group consisting of Kassala town, Kilo 26, Khashm al Girba; (2) Showak group: Um Gargur, Karkora, Um Ali, and Abuda settlements; (3) Gedaref group: Gedaref, Tawawa, Um-Gulja; (4) Al Hawata group: Um Rakouba, Qala En Nahal, Al Hawata, Wad Awad, Abu Rakham, Teneidba; 5) Suki group: Fath El Rahman, Awad Es Sid, Kilo 7.
3. In late 1981 Commissioner Al-Bashir left his post and was succeeded by Ambassador Ahmedi, who was less experienced and less critical of the influence of external agencies.

ment in the implementation of the projects to avoid future conflict and overlap between the existing government management and the new ILO structure. COR officials also called for accountability criteria to be written into the agreement, and asked that the organisation of income-generating activities be extended to include the Sudanese population in the refugee-affected areas, as was originally envisaged (COR Memorandum 10/C/1, March 1984).

As a result of these comments, the role of COR and other government partners was re-established at the top of the organisational structure, that is, at the level of what was called the Advisory Board for Income Generating Activities for Refugees (ABIGAR), which first met on 18 September 1984. ABIGAR also included representatives from ILO, UNHCR and the Labour Department. The original structure was left as it was. This adjustment led to delays in implementing the programme of income-generating activities.

The actual implementation was further delayed by ILO's procrastination in selecting the Chief Technical Adviser until June 1984. ILO failed to find a suitable expert, and the delay was compounded by difficulties in finding office space in Khartoum. As a result, the Chief Technical Adviser could only arrange the first meeting for ABIGAR in September 1984. By then, according to the ILO adviser, the income-generating projects suggested in 1983 needed substantial revision due mainly to the huge influx of famine-affected refugees from Tigray and Eritrea which obliged UNHCR to divert money to fund the necessary relief operation. The ILO income-generating activities suffered as a result. Both the organisational structure of the income-generating activities and the activities themselves were revised. Eventually the total number of 'federations' was reduced to four instead of ten, and the number of income-generating associations and women's production groups was also reduced. There were also cuts in staffing levels. In all, only five out of the original seventeen projects were actually implemented.

The NGOs working in Sudan were reluctant to get involved in the ILO project because of the complex technical and financial procedures demanded by UNHCR (Es Sayed 1987: 9). Even those involved in the implementation of the four projects were faced with a sharp warning by UNHCR in September 1985, when the latter announced its budgetary constraints and requested agencies to finance the projects themselves until other funds were available (ibid.: 17). Five years after its conception, the UN technical teams of ILO and UNHCR gave birth to a feeble programme of income-generating activities which was completely incapable of meeting government expectations. For example, only 84 refugees benefited from the brick making project and 105 from the soap making project (for details see Idris 1987).

The Third Follow-up Mission on Education and Social Services

The third UN follow-up mission, which comprised UNECA, UNESCO, UNICEF, and UNHCR, arrived in Sudan in January 1982. The mission was expected to carry out feasibility studies with the objective of strengthening or establishing education and social development services for refugees (Inter-agency Mission 1982). During its three-week stay in Sudan, it concentrated on two themes: the objectives of education under the prevailing political, socio-economic and cultural trends in Sudan and the assessment of the need, and its financial and human resources implications (ECOSOC 1982). The mission decided that no action could be taken unless accurate data were collected. It recommended further extensive research to be conducted by UNESCO which should include a study of the education sector in view of the new policy of decentralisation then being implemented in Sudan (ibid.: 7). The mission further stressed that it was impossible to carry out feasibility studies for viable projects in the social services sector, due to lack of demographic and sociological data (ibid.: 8). In general, the UN experts warned against the government policy of establishing refugee settlements, because refugee settlements might impede the 'social osmosis' which would pave the way for possible refugee integration in their country of asylum (ibid.: 10). Hence, the social services projects, designed for both Sudanese and refugees, should be geared towards solving the issue of social unrest and inter-community friction attributable to diverging social attitudes, cultural values and traditions (ibid.). The mission then went on to recommend that COR should be assisted by a special UN expert to follow up the mission recommendations. He would help with conducting socio-economic surveys and initiating contacts with interested parties to bring about a 'well-conceived and co-ordinated global approach for the refugee development programmes' (ibid.: 14). Despite the urgent financial needs of the education sector mentioned in the 1980 government plan and estimated at US$35 million, the mission concluded by recommending a small package of proposals which would only cost US$6 million.

Overall, the 1980 international campaign did not produce the positive response expected by the government. As the fate of the government's plans rested mainly with the UN system, it appeared that there was little that could be done without the involvement of UNHCR.

At the same time, the UN questioned the work of the Sudanese agencies. The UN inter-agency missions not only raised doubts about the technical soundness of the government's plan but also questioned the principles on which the plan was based, including the refugee settlement policy which was its cornerstone. In spite of the fact that the government had taken the precaution of appointing an experienced 'technical team' to prepare its 1980 proposals, the UN missions also questioned the expertise of the government, and their reports emphasised the need for intensive alternative research as a prerequisite for sound planning. Another feature of the UN missions was that they reported back to the UN General Assembly which again re-channelled the demands of the Sudanese Government to UNHCR, as the other agencies seemed reluctant to be occupied with refugee aid, because of constraints of mandates. The government's request for additional funds remained as a fixed item on the agenda of ECOSOC and the UN General Assembly.[4]

Establishing the Refugee Fund

The leading UN agency in charge of refugee assistance policies, UNHCR was not sympathetic to the government campaign in 1980. It complained that the government had overplayed its role by calling for the international conference. In particular, UNHCR was sceptical about the main proposals to raise extra finance and to establish a special fund to pool that finance partly under government control. In objecting to the idea of the Refugee Fund, UNHCR used the same arguments which the government had used to justify its establishment. For UNHCR, the Refugee Fund was 'unwelcome as it was liable to lead to duplication of funding and a division of authority, in practical terms over the allocation and accounting of such contributions' (Betts 1982: 34). In addition to opposition from UNHCR, other factors contributed to a complete change in the functions of the proposed Refugee Fund and of the National Refugee Council. In the original proposal, the National Refugee Council was intended to be a national umbrella group, comprising representatives of different government ministries, who would co-ordinate refugee policy in

4. See the following UNGA Resolutions on the refugee situation in Sudan: Res. 35/181 (15.12.1980); Res. 36/158 (16.12.1981); Res. 37/173 (17.12.1982); Res. 38/90 (16.12.1983); Res. 39/108 (14.12.1984); Res. 40/135 (16.12.1985).

Sudan. The Refugee Fund would be administered by a separate body, including representatives of the UN and other donor agencies. After the reattachment of COR to the Ministry of Internal Affairs in June 1980, and the departure of the Commissioner for Refugees who had articulated the 1980 proposals, these two separate bodies were redefined and merged together.

The National Refugee Council was now given a limited role, in administering a special fund (COR 1984). Nevertheless, the Refugee Fund Bill was discussed and approved at the People's National Assembly in its 38th session on 10 June 1982. On 29 June it was approved and signed by the President of the Republic as an act of law. According to the Refugee Fund Act (1982), all funds and property related to refugee services should be pooled in the Refugee Fund. This would include the contributions received from UNHCR, WFP and other UN agencies, as well as bilateral and NGO contributions (Refugee Fund Act Ch.5 para. 5). The National Refugee Council would prepare its own budget and would have its own bank accounts which would be subject to the auditing regulations of the government of the Sudan. The National Refugee Council would formulate general policies for the financing of refugee relief and rehabilitation and define guidelines for the execution of these policies. The Council was also entrusted with the task of concluding agreements with financial donors (ibid. Ch.3 para. 16).

Nimeiry approved the nomination of the twenty-three members of the National Refugee Council on 27 October 1982. They represented mainly government departments: the UN agencies and NGOs were not represented. It held its first meeting on 8 January 1983, almost three years after it was proposed by COR (1984: 3). In the seven sessions held between January 1983 and December 1984, one constant issue was the concern over funding. At the first meeting a decision was taken to delegate the right of making agreements on funding to COR.

In consequence of this decision, the UNHCR annual refugee assistance programme continued to be beyond the National Refugee Council's control. The Special Fund was completely dependent on funding provided by the Islamic Co-operation Fund, which contributed $765,880 in cash, and the Islamic Development Bank, which provided the Special Fund with $1.2 million for building schools in Eastern Sudan and $650,000 for the consolidation of health services for Ugandan refugees. The Minister of Internal Affairs paid a special visit to Saudi Arabia for discussions with Islamic financial institutions. The meetings were also attended by COR and the Islamic African Relief Agency (controlled by Muslim Brothers in Sudan); see COR 1983.

The National Refugee Council hardly had any impact on refugee policy. On the few occasions when the members raised queries about seminal issues, the questions were either avoided, or dismissed, on the grounds that further research was needed. For example, in 1983 there were recommendations that the Commissioner should consider the effects of drought in neighbouring countries and the possibility of an influx of large numbers of affected people into Sudan. Another issue raised during the sessions of 1983-1984 was the role of NGOs and the need to reorganise their work with the recommendation that Sudanese expertise should be used, and that expatriates should be employed only when necessary. Also, in 1984, queries were raised about the political implications of the American Refugee Resettlement programmes. The Resettlement Programme introduced by 1981 to send 3,000 refugees for resettlement in the United States was criticised by different quarters. There was the suspicion in 1984 that it was used as a camouflage to smuggle the Ethiopian Falashas to Israel via intermediate countries. In all these cases the Commissioner never provided adequate answers, nor did he suggest ways to tackle the issues satisfactorily. The National Refugee Council failed, therefore, either to raise substantial funds or to influence national policy on refugees.

Pressure for Additional Assistance through Collective Action by African Countries

The 1980 conference was seen by the participants as adding to the momentum that was generated at the Arusha Pan-African Conference in 1979, which put pressure on the donors to increase aid for African refugees (see Vol. 5 of the conference documents). In the ensuing years, two major encounters between the African countries and the financial donors took place (ICARA I and ICARA II), at which the African countries tried to emphasise the concept of international obligation, burden-sharing and development-oriented refugee assistance. The financial donors tried to contain the pressure, by arguing that the provision of additional aid should be subject to certain conditions.

The International Conference on Assistance to Refugees in Africa (ICARA I)

As a result of the report produced by the Arusha Pan-African Refugee Conference, the OAU Summit Conference held at Freetown (Sierra Leone) in July 1980, endorsed a proposal to organise an International Conference on Assistance to African Refugees (OAU-CM/Res. 814[XXXV]). The proposal was also endorsed by the United Nations General Assembly. The objectives of the conference were to focus public attention on the plight of refugees in Africa in order to mobilise additional resources for refugee programmes, and to assist the affected countries to cope with the burden of large numbers of refugees by strengthening their meagre services and facilities (UNGA Res. A/35/42 25 November 1980).

As it was conceived as a fund-raising forum, the conference's success depended mainly on the response of the donors. To advise and assist the OAU General Secretaries to organise the conference, a task force was set up including members from UNHCR, UNECA, UNESCO and AACC. Even before the conference was held, a problem arose concerning one of the fundamental objectives of ICARA. While the theme of the conference aimed at additional assistance over and above the funds contributed for the programmes of UNHCR, it appeared that the prospective donors wanted the funds approved for 1981 UNHCR programmes to be included in their pledges to ICARA.

Pressure was brought to bear on the Council of Ministers of the OAU at its regular session in Addis Ababa in February 1981 to accept the donors' position (Birido 1982: 4). In the period of the four months between the decision of the UN General Assembly and the actual convening of the conference in April, the donors were faced with projected estimates by African countries amounting to US$893,126,792 in addition to the current programme by UN agencies of US$260,853,500. Sudan, which rated only second to Somalia, projected its need for additional assistance at US$268,120,000, including an approved current programme of US$41,481,000.

ICARA was held in April 1981 and attended by 99 governments and more than 120 intergovernmental and non-governmental organisations. Despite this high level of attendance, the participants initially pledged a sum of US$560 million dollars, subsequently increased to US$574 million which was much below the totals of projected need. Of this total, the United States alone pledged US$285 million dollars.

During the conference, it emerged that the financial donors' immediate response was to reject the African governments' projections on the grounds that they were exaggerated. Moreover, the donors believed that most of the projects proposed should fall under the auspices of UNHCR. This meant that if there was a need for additional pledges, the money raised should be channelled through

Table 6.3 *ICARA Pledges and Channel of Distribution (in US$1000)*

UNHCR	222,915
UNICEF	8,006
WFP	104,380
ICRC	21,536
Special Trust Fund	396
OAU	1,000
Others	28,221
Bilateral	175,448
To Be Specified	12,041
Total	573,943

Source: ICARA Report of the Secretary General E/1982/76.

UNHCR. This latter option seemed the most desirable as UNHCR itself announced on the second day of the conference that its on-going annual programmes for refugees were threatened by lack of finance. The objectives of ICARA were, therefore, pushed to the background in favour of financing the annual programme of UNHCR and other agencies. This position was confirmed by the UN Secretary General in his report to ECOSOC, where he confirmed that a number of projects submitted by the African countries to ICARA were found to fall within the UNHCR programme (Secretary General 1982). He gave the breakdown of the distribution of ICARA money between the different agencies (see table 6.3). But neither the agencies to which the contributions were channelled, nor the Secretary General, explained whether the ICARA contributions were in fact 'additional' assistance.

As to the fate of projects requiring additional assistance outside programmes of multilateral agencies, a special working group was formed to select a list of priority projects. In the aftermath of the conference, the steering committee selected certain priority projects costed at only US$38 million. This amounted to additional assistance of US$2 million for each of the asylum countries. In December 1981 it was left to UNHCR to submit to potential financiers a summary of the priority projects for funding. But even with the projections of African countries reduced to a mere US$38 million there were problems. As the UN Secretary General explained:

> In attempting to obtain donor funding for priority projects, a number of difficulties were encountered. One such difficulty arose from the lack of clarity concerning pledges made at ICARA. (Secretary General 1982 in Birido 1982: 5)

ICARA thus failed to generate additional assistance: instead, the UNHCR allocations to Africa fell steadily from US$173 million in 1980 to US$168 million in 1981 and only US$158 million in 1982 (Birido 1982: 7). The pledges made at the conference therefore were not new money, but allocations made regularly by some donors to UNHCR and other UN programmes. Despite the failure to generate additional funds, the Conference was considered a landmark in so far as it succeeded in bringing attention to the magnitude of the African refugee problem at the international level. This was expressed by the UN Secretary General in his concluding statement to ICARA:

> The world now clearly recognises that one half of the entire world refugee population is to be found in the African continent, that five mil-lion homeless persons are living in conditions of destitution and that a small number of host countries, who are themselves economically disad-vantaged, are bearing the greatest share of the burden. (Ibid.: 3)

The demand for another conference was born directly from the African dissatisfaction with ICARA I, as it came to be known (ICARA/81/STA/4: 7). In December 1981 the UN General Assem-bly requested the Secretary General to keep the African refugee sit-uation under close scrutiny. It asked him to submit a report (UNGA Res. 36/124, 14 December 1981) to the ECOSOC regular session in 1982 to facilitate the review of the situation by the General Assem-bly in its 37th session, and to assess the need for further action after ICARA I. This report confirmed that ICARA had fallen short of its expectations (Secretary General 1982: para. 36).

Another forceful move to support the demand for a further inter-national conference was made by the OAU Council of Ministers. In its 38th ordinary session of February 1982 it observed that:

> … having reviewed the pledges made at ICARA in relation to the urgent needs of the refugees and the economic constraints confronting countries of asylum, … ICARA's objective of mobilising additional resources for refugees programmes in Africa has fallen short of all expectations.

The Council of Ministers requested the Secretary General of the OAU to undertake a thorough evaluation of ICARA I and its results so that after appropriate assessment of the situation, accurate data collection, and feasibility studies on project proposals, the desirabil-ity of another conference could be considered (Birido 1982).

In April 1982 the OAU secretariat suggested that UNHCR should examine the list of projects submitted for additional funding at ICARA

I to identify the ones falling within its competence. The remainder should constitute the basis of a list to be submitted to the international donors, including the UN development agencies. The OAU also suggested that the appropriate agencies should help with preparing project documents in order to meet the donor demand for feasibility. Moreover, the additional assistance should not be made at the expense of the African countries' own development needs. The OAU also suggested that if and when the UN General Assembly approved the holding of another international conference, every support should be given to its organisation by the UN agencies (ibid.: 9; Secretary General 1982).

Through their persistence in the UN, the African countries maintained the pressure on donors. The demand for another conference for assistance to refugees in Africa was confirmed by the General Assembly a year after ICARA I. Resolution 37/197 of 18 December 1982 requested the Secretary General, in close co-operation with the Secretary General of the OAU and UNHCR, to convene at Geneva in 1984 a second International Conference on Assistance to Refugees in Africa (ICARA II). A steering committee was formed of representatives of the UN Secretary General, the OAU Secretary General, UNHCR and UNDP to prepare for the conference. The inclusion of UNDP was of particular significance, since emphasis was given to the role of development assistance in support of ongoing refugee assistance programmes. The Steering Committee was also supported by a technical team comprising OAU, UNO, UNHCR and FAO, established to consult with affected countries on the nature and extent of assistance needed to strengthen their capacity to deal with the refugee situation.

Additional Assistance and the Need for Clarification of the Principle and the Role of Parties Involved

The interlude before ICARA II was significant for donors, recipients and aid organisations as they attempted to study the principle of additional assistance to refugee-affected countries and ways to handle it. It appeared that with the whole refugee assistance structure so influenced by a relief approach, no refugee agency was ready to engage in the provision of long term development aid. Obviously, it had not been envisaged that development agencies such as UNDP would provide assistance to refugees. The donor countries had entrusted the responsibility of relief and development assistance to separate departments. NGOs were generally oriented towards relief assistance to refugees; but even those which engaged in development work had a completely different approach from intergovernmental and governmental development agencies.

Drawing on the experience of the ICARA I projects, UNHCR took the initiative in 1983 to organise a meeting of experts on 'refugee aid and development'.[5] In that meeting UNHCR recognised the need to provide long term assistance to affected countries, but it defined its role as one of a 'catalyst' and a 'broker'. It suggested that there was still the need for a mechanism to formulate and implement projects of assistance which had a developmental character (Goodwillie 1983: Annex 11: 18). However, UNHCR would not itself change its mandate to include development assistance but would present projects of additional assistance defined by refugee-affected countries to prospective donors (ibid.: 19).

The Executive Committee of UNHCR responded by requesting the views of non-governmental and intergovernmental organisations. UNHCR was also asked to conduct a study of issues and problems relating to the question of additionality before EXCOM was asked 'to commit itself on principles or courses of action' (UNHCR/EXCOM 1983: para. 112). The NGOs and intergovernmental organisations approved the coordinating role of UNHCR while maintaining their different conceptions of the development approach.

The NGOs were notable for their small scale project approach, concentrating not only on economic returns but also legal protection and psychological security of the refugees (UNHCR 1983: Annex III). The intergovernmental organisations, however, were more concerned about inter-agency co-operation and the source of funding for additional assistance. In their meeting with UNHCR, intergovernmental organisations commended the agreements between UNHCR and agencies such as ILO in Sudan and UNDP and World Bank in other places. As to generating additional funds, the intergovernmental organisations suggested that this could be done either by adjusting the budgets of development agencies or by a combination of grants and concessionary credits (UNHCR 1983). Although no specific formula was agreed upon, it was generally recognised that the presence of refugees should be taken into consideration as a criterion in the allocation of national development assistance by bilateral and multilateral aid donors.

The Second International Conference on Assistance to Refugees in Africa: July 1984

Almost all the donor contributions to ICARA I were channelled through UNHCR and WFP in order to finance their ongoing pro-

---

5. This meeting, held at Mont Pélérin, Switzerland, 23-30 August 1983, was attended by 24 participants, three of them from African countries: Algeria, Sudan and Tanzania.

grammes. Since the UN Secretary General's report on the status of ICARA I contributions, there had not been any noteworthy increase in the size of donations (UNGA n.d.: 10). The steering committee for ICARA II therefore had to engage in a completely new and separate effort to redesign projects according to special guidelines which had evolved after ICARA I. Accordingly the Steering Committee concerned itself mainly with only two of the objectives of ICARA II set out in General Assembly Resolution 37/197. These were included in article 5(b) which stated that the conference should consider additional assistance for refugee and returnee programmes, relief, rehabilitation and resettlement. Article 5(c) was concerned with the impact of refugees and returnees on the economies of affected countries and the aim of the conference was to provide assistance to strengthen their social and economic infrastructure.

During its preparatory work, the Steering Committee tried to prepare projects that would satisfy the donors. Preparation of projects subject to article 5(b) were left to UNHCR as they were considered part of the normal UNHCR programme. The projects relating to 5(c) were to be prepared by the UN Secretary General with the help of UNDP (ibid.: 19 para. 42). In 1983, UNHCR distributed guidelines to its branch offices in Africa, to prepare the 1984 budget of US$155 million within the context of article 5(b) of the General Assembly Resolution 37/197. A total of US$125 million was allocated to relief, settlement and maintenance, with US$30 million for returnees and refugee students. UNHCR also submitted ten projects for funding, costing US$10.9 million, to ICARA II (ibid.). For financial reasons, the figure for the total number of refugees in Africa was cut down to three million (ibid. 2: 11, based on UNHCR estimates) instead of the five million recognised before. The reduction of numbers was also related to the donors' accusation of exaggeration by affected countries, with the US Committee for Refugees suggesting an even lower figure of 1,904,200 (Gallagher and Stein 1984: 5).

Twenty-two African countries which received refugees and returnees were invited to submit projects under article 5(c). They were requested to observe the guidelines, and the technical team helping the Steering Committee was deployed to ensure that the projects were viable. The guidelines sought to ensure that projects were related to refugees and that they were based on a realistic assessment of need. Projects were expected to be adequately costed: the host country should have the capacity to implement them and to manage their future running costs. The projects should also be consistent with the country's national development efforts (Smith 1984) and clearly justified by their intention to ameliorate the problem or to facilitate long term solutions. The guidelines also requested a clear statement of the governments' policies regarding refugees or returnees, and particularly, where relevant, prospects for a lasting solution (Gallagher and Stein 1984).

Between July and December 1983, the technical teams visited fourteen African countries to finalise and adjust the proposals. Sudan was visited from 21-29 August. The teams identified 128 projects considered as priorities for infrastructure development which would benefit refugees, returnees and other nationals. It was estimated that the implementation of these projects would cost US$362 million. The distribution of these projects by sector indicates that 28 per cent related to transport and road improvements, 24 per cent to agriculture, forestry and fishery projects, 20 per cent to education, 16 per cent to health, 10 per cent to water supply and two per cent to social development (UNGA n.d. 2 :23, para. 69).

As far as Sudan was concerned, its government was first requested to limit its projects to a total cost of US$75 million. During the technical team's one week visit to Sudan, which included visits to the refugee affected area, the ceiling was raised to US$95.7 million (ICARA II Technical Team 1983) (see tables 6.4 and 6.5). Thus, between 1980 and 1983, Sudan had to rewrite its priorities three times. By accepting the arbitrary ceiling figure of US$95.7 million the government was made to scale down its US$230 million proposal submitted to the Khartoum International Conference and the request for US$268 million submitted to ICARA I.

In March 1984 the Steering Committee produced a report containing detailed information on the refugee situation and an outline of the projects in the different African countries. It then approached the donors, to encourage them to attend the conference.

Table 6.4 *Projects Proposed for the Consideration of ICARA II by Region*

Region	Province	No. of Projects	Amount (US$)
Eastern Region	Kassala	4	10,110,000
	Red Sea	12	48,423,000
Central Region	Blue Nile	3	2,240,000
Equatoria Region	Equatoria	10	34,500,475
Khartoum		1	500,000
Total		30	95,773,475

Source: COR, Khartoum, 1983.

Table 6.5 *Projects Proposed for the Consideration of ICARA II by Sector*

Sector	No. of Projects	Amount (US$)
1. Education and Vocational Training	11	26,660,000
2. Environmental Health and Hospital	6	19,300,000
3. Demonstration Projects for Agriculture and Forests	6	19,603,475
4. Roads, Bridges and Electrical Power	4	25,200,000
5. Water Development Projects	3	5,010,000
Total	30	95,773,475

Source: COR, Khartoum, 1983.

Until then, ICARA II had not been a high priority issue for donor governments, particularly the United States. Evidently, there was a difference in the perspectives of the African countries and donors, exacerbated by their respective positions in the global system. The Africans portrayed the burden which was already there. They admitted their poverty and incapability. They agreed to scale down their demands and to allow others to mediate and to define their needs. Although the criticisms of the African countries which characterised ICARA I were avoided in ICARA II, donors were still unwilling to accept, unreservedly, an obligation to share the burden.

When ICARA II was convened in Geneva on 9 July 1984, it was not intended to be a pledging conference. To the dismay of the African countries, the conference was to concentrate on issues such as the principles of burden sharing, refugee aid for development and the end-goal of durable solutions. A hundred and two governments and 147 intergovernmental and non-governmental organisations attended. Although the conference was, in theory, a gathering of African countries, donor governments and aid organisations, the dialogue in practice was one between the donor governments themselves and their conduit organisations. After repeatedly stressing the plight of their countries, and the refugee/returnee crises, the African representatives sat and watched the response of the donors. There was a general consensus on international responsibility for the provision of relief assistance to address refugee crises in Africa. However, the donors rejected any notion of obligation to fund ICARA II projects. In fact one donor government representative was particularly critical of the tendency to expand the concept of burden sharing to involve the international non-African parties. The British representative recognised the burden some countries were bearing on behalf of 'us all' but he reminded the conference of the political causes and consequences of the refugee problem. He argued that:

> ... of course the international community has a clear responsibility for contributing to the relief of needs among refugees in Africa. *But it is not we ultimately who can find solutions to African problems.* As President Nyerere said at the meeting last March in Arusha of the OAU secretariat and voluntary agencies, we are talking today 'about a problem which rightly belongs to the African people and African governments'. (Raison 1984; emphasis added)

The US joined the British in reminding the Africans of the need to seek political solutions and requested the OAU to make it their priority to resolve the root causes of the refugee problem. The US delegate urged that:

> Serious and carefully planned regional and bilateral negotiations could pave the way towards the safe return home of many more refugees. Such negotiations could also help prevent additional destabilising flows of refugees. (Smith 1984)

The major donors not only rejected the notion of the duty to provide additional aid but also any claims that the African governments had a corresponding right to demand it. If and when additional funds became necessary, the donors believed that the argument of obligation should be applied to the African governments themselves. Accordingly, additional assistance should be made on conditional terms: burden sharing which involved additional capital aid for development, should be balanced by a commitment on the part of the recipients towards durable solutions to the refugee problem.

Durable Solutions

The emphasis on durable solutions had the effect of weakening the claims of host countries receiving large numbers of refugees. Host countries were required to take permanent responsibility for an unpredictable and dynamic refugee situation. If they were not able or prepared to make this commitment, they risked losing the support of the donors. The only other option favoured by the international community was the voluntary repatriation of refugees to their country of origin. The legitimacy of this option could not be denied as it had been approved as the best solution to the refugee problem even by the host countries themselves. For the countries of origin, the return of the refugees would signify a political success, and the prospective international aid would be only too welcome.

By stressing voluntary repatriation and the provision of aid for returnees as a first priority, the international donors could easily economise by exploiting the competitive claims of the African governments concerned: the claims of a host for additional assistance could easily be set against the claims of the country of origin for assistance for the repatriating refugees. This was exactly the strategy adopted by the donors after 1980 in the case of Sudan and Ethiopia. It should be noted that while discussing these two options - integration in the host country or reintegration in the country of origin - the conference did not involve the refugees themselves as full partners whose views on either solution were crucial.

Declaration and Programme of Action for ICARA II

Like its predecessor, ICARA II did not result in immediate commitments for financing the proposed projects. Out of the 128 projects, donors expressed their willingness to contribute towards partial funding for only 30 projects. The donors made pledges of US$80 million, approximately a fifth of the total projections of US$362 million. Of the US$80 million, US$61 million were for projects affecting national economies, while the rest went to UNHCR programmes (Gorman 1985: 14).

However, at the end of the conference, a declaration was produced which synthesised the principle of international responsibility and the specific commitments of the African countries towards protection and assistance of refugees. Internationally it was declared that the conference:

> ... recognises that the condition of refugees is a global responsibility of the international community and emphasises the need for equitable burden sharing by all its members, taking into consideration particularly the case of the least developed countries. (UNGA 1984: A/CONF.125/L.1)

As for continental responsibility, the declaration emphasised the need to take special account of the OAU Convention Governing Specific Aspects of the Refugee Problems in Africa of 1969, the recommendations of the Arusha Conference (subject of OAU/CM.Res. 727 (XXXIII) and UNGA Res. 34/61 and 35/41), the recommendations of the OAU secretariat and NGOs of 1983 and the OAU Charter on Human and Peoples' Rights.

The declaration emphasised the two approaches accepted as solutions to the African refugee problem: voluntary repatriation of refugees or settlement in a host country. However, the declaration stated that for solutions to last, assistance to refugees must be development-oriented and aim at enabling refugees to work towards durable self-reliance (UNGA 1984: A/CONF.125/L.1 p.3). At the same time, international co-operation should be strengthened to avert new refugee flows. The declaration urged states to refrain from taking measures that would create or aggravate the refugee problem (ibid.: 1).

Apart from the lip-service paid to the necessity of international co-operation to avert new refugee flows, all the principles concerning the continental responsibility were a repetition of what had been agreed before. However, the most significant part of the declaration was the second part on the Programme of Action which recommended practical steps to facilitate voluntary repatriation. The programme of action not only stressed the mandatory role of UNHCR to facilitate and guarantee the safe return of refugees to their home country, but urged UNHCR to take all measures deemed appropriate and feasible to promote such voluntary return. The declaration indirectly endorsed the steps taken by UNHCR in Djibouti and Ethiopia by stating that: 'whenever appropriate, tripartite commissions composed of representatives of the country of origin, the country of asylum and UNHCR should be established' (ibid.: 4). Including representatives of refugees in the commissions was not mentioned.

Despite the highly political nature of voluntary repatriation as a durable solution, the declaration paradoxically urged that care should be taken to respect the 'entirely non-political character of UNHCR' (ibid.). The declaration approved of support for the infrastructure in countries affected by the refugee problems, to counteract the adverse effects of the presence of refugees on the national economies, and stressed that support should be additional to other development programmes. Recognising the existing gaps between refugee and development structures, it called for closer coordination to ensure that assistance to refugees complemented development-oriented assistance.

In this context, UNDP was expected to play a central role in the coordination, implementation and monitoring of refugee-related infrastructure projects. NGOs were also expected to play a role in the assessment, planning and execution of development-oriented projects. In addition, UNHCR was still expected to play a leading role in relief and post-relief activities, both in the host countries and in the countries of origin (ibid.).

Conclusion

Like the Khartoum conference, the two international conferences for assistance to African refugees failed to provide the funds requested by African countries. As the last major initiative, ICARA II was dominated by a discussion of issues relating to international responsibility and additional assistance to relieve the burden caused by refugees. Facing pressure from countries affected by the presence of refugees, the donors accepted the responsibility to provide relief, but they rejected any notion of obligation to provide additional assistance to relieve the burden on the affected countries.

The message that came out of ICARA II was that when the need for additional assistance was justified, it would be conditional on a commitment on the part of refugee-affected countries to 'durable solutions'. 'Durable solutions' for refugees were specifically defined as voluntary repatriation or integration into the host country. Theoretically, the two durable solutions cancel each other out: when the voluntary repatriation of a particular group justifies the claims of the country of origin for additional assistance, it disqualifies the claims of the host country for additional assistance for the same group.

In practice, the two durable solutions were dependent on the state of the conflicts that generated the refugees. The ability of the countries of origin and host countries to implement either of the two durable solutions depended on other parties such as political opposition groups, the refugees themselves, and, not least, the local population in the host country. In the case of Sudan and Ethiopia, the internecine conflict militated against repatriation, as the Ethiopian Government did not control the areas from which the refugees had come. Refugee and indigenous sentiment also militated against a commitment by any Sudanese government to the permanent integration and naturalisation of all refugees. The conditions established at ICARA II for additional assistance, therefore, allowed more options for the donors, whilst failing to deliver real solutions to the refugee problem. The position of the African governments was weakened as their competitive claims were set against each other.

However, one of the most important results of the encounters between the refugee-affected African countries and the donors was the interest generated in the suggestion of linking refugee assistance to development. These proposals were of interest to the aid agencies in particular. Despite their varying approaches, the aid agencies emerged as powerful actors who considered their role as indispensable. Through involvement in assistance beyond relief, they worked to consolidate themselves as the intermediaries between the donors, the recipient governments and the refugees. The multilateral agencies worked to improve inter-agency co-operation. UNHCR defined its role as both a central agency concerned with refugees as well as a 'broker' between recipient countries and development agencies.

Closer co-operation was sought with UNDP, ILO and the World Bank. UNDP also established a special fund of US$5.6 million raised from ICARA contributions, in order to help with ICARA projects.

The consequences for Sudan were twofold. Firstly, the government failed to obtain additional assistance from international donors. Secondly, the government's ability to control policy and to manage the assistance programme was weakened further, as more aid agencies were empowered to introduce their own policy priorities in Sudan, and to apply them more or less autonomously. COR's attempt to end the fragmentation within the government, and to challenge the position of UNHCR, culminated in the re-evaluation by UNHCR of its own policies, claims and interests. Altruism and expediency had become indistinguishable.

References

Abd Alla, S. M. (1983) 'Military Expenditure during May Revolution Regime', Dissertation, National Defence College, Khartoum (Arabic).

Amate, C. O. C. (1986) *Inside the OAU: Pan-Africanism in Practice*, London: Macmillan.

Betts, T. F. (1982) 'Spontaneous Settlement of the Rural Refugees in Africa: Research Project 111, Sudan', Euro-Action ACORD, London.

Birido, O. Y. (1982) 'International Conference on Assistance to Refugees in Africa (ICARA) and its Aftermath', paper submitted to the Khartoum Refugee Seminar organized by COR, 11-14 September, Khartoum.

COR (1979) 'The International Fund-raising Campaign for Refugees in Sudan', Memorandum No. CR/20/F/1, 21 November.

— (1983) 'A Report on Refugees' (Arabic) No. 57/A/1, 30 November.

— (1984a) 'Observations on Agreement 83-84/AP/SUD/LS/50/ILO', Memorandum No. 10/C/1, Khartoum, March (Arabic).

— (1984b) 'The Refugee Special Fund' (Arabic), Memorandum, December, COR, Khartoum.

ECOSOC (1980) 'Special Economic and Disaster Relief Assistance', Report, Second Regular Session, E/1980/L.53.

— (1982) 'Assistance to Refugees in the Sudan: Report of the Secretary General', A/87/178, UNGA 37th session, New York, 5 April.

Es Sayed, F. (1987) 'Organization Structure Project', Progress Report, ILO Project Coordinator's Office, Showak, March.

Gallagher, D. and Stein, B. (1984) 'ICARA II: Burden Sharing and Durable Solutions', Washington: Refugee Policy Group, April.

Goodwillie, S. (1983) 'Refugees in the Developing World: A Challenge to the International Community', Report of UNHCR to the 34th session of the Executive Committee.

Gorman, R. F. (1986) 'Beyond ICARA II: Implementing Refugee-Related Development Assistance', *International Migration Review* 20(2): 283-297.

ICARA II Technical Team (1983) *Sudan: The Infrastructure Burden of Dealing with Large Numbers of Refugees*, Report of the United Nations Technical Team for ICARA II, September.

Idris, Y. A. (1987) 'Income-generating Activities among Refugees in Eastern Sudan', M.A. Thesis, Afro-Asian Studies Institute, Khartoum University.

NCAR (1980a) 'Introduction to Donors', in *Economics and Project Implementation*, Documentation to the Khartoum Conference Vol. 2, Khartoum 20-22 June.

— (1980b) 'Final Report', Documentation to the Khartoum Conference Vol. 5.

Neldner, B. (1981) '?' in Erikson, E.G., Melander, G. and Nobel, P. *An Analysing Account of the Conference on the African Refugee Problem, Arusha 1979*, Uppsala: Scandinavian Institute of African Studies.

ILO/UNHCR (1984) *Towards Self-Reliance: A Programme of Action for Refugees in Eastern and Central Sudan*, Geneva: ILO.

ILO/UNHCR/COR (1983) 'Organizational Structure for the Promotion of Self-Reliance among Ethiopian Refugees in the Sudan', Agreement under the programme of UNHCR No. 83-84/AP/SUD/LS/50/ Geneva: ILO.

Inter-Agency Mission (1982) Report of the Inter-agency Mission on Education and Social Development and Welfare Services for Refugees in Sudan (Draft), COR, Khartoum.

Raison, T. (1984) 'The British Response to ICARA II', speech by Rt. Hon. Timothy Raison, UK Minister of Overseas Development, at ICARA II, Geneva, 9-11 July. See British Refugee Council Briefing Paper.

Secretary General (1982) ICARA, Report of the Secretary General E/1982/76, 10 June.

Smith, W. F. (USA Attorney General) (1984) 'Statement to ICARA II', Geneva.

UNGA (1980) 'Assistance to Refugees in Sudan', Report of the Economic and Social Council 1980/10.

— (1984) 'Declaration and Programme of Action of the Second International Conference', No. A/CONF.125/L.1. 10 July.

—— (n.d.) 'Detailed Description of Needs, Project Outlines, and Background Information Report of the Secretary General', ICARA II, No. A/CONF.125.

UNHCR (1983a) Report of the meeting with non-governmental organizations, 24-25 November 1983, AC/AC.96/635.

—— (1983b) Report of a meeting of inter-governmental organizations, 5-7 December 1983, AC/AC.96.653.

UNHCR/COR (1980) 'Planned Rural Refugee Settlements in Kassala Province: Report of a Technical Appraisal Mission', Khartoum, December.

UNHCR/EXCOM (1983) 'Report of the Thirty Fourth Session of the Executive Committee of the High Commissioner for Refugees', No. A/AC.96/631, Geneva: UNHCR, September.

UNHCR/ILO (1982) 'Income Generating Activities for Refugees in the Sudan', Report of the UNHCR/ILO Disciplinary Mission on the Employment, Income Generation, and Training of Refugees in Sudan, Geneva: ILO.

7

The Active Role of UNHCR in the Development of Refugee Policy: The Promotion of Voluntary Repatriation as an Option

After the exchanges between the Sudanese Government and external donors between 1980 and 1983, the government lost its ability to control refugee policy, or to direct its implementation. As the government successfully sought more assistance from foreign donors, the aid organisations, and in particular UNHCR, were more able to dominate government policy. After 1983, there were even some extreme cases of intervention by foreign organisations and governments to assist particular refugee groups and dissident political fronts directly. Examples of these extreme cases were the secret operations to help the Falasha (Ethiopian Jews) to leave Sudan, and the direct assistance given by some European NGOs to political fronts such as the TPLF, the ELF and the EPLF.

However, without minimising the importance of these developments, this discussion is confined to the role of UNHCR, the main partner of the government in dealing with the consequences of the refugee influx. The role of COR declined, while UNHCR emerged as the more active agent, which imposed its own priorities, particularly with regard to settlement policy and its attempts to promote the repatriation of refugees to Ethiopia.

The Decline of the Role of the Commissioner for Refugees

After 1980, political developments inside Sudan led to a change in the status and role of COR. When it was transferred to the Ministry of Internal Affairs in June 1980, COR's authority was weakened, particularly in relation to the regional governments which now had greater constitutional powers than the central ministries.

However, it was the appointment of the new Minister of Internal Affairs that had a greater significance for COR. The new minister was a leading member of the Muslim Brothers, who joined Nimeiry's regime after a further reconciliation initiative similar to the national reconciliation of 1977. From his position at Internal Affairs, he used every opportunity to consolidate his own power, and that of the Muslim Brothers within the regime. The refugee work, with its possibilities of external links, was a useful vantage point. The minister worked to bring COR under his own authority, and also reinterpreted the role of the proposed Refugee Fund and National Refugee Council discussed earlier.

Conflict soon erupted with the Commissioner for Refugees, who was attempting to establish his own mechanisms of control over refugee policy. The potential for conflict was exacerbated by accusations from other government authorities, particularly the security organisations, which complained that the Commissioner was implementing refugee policy in isolation from other government departments, in spite of the establishment of the National Council. Parallel criticisms came from the aid organisations.

Problems between the Commissioner for Refugees and the Minister of Internal Affairs began to unfold immediately after the 1980 Khartoum conference. The minister's first step was to reorganise the different departments to work under an under-secretary selected by himself. The commissioner objected to working with an under-secretary on the grounds that this would create a cumbersome bureaucratic structure involving the minister, the under-secretary and COR. When the new structure was imposed in 1981, the commissioner and the minister came into direct conflict over policy issues and working methods.

As mentioned, the minister worked to change the outcome of the proposal to establish a National Refugee Council, and made himself chairman of the council. He used the council to create a forum through which he could create links and obtain funding from Islamic organisations. This, and the new administrative structure itself, allowed UNHCR as well as the NGOs to deal with the Minister directly, and therefore to bypass COR.

COR continued to adopt an uncompromising attitude towards both UNHCR and the NGOs. It tried to regain control over the refugee assistance programme, and argued that NGO programmes should be complementary to the UNHCR-financed programmes, with additional funds from the NGOs themselves. In late 1981 the

Commissioner was also outspoken in his criticism of the American programme for the resettlement of Ethiopian refugees in the United States, arguing that this would be of limited benefit to the majority of refugees. He saw the minister's conciliatory attitude towards the expatriate agencies as indicative of the dependence of the regime generally, and the Muslim Brothers in particular, on the United States and its western allies.

The interests of the minister and of the assistance organisations converged against the Commissioner for Refugees. In February 1982, he was forced to leave his job and a new commissioner was selected by the minister. The new commissioner was a diplomat - selected on secondment from the Ministry of Foreign Affairs - with no specific experience of refugee work. This is indicative of the priorities of the minister, who attached great importance to the role of foreign aid organisations, and to the policy of externalising responsibility for refugees.

After the new commissioner had been appointed, the minister selected a new team to augment the staff of COR, as had been suggested in 1980. The new deputy commissioner and staff, who were organised in six 'specialised' units, were selected often through favouritism rather than merit or experience. By 1982, as a result of the new appointments, COR in Khartoum was run by a group who had no previous experience of refugee work, and had no idea of the complex relationship between COR and UNHCR. The changes in COR only applied to the Headquarters in Khartoum. The regional offices in Gedaref and Showak were left as they were, with the same senior staff who had worked there since 1976. As the new commissioner did not have any new plan or policy to replace the 1980 policy objectives, the staff in the regions were left to work without any clear policy directives.

UNHCR welcomed the changes at COR headquarters, and even helped to fund the new developments. It helped to finance the establishment and equipment of the new offices, and, in its budget for 1982, approved the payment of 50 per cent salary increments to the staff, as well as provision for vehicles and equipment. A UNHCR senior programme officer was placed in COR's office to help the new Commissioner to coordinate with UNHCR and to help with the in-service training of the staff. For these reasons the new commissioner, unlike his predecessor, willingly followed the guidelines established by UNHCR for the planning and management of refugee assistance.

The only role left to COR was to assess and publicise the impact on the refugee-affected areas. After 1983 the Commissioner for

Refugees began a series of attempts to quantify the costs that were thought to be incurred by the local authorities, in assisting refugees who lived outside UNHCR-financed assistance programmes. However, UNHCR was unwilling to address this problem directly, and would only act as a 'catalyst' on condition that the government committed itself to offering permanent and durable solutions. As COR'S position within the government became weaker, and as the refugee situation itself deteriorated, it was clearly unable to guarantee any such commitment.

The Active Intervention of UNHCR in Government Refugee Policy

When the government requested financial assistance from international donors, the donors did not deny categorically the claims that the refugees were having a detrimental impact on the Sudanese economy; instead, they questioned the validity of the solutions proposed, particularly those which related to government control over refugee policy and its implementation (see for example the *Guardian*, 9 February 1981; *Horn of Africa* 1984). Subsequently, representatives of some donors made various attempts to break the government's monopoly over policy. UNHCR in particular ended its longstanding policy of non-operationalism and applied drastic changes to its strategy for handling the refugee situation in Sudan. The government monopoly was also broken by NGO involvement in the implementation of projects through tripartite agreements, as well as working alone without agreement in the case of resettlement programmes. By virtue of its internationally acclaimed position, trusted by donors and needed by host countries, and its command over funds allocated for refugees, UNHCR emerged in 1982 as a stronger actor than any single government or non-government organisation. UNHCR aimed not only to reduce the monopoly of the government but also to act as an ombudsman between the different organisations involved in refugee assistance.

COR was useful and necessary to UNHCR, as an acceptable representative of the government. Therefore, UNHCR employed different methods to mitigate what was considered to be the dominance of COR over refugee policy, without eliminating its nominal authority. The field management staff in Khartoum, Gedaref, and Port Sudan were augmented to ensure that UNHCR guidelines were closely adhered to, and that the government's project management staff worked alongside UNHCR in every area. Moreover, UNHCR introduced new measures aimed at ensuring that the UNHCR branch office in Khartoum had control over the disbursement of funds. Previously, UNHCR allocations had been transferred directly to the COR account, but under the new system, the UNHCR branch office was able to adjust the budgets by making amendments in the programme during the same year. In 1983 it was able to deposit the money with a foreign bank, apparently to benefit from the higher value of the foreign currency at a time when the Sudanese pound was devalued considerably.

To further reduce the government's control over refugee funds, UNHCR improvised the idea that COR's role should be to have 'overall responsibility' for the refugee programmes. This implied that it should not be involved directly in the implementation of refugee projects. In fact, the task of implementing refugee programmes was to be transferred to the NGOs; after 1982 it became common practice for UNHCR to provide partial funding for NGOs to implement particular projects. This pattern, which had been inconceivable in the 1970s, was applied without resistance in southern Sudan and in Darfur where COR was particularly weak, although it proved difficult in eastern Sudan where the administrative structure was stronger.

As a result of these developments, after 1982 COR in Khartoum was unable to articulate a policy that would effectively reconcile the positions of the government authorities and UNHCR. The government increasingly stigmatised the refugees, and was unable and unwilling to make a permanent commitment to 'durable solutions' without massive assistance from external donors; UNHCR, on the other hand, continued to press for cost-effective programmes which partly depended on a permanent commitment from the government. Consequently, UNHCR not only succeeded in defusing the pressure created by the 1980 international campaign, but was even able to question the viability of the settlement policy itself.

Review of Settlement Policy

In spite of the fact that UNHCR had financed seven more refugee villages in Eastern Sudan between 1980 and 1983 (COR 1983), it began to express doubts about the viability of these settlements, and the advisability of pursuing the settlement strategy. UNHCR not only rejected the government's proposal to settle all refugees in new settlements, but also considered it inconceivable that spending on existing settlements could continue indefinitely. In order to justify withdrawal of assistance from the settlements, it attempted to rede-

fine its objectives, which primarily related to the concept of 'self-sufficiency' of the refugees (Johnson and Cree 1982).

In 1982, UNHCR devised a standard definition of the relative
concepts of 'self-sufficiency' and 'self-reliance', based on three parameters which were necessarily interdependent, and all fundamentally dependent on surplus production by the refugees. The first
parameter for self-sufficiency was the surplus production of a staple
food crop: sorghum. Sorghum self-sufficiency presupposed that an
average family of 5.2 members could produce a sufficient quantity
from the allocated land to pay for all costs of production, yet still
have ten sacks of sorghum to meet the annual consumption needs
(ibid.: 2). Basic food guaranteed, the second parameter for
self-reliance was 'family self-reliance'. This meant that having
achieved sorghum self-sufficiency, a refugee family should be able to
generate from other sources enough income to cover minimum
household requirements such as additional food, clothing, bedding,
and shelter. The third parameter was the settlement's self-reliance.
When family self-sufficiency was reached, an overall income surplus
should be generated to cover operating costs and the minimum
infrastructure requirements of the settlement itself, including administration, water supply, education, health care and sanitation (ibid.).

These parameters applied only to those settlements where land
had been distributed to refugee families, and not to settlements
which were dependent on agricultural wage labour or on urban centres for income generation. Special criteria for self-sufficiency were
improvised for wage-earning settlements, whereby families were
expected to generate income not only to cover basic food and household needs, but also the running costs of the settlement as a whole
(see Johnson 1982; Johnson and Cree 1982: 46-47).

Of the nine[1] settlements surveyed in 1982, only three were considered capable of achieving sorghum self-sufficiency. The failure of
the remaining land settlements was attributed to the location of some
settlements in marginal rainfall areas, the exhaustion of the soil and
the insufficiency of arable land allocated to refugee families.

Although the report on the settlements called for more investigation into food production and the minimum family requirements,[2]
the point was made that they could not attain self-reliance without

---

1. These were Um Gargour, Karkora, Teneidba, Wad Awad, El Hawata, Abu
   Rakham, Um Ali, Abuda, Um Rakouba. The survey did not include the six land
   settlement villages in Qala en Nahal.
2. Johnson and Cree roughly estimated minimum requirements per annum as
   £S600-£S720 compared to the estimated family income of £S112-£S235
   (1982:29).

UNHCR support for services and running costs. The potential for agricultural self-reliance had been reduced by the introduction of mechanised farming methods. The report showed that agricultural machinery had been purchased at the special exchange rate ($1 = £S0.9) offered by the government to the UN, and that import duties had been waived. However, if the refugees were expected to become self-reliant, they might have to purchase from agricultural machinery importers at the higher exchange rate of $1 = £S1.35. Also, there was the possibility that the government would restrict imports for several years, as was the case in 1982. This would result in the prolonged use of inefficient equipment operating at less than full capacity. According to the report, 'the refugee settlements could therefore be faced in the future with considerable difficulty in replacing their agricultural machinery' (Johnson and Cree 1982: 5).

The situation was considered worse in the wage-earning settlements where the refugees were landless peasants. In four settlements in Suki and New Halfa, the refugees were supposed to live on incomes generated from agricultural labour in the neighbouring Sudanese schemes. Due to the seasonal nature of agricultural labour, unfamiliarity with agricultural activities, and the general physical health of the refugees, incomes generated from wage-labour were not sufficient to guarantee family self-sufficiency. Also, employment opportunities themselves were limited, leading to a high percentage of unemployment in the settlements: 30 to 40 per cent (Johnson 1982: 13). The UNHCR consultants estimated the income from four months' seasonal agricultural work to be £S120, and this was also considered to be the income for the whole year (ibid.: 12).

The UNHCR findings cast even more doubt on the prospects for settlements achieving self-reliance. A survey of the Suki wage-earning settlement compared family incomes with UNHCR assistance. The total disbursements of UNHCR and WFP were estimated at more than $3 million since the establishment of the settlement in 1978 (an average of $2,700 = £S2,430 per household). The operational costs were seen as the most costly factor; these constituted 30 per cent of the UNHCR budget in 1981-1982. In this particular area the report recommended:

> ... considerable cuts in the settlement budgets, i.e., on staff, 'temporary' constructions instead of 'permanent', employment of refugee labour in 'self-help' constructions and projects, introduction of small charges for water, medicines and educational materials. (Johnson 1982: 23)

In the wage-earning settlements, UNHCR believed that the best way to achieve self-reliance was to distribute the costs between the

refugee community and the Sudanese hosts. The UNHCR consultants called for land plots to be offered to refugees for rain-fed farming. This was recommended despite an acknowledgement that the
only land available was 60 km from the settlement, and that the
refugees had been found to be in poor physical health (ibid.). The
popular concept of 'participation' was invoked as a means of reduc-
ing the high operational costs. The population was to be organised
and mobilised to contribute to the running of the settlements.

It was becoming very clear that UNHCR was preoccupied with
finding 'a course of action which could lead to the phasing out of
UNHCR material assistance' (Cuénod *et al.* 1983). A mission led by
the Director of Assistance was sent from Geneva in November 1982,
to review the programme of assistance to refugees, and to identify the
obstacles to self-sufficiency. The mission was also entrusted with the
responsibility of reviewing the implementation of UNHCR-financed
projects, bearing in mind the possible role to be played by the UN
development agencies, bilateral aid, and non-governmental organisations (ibid.: 2). Significantly, a member of the review mission subsequently remained in Sudan to work with the ILO mission which
arrived on 17 November (UNHCR/ILO 1982: 5).

This report, produced in early 1983, carried the strongest attack
on the existing patterns of refugee assistance. It was a forceful
attempt to shape the government policy, and to suggest alternative
management structures. The report argued that in continuing to seek
external assistance, the government was hampering the prospects of
self-sufficiency for refugees. The implication was that the Sudanese
Government had a vested interest in overplaying the refugee crisis:

> As the economic conditions of the Sudanese have grown worse, the
> immigrant population tends to become a scapegoat. Complaints about
> the inadequacy of public services and the limited urban employment
> opportunities are followed by questions about the ability of the Sudanese
> infrastructure to support these aliens. (Ibid.: 18)

The formation of the National Council for Refugees was inter-
preted in this light; it was cited as evidence of the 'recent activity in
the country [which] indicates that the refugee issue has acquired
greater significance among government circles ' (ibid.: 19).

The report also paid particular attention to the amount of assistance provided to Sudan outside UNHCR channels. It argued that:
'In view of the present geopolitical situation of Sudan in the region,
the country has been receiving substantial bilateral aid for refugees
during the last two years' (ibid.). The implication was that Sudan was
perhaps receiving these funds unjustifiably.

UNHCR's real objection was that it had no control over funds provided by bilateral donors. It had strongly opposed the establishment of the Refugee Fund proposed in 1980. Nevertheless, in 1982, the UNHCR mission recognised the need for a 'co-ordinating mechanism' to oversee funds given to Sudan from bilateral sources. The report enumerated some of the contributions pledged to the government after 1980 and added that 'there is no structure for co-ordinating bilateral contributions with multilateral aid' (ibid.). But as the special fund already established was theoretically under the control of the National Refugee Council, UNHCR aimed at the establishment of another fund which would lie outside the government's control.

The review mission then severely criticised the settlement programme, pointing out the drawbacks of the different types of settlement which had been established in Eastern Sudan. It echoed Johnson's hypothesis that the settlements would never be self-reliant. It was particularly critical of the settlement in Port Sudan which accommodated only 3,500 of the 50,000 refugees in the town. In an attempt to justify UNHCR's involvement, it argued that the primary reason for advocating such a settlement had been to comply with the presidential decree which required all refugees to be relocated outside Sudanese towns (ibid.: 22).

The report recognised that, in 1982, the UNHCR-sponsored settlements in Eastern Sudan catered for only 110,000 of the 440,000 refugees who were mostly scattered along the border and in towns, thereby putting pressure on the already fragile infrastructure. In other words, it agreed with the Sudanese Government that the refugees were having a negative impact on the local infrastructure. However, it rejected the government's policy of establishing more settlements, and in fact recommended the opposite course of action. The mission reiterated the argument that 'any solution to the refugee problem should be viewed within the wider perspective of the Sudanese economy as a whole' (ibid.: 25). In paying lip service to this argument, the mission was fully aware that UNHCR had a limited role to play in the provision of development aid (ibid.: 'Summary and Conclusion' p.9). The report was thus paving a way for the gradual withdrawal of UNHCR, and a transfer of responsibility to other agencies. These ideas were developed and presented to the international forums in 1983. To limit the growth of its own programme, UNHCR had to suggest alternatives. Although it had recently increased the number of staff employed in its own offices, it now argued that the existing pattern of management was highly centralised and there was a tendency in COR to recruit specialists with UNHCR funds instead of giving technical jobs to technical ministries. Consequently, it was suggested:

... there is a need to decentralise and to allow more involvement of technical ministries in project planning and of refugees and voluntary agencies in project implementation. In fact, such measures are a prerequisite
for the settlements to achieve self-sufficiency. (Ibid.: 26)

This was a shift from the previous position, which had called for the
strengthening of COR regional offices with technical expertise. Even
the income-generating activities in the settlements were categorically
denounced. 'The vegetable gardens and poultry units are not providing the expected services; they run like public services with personnel hired by COR' (ibid.: 36).

UNHCR thus decided that the function of COR should be one of
overall responsibility and coordination, and that it should not be
involved in the implementation of projects. In cases where funds
were channelled through COR, UNHCR should be entitled to monitor that assistance (ibid.: 29).

Consequences of the Review of Settlement Policy

The serious criticisms of government policy in the UNHCR reports
indicated that the priorities of the government and of UNHCR were
incompatible. UNHCR's concern about the continuing dependence
of the refugee settlements on external aid was understandable when
viewed from the donors' point of view. However, it was absurd to
expect the Sudanese and refugee communities to pay for the running
costs of the settlements, when, in some cases, even the basic goal of
self-sufficiency in food had not yet been reached.

The preconditions identified as necessary for the attainment of
self-sufficiency could not be conceded by the government, given the
circumstances described in Chapter 4. Both the government and
UNHCR were facing a dilemma as far as assistance was concerned.
While UNHCR continued to seek ways of cutting its budget, the
government thought it justifiable to ask for more financial assistance.

In the face of these dilemmas, UNHCR's first strategy was to seek
ways to rationalise its gradual withdrawal. Paradoxically, it simultaneously advocated a reduction in government intervention; the
review mission report specifically recommended that COR should
'avoid direct involvement in planning and implementation of refugee
projects'. Between 1984 and 1985 as war, drought and famine
brought an unprecedented influx of 300,000 refugees from Tigray
and Eritrea, an even more drastic solution was recommended. As we
have seen, 'voluntary repatriation' was universally recognised to be,

at least in theory, the ultimate solution to the refugee problem. In 1984, when all other alternatives seemed to have failed, UNHCR actively began to promote the repatriation of refugees to Ethiopia.

The Development of an Alternative Strategy: The Attempt to Promote Repatriation

Voluntary repatriation is a term which has been used in refugee law and practice to indicate the safe return of refugees to their country of origin. Its precondition of voluntarism makes it contingent upon the elimination of the factors that caused the refugee exodus in the first place. In theory, it is considered the ideal solution when associated with stability in and between countries of origin and asylum. This solution is believed to have a positive effect on the economic and political conditions of the entire region, as well as leading to the decline of demands for financial assistance from the international community. Therefore, voluntary repatriation has been constantly advocated in international, regional and national forums, as the ideal solution to the refugee problem (Karadawi 1977: 148-151).

In practice voluntary repatriation depends on the specific characteristics of the conflict which generated the refugees, and on the way this conflict is resolved. Administrative and technical interventions by international agencies have rarely played a significant role in the resolution of such conflicts. Furthermore, refugees rarely return simply as a result of bilateral agreements between states. Massive voluntary repatriation only occurs when there is a substantial shift in the attitude of the regime in the country of origin, or even a complete change of regime. For example, the return of southern Sudanese refugees in 1972 and 1973 occurred as a result of a political settlement and the formal agreement signed between Nimeiry's regime and the southern Sudanese liberation movements in Addis Ababa in March 1972. Similarly, the return of the Ansar fighters and other members of the opposition in 1977 and 1980 was a direct result of the reconciliation between Nimeiry and the Sudanese National Front. This was also the case with the refugees from Uganda and Chad. For the Chadian supporters of Hussein Habre, return became possible only when their leadership was returned to power in 1982-1983. The Ugandans who fled the repression of the Amin regime returned only after the overthrow of Amin in May 1979. In all these cases of large scale repatriation, the intervention of UNHCR and refugee aid organisations was only significant as a complement to the political changes in the country of origin.

By its mandate, UNHCR was always constrained from interfering in the 'internal affairs' of the country of refugee origin (Karadawi 1983: 540). Therefore, it could not even work to create conducive conditions for voluntary repatriation (e.g., by putting political pressure on the contending parties, or by trying to influence the position of the regime in power). In the absence of major political shifts, attempts to promote repatriation were of dubious value. It was always possible that amnesties would be violated and returnees would have to experience flight into exile once again. This may explain why, until 1980, UNHCR continued to uphold a policy of settlement in countries of asylum, particularly in Sudan, and did not attempt to facilitate voluntary repatriation unless the circumstances in the country of origin changed significantly.

In 1980, there was, however, a significant shift in UNHCR policy. Voluntary repatriation became a major priority, especially in the Horn of Africa. Ironically, this occurred at a time when there was no significant change in the circumstances which had generated the refugee flights. In fact, the numbers of refugees arriving in host countries were constantly increasing. When applied to the refugee situation in the Horn of Africa, the new emphasis on voluntary repatriation necessitated a fresh interpretation of the refugee phenomenon, and consequently, a reconstruction of the international refugee policy.

According to the new interpretation, the previous attempt to provide assistance to refugees in the countries of asylum had not resulted in durable solutions (UNHCR 1986). There were serious doubts about the ability and the willingness of host countries to offer favourable treatment to the refugees; the long-standing tradition of African hospitality had been put at risk (Crisp 1984: 21). Furthermore, as refugee programmes were dependent on financial assistance from international donors, the refugees had become a liability for them. According to UNHCR:

> While being a refugee should be a temporary state of affairs, there is a real danger of refugee situations and the problems of refugees being institutionalised and of people remaining refugees forever. The foremost challenge facing the international community today is to reverse this trend. (UNHCR 1986)

These arguments in themselves did not justify the new emphasis on voluntary repatriation, and nor could it be proved that repatriation would offer a permanent solution to the refugee phenomenon. Therefore, additional arguments were improvised to cast doubt on the status of the refugees themselves. Contrary to all the evidence that refugee movements were caused directly or indirectly by political conflict, UNHCR now argued that the majority of African refugees were persons who did not fall within the 'classic' definition in the UNHCR statute (ibid.). This interpretation was indicative of a tendency to deny that the international community had a responsibility towards African refugees. This is in spite of the fact that ever since 1957, UNHCR had provided assistance without applying the 1951 definition to the dynamic African refugee situation.

In order to deny the majority of African refugees their legal status, thereby denying them material assistance, UNHCR argued that the movement of many refugees from their countries of origin had been caused by the assistance programmes in the countries of asylum, in that they gave people an incentive to leave their homes. Moreover, the concentration of assistance in the country of asylum discouraged repatriation (US Committee for Refugees 1984: 29-32; Crisp 1984: 19-21). Consequently, any attempt to promote voluntary repatriation would necessarily involve limiting the amount of material assistance provided to refugees in the country of asylum.[3] Furthermore, less emphasis would be placed on the need to create politically conducive conditions in the country of origin. By providing 'incentives' for refugees to go home, UNHCR hoped to influence, in an unprecedented way, the return movement of massive numbers of refugees, in spite of the fact that there had been no significant political change in the Horn of Africa that would justify such return.

The Competitive Demands of the Ethiopian Government

From the donor's perspective, the claims of a host country for additional assistance are negated at the moment when the country of origin begins to promote repatriation. Moreover, if the refugees are able to return home, assistance to refugees in the host country becomes harder to justify. Furthermore, as the international community is also expected to finance resettlement programmes for returning refugees, repatriation programmes make competitive demands on scarce resources.

In the case of Ethiopia, attempts were made from 1980 onwards to persuade international donors to finance the repatriation of refugees from Sudan, thus undermining Sudan's campaign for more assistance. In April 1980, just before the international conference in Sudan, the Ethiopian Government declared that a population of

3. Crisp stated that as a result of these pressures on refugees in Djibouti it 'seemed preferable to live in poverty and danger in their own country than to remain unwelcome guests in a foreign country which offered few, if any, prospects of advancement'.

over five million in nine administrative regions, including Eritrea and Tigray, were affected by drought at a time when the country was suffering from acute food shortages. In the same month, a UNICEF official reported that the Ethiopian Government:

> ... strongly feels that the UN system is taking a one-sided view of the situation by launching a large scale assistance programme in Somalia and doing almost nothing in Ethiopia. They feel that this will only aggravate the situation by attracting a large number of people to cross the border. (Hassan 1980: Annex 11)

The Ethiopian Government chose to emphasise the case of Somalia because it saw itself as a victim of aggression in the war with Somalia (1977-1978). It was therefore considered justifiable to request assistance for areas which were affected by the war. However, it also requested assistance for people and areas affected by its civil war.

UNHCR did not in principle reject the possibility of providing assistance to this government, even where it was directly responsible for the displacement of the population. According to the UNICEF report:

> The UNHCR representative broadly agrees with the [Ethiopian] government perception of the situation, and feels that both on humanitarian and pragmatic grounds a comprehensive approach is needed; this would include assistance for the displaced and affected population in Ethiopia *thus reducing the incentive to swell the number of refugees in neighbouring countries.* (Ibid.; emphasis added)

This argument of increase in refugee numbers because of the incentive created by assistance is certainly untrue in the case of the civil wars in Eritrea and Tigray. The escalation of fighting was the main reason.

In May and June 1980, a mission composed of UN agencies and representatives of donors visited Ethiopia at the government's request, to consider assistance for drought-affected areas in Eritrea, Tigray and Harerge as well as in the southern regions. The mission was led by UNDRO accompanied by representatives of France, Sweden, USA, EEC, UNDP, WFP, ILO, FAO, WHO. Reporting roughly at the same time as the June 1980 conference in Sudan, a UNDRO mission to Ethiopia projected the situation in the following terms:

> The problem in Ethiopia (as indeed elsewhere in the Horn of Africa) is made more difficult by the presence of people in the same drought affected areas who are displaced by reasons of civil conflict. The assistance provided to those people by UNHCR under the terms of its general mandate and the specific authority of ECOSOC resolutions ... must

of necessity be combined with that given by other donors within and outside the UN system. (UNDRO 1980)

This mission report argued that co-ordinated action was necessary to provide both relief and development aid for those people affected by civil conflict and/or drought. However, the UNDRO mission assessed only the food needs and logistical support required to augment the government efforts. These were estimated at 151,000 tonnes of cereals, 27,000 tonnes of supplementary food, 4,300 tonnes of butter oil and 650 tonnes of tea in addition to a sum of $34,743,400 for transport.

Under pressure from the Ethiopian Government, a second UNDRO mission led by UNDRO Co-ordinator F. Berkol was then dispatched to assess the long term assistance needs. The second mission endorsed the government programme of rehabilitation and reconstruction in war affected areas. This programme was to extend for three to five years and was estimated at a cost of $1.2 billion, in addition to 800,000 tonnes of food (ECOSOC 1980; UNHCR/RRC 1981: iv). The two reports were endorsed by ECOSOC at its regular session in 1980, and by the UN General Assembly at its 35th session. Both bodies appealed to the international community to support the rehabilitation and economic assistance programme.

The significance of these developments is that they coincided with the efforts by Sudan to claim more assistance. ECOSOC endorsed the demands of both countries and appealed to the international community for support for both sets of proposals (UNHCR/RRC 1981: v).

In fact, the international response to Ethiopia's request was very similar to the response to the Sudanese Government campaign. A number of UN organisations said that it would be helpful to identify the most urgent short term needs. In March 1981, a document produced jointly by the Ethiopian Relief and Rehabilitation Commission and the United Nations Coordinating Committee for Relief and Rehabilitation attempted to identify what was needed to cover only the period between April and September 1982. The proposals were to provide for 1.5 million people at an estimated cost of $215 million to cover food, water, health, and education provisions. The document made it clear that the package applied only to people displaced inside Ethiopia (ibid.). Nevertheless, Ethiopia continued to press for assistance for returnees. In September 1981, the Ethiopian Government produced another document which called for assistance from UNHCR. In carefully designed language, it avoided mention of the causes of the refugee exodus and did not even assess the possibilities of return. Refugees, according to this report, had been 'forced to move with a view to lure international assistance' (Ethiopian Relief and Rehabilitation Commission 1981: 3). The implication was that it was the Sudanese Government who had encouraged the exodus. On the other hand, the government document blamed the refugees themselves for the problems facing host governments, the country of origin and the international community:

> A refugee is a destitute person, and as such he creates problems for many parties of the international community. He becomes a burden to the host country by perhaps sharing its meagre resources, thus impairing development. He poses problems to the international community which has the moral responsibility of clasping him and reinstating him to his former condition. (Ibid.: 2)

The refugee, according to the RRC document, was also to blame for the problems back at home:

> ... by dislocating himself and his family, he withdraws his essential labour which is so vital for the development of his country's economy. It is therefore incumbent upon the country of refuge, the international community, and the country of origin to help refugees return home. A redoubled effort must be made by all groups to change the deplorable situation of refugees everywhere. It is then, and only then, that the world, which is increasingly getting interdependent economically among other things, will be able to produce more and distribute the production effectively to alleviate the general problem of countries which are faced with the puzzle ... the puzzle brought about by the refugees. (Ibid.)

Despite the fact that the political conditions which originally caused the exodus of refugees remained unchanged, the Ethiopian Government insisted that:

> Ethiopian refugees in Sudan are also returning home mainly to reception areas in Eritrea and Gonder. Over 5,000 family heads and 17,000 members are receiving assistance in and outside shelters in Eritrea. In Gonder 720 returnees are being cared for in a shelter in the town. 318 more refugees from Sudan have come back through Addis Ababa. (Ibid.: 3)

Moreover, the Ethiopian Government claimed that some 542,000 refugees were expected to return from Sudan in the next four years. The assistance from UNHCR was sought to meet the needs of 340,000 Eritreans then residing in Sudan, in addition to the 22,000 who were alleged to have returned. As for (non-Eritrean) Ethiopian refugees in Sudan, the Ethiopian Government projected that 58,000 would return soon, in addition to the 720 who had allegedly arrived in Gonder. The total cost of the returnee programme for 1982-1986 was estimated at $116,194,802 (ibid.).

The UNHCR Response

After late 1980, UNHCR expressed a willingness to assist a returnee programme on the grounds that it had been urged to do so by the ECOSOC resolution 1980/54. In 1980-1981 UNHCR made allocations of $1.3 million to assist 10,000 returnees (as opposed to $15.89 million allocated to the Sudanese Government for its 441,000 refugees). Moreover, in November 1981, two months after the publication of the RRC document, UNHCR distributed a report to the members of its Executive Committee in which it expressed its intention to continue this pattern of assistance over the ensuing years.

In this report, UNHCR claimed that 151,000 refugees were expected to return to Ethiopia. This figure exceeded even the number given by the Ethiopian Government two months earlier. The report stated:

> Refugees are returning in their thousands, particularly in the northern province of Eritrea. The 10,060 caseload figure set for this initial period has long been exceeded. In the north, for example, nearly the totality of the population of Keren and its suburbs (estimated to be 10,000) who fled to Sudan to avoid severe military activity, are reported by government officials to have returned, while another group of some 20,000 are said to have found their way back to Tessenei, mostly from the neighbouring town of Kassala in Sudan. (UNHCR 1981: Report 1)

Neither the UNHCR branch office in Khartoum nor the Sudanese Commissioner for Refugees agreed on the number of returnees mentioned in the report. Clearly, if such a large number of refugees had moved out of Kassala town, this could not have passed unnoticed.

When Sudan's permanent mission in Geneva challenged the UNHCR report, UNHCR's Director of External Affairs admitted that there was a contradiction between the information provided by the Ethiopian authorities, and the reality of the situation of the Ethiopian refugees in Sudan and elsewhere. The Sudanese Ambassador asked for an explanation of UNHCR's adoption of 'false' information that might distort the reality in the minds of other members of the Executive Committee (Birido to Wolfgang quoted in Under-secretary Foreign Affairs to COR, 19/1/A/739 conf.). UNHCR, in reply, simply said that it did not usually challenge information provided by governments. This did not explain the discrepancies between the Ethiopian Government's report in September 1981 and the UNHCR report in November.

The Sudanese Government therefore requested that missions should be sent to the reception areas to provide UNHCR with properly researched information on the returnees. UNHCR simply ignored this request, and proceeded with its plans for the 1982 returnee programme as discussed at the Executive Committee's 32nd session. The Sudanese diplomats speculated that persistence in repatriation was a manifestation of a growing *rapprochement* between Ethiopia and the western countries. Given UNHCR's insistence on research to justify the Sudanese Government's proposals in 1980, their refusal to allow the missions to investigate repatriation can be seen as indicative of their determination to proceed.

In April 1982, UNHCR distributed an *aide-mémoire* to donors requesting them to provide $20.3 million for the repatriation programme in Ethiopia (Hartling 1982). In 1983, UNHCR entered into a tripartite agreement with Ethiopia and Djibouti. From that time promotion of repatriation became a cornerstone of UNHCR policy.

Attempts to Promote Repatriation in Sudan

Throughout 1982, the Ethiopian embassy in Khartoum, in co-operation with UNHCR, tried to step up repatriation operations by gathering individual refugees, mainly from Khartoum, Port Sudan and Gedaref. The number of refugees willing to return was small: in 1982 COR records indicate that only 424 refugees declared their willingness (COR File 35/A/3, Voluntary Repatriation 1982-1983).

However, as the returnees were allowed to fly from Khartoum airport, it is arguable that some refugees who registered for repatriation from Eastern Sudan were merely seeking an opportunity to go to Khartoum. Dismayed by the fact that refugees were breaking travel restrictions by travelling to Khartoum with the excuse that they intended to register for repatriation, the Assistant Commissioner in Gedaref argued that the repatriation of Ethiopian refugees should be arranged directly from the Eastern Region, and that they should travel overland via Hamadaiet to Homera. This would ensure that the number of refugees who returned was carefully monitored (Assistant Commissioner for Refugees, Gedaref to COR, Khartoum, ACRG/35/C/A/conf., 16 August 1982). However, the proposal was not pursued as the military offensives in both Tigray and Eritrea made any sizeable repatriation inconceivable. Throughout 1983, the number of refugees expressing the wish to return home remained embarrassingly low. In June 1983, only 142 refugees repatriated, according to COR records (COR File 35/A/3 1982-1983). These numbers were only indicative because it was difficult to check which refugees actually left Khartoum.

UNHCR and the Ethiopian Embassy subsequently improvised an ambiguous proposal to repatriate those who were not residing in the Eastern Region, and sought approval to send them overland. In a letter to COR, the UNHCR representative in Khartoum wrote:

> As you know, until the present date *official* repatriation to Ethiopia has always taken place through Khartoum by air to Addis Ababa. Recently, however, the Ethiopian Ambassador has proposed to UNHCR to repatriate refugees from Wollega Province directly overland to Gambella. (Muller 1983; emphasis added)

This demand was considered by COR as an attempt to embarrass the Sudanese Government and to divert attention from the failure of the repatriation attempts. Approximately 3,000 of the refugees who resided in Upper Nile were members of the Anuak tribe who lived on both sides of the border. Since their arrival in Sudan, neither UNHCR nor COR had established any special programmes of assistance for them, and only scant information about them was available. Moreover, this area was experiencing growing instability as southern Sudanese anti-government forces were operating in the Nasir district neighbouring Gambella in Ethiopia. Because of this, COR calculated that any attempts to repatriate refugees overland would be hampered by the unstable conditions in the area. Consequently, it responded by calling on both UNHCR and the Ethiopian embassy to agree to allow COR representatives in the Eastern Region, UNHCR sub-offices in Gedaref, and the Ethiopian consulate in Kassala to monitor and coordinate the repatriation initiatives as originally envisaged (Assistant Commissioner, Gedaref to COR, ACR.G/35/A/1.conf., 5 April 1983).

In spite of COR's reservations, some of the Anuak were brought to Khartoum for repatriation. Because of the deteriorating security situation in Upper Nile, state security in Khartoum subjected these Anuak refugees to thorough investigation. This led the Ethiopian Government to accuse the Sudanese authorities of obstructing the repatriation initiative. In early September 1983, they began to exert pressure through UNHCR. On one occasion, when the departure of 37 refugees was delayed, UNHCR urged the Commissioner for Refugees to intervene and obtain exit visas. Ethiopia threatened to raise the issue of Sudanese obstruction of the repatriation effort at the 35th Executive Session in Geneva in October 1983 (Abd al Majid al-Ahmadi to Chief of State Security, 35/A/3, 7 September 1983).

Attempts to Involve Sudan in a Tripartite Commission for Repatriation

As noted, in 1983, amid much controversy, UNHCR developed a more active role in promoting voluntary repatriation in the Horn of

Africa by establishing a tripartite agreement between UNHCR, Djibouti and Ethiopia. It was believed that this strategy could be repeated in Sudan. As the ability of the Sudanese Government to cope with refugee influxes was stretched to breaking point, Sudan would inevitably agree to sign a similar agreement with UNHCR and the Ethiopian Government.

The idea of establishing a tripartite commission was raised by the UNHCR representative in Ethiopia with Vice President al Tayeb during his visit to the OAU Summit in 1983. UNHCR followed up the initiative by approaching the Sudanese Embassy in Addis Ababa in July 1983 (Chargé d'affaires, Sudanese Embassy, Addis Ababa to Under Secretary of Foreign Affairs, Khartoum, conf. 1/5/7, 21 July 1983). In letters exchanged between the Sudanese Embassy, the Ministry of Foreign Affairs in Khartoum, and COR, Sudanese officials agreed to resist the proposal for two main reasons. Firstly, the attempt to encourage repatriation was thought fundamentally incompatible with the Sudanese strategy of seeking assistance for refugees in Sudan (Permanent Mission, Geneva to Under Secretary of Foreign Affairs, PMG/8/1/4/3/1, 2 December 1981). Secondly, the moves to promote repatriation could not be based on humanitarian considerations as the situation in Ethiopia had not improved (Ambassador to Djibouti 1983). There were obvious similarities with the model of Djibouti, Ethiopia and UNHCR which, according to Sudanese officials, amounted to forcible repatriation (Under Secretary of Foreign Affairs to COR, MFA/8/1/4/3/6, 7 August 1983).

The initiative was seen to be part of a political strategy devised by donor countries, particularly by the US and Canada, to create an impression of stability in Ethiopia and to improve its international image (ibid.). The link between the changing US policy towards Ethiopia and the active promotion of repatriation was noted by Sudanese officials during the visit to Sudan in March 1983 of Eugene Douglas, the US Presidential Advisor. Douglas conveyed his view that much of the refugee influx in the area was casual migration, rather than a response to persecution. Accordingly:

> ... [he] wondered whether UNHCR could not take steps (as they had been taken elsewhere) to discourage the wholesale flow. He suggested that the UN, US, and the Sudanese Government were not yet talking about the hard questions, e.g., how to limit new arrivals humanely. (Crisp 1984: 20)

In the same month, reports of the Sudanese Ambassador in Djibouti expressed concern about the persistence of the Djibouti and Ethiopian Governments and UNHCR in repatriating the Ethiopian refugees, despite evidence of malpractice on the part of the Djibouti Government. For example, the Ambassador referred to the harassment of refugees and the outright refusal to allow them to stay in Djibouti: if they were unwilling to return to Ethiopia, they were told to go to Somalia instead. In spite of this, the Sudanese Ambassador reported that the US officials in Djibouti were in favour of repatriation under the tripartite commission. The US apparently preferred to transfer material assistance to Ethiopia, rather than to the refugee programme in Djibouti. The Sudanese Ambassador warned that if this was part of a shift in US foreign policy, there was a danger that the same emphasis on repatriation would be applied in the case of Sudan.

On receiving this warning, the Sudanese Government set out new arguments to justify its opposition to UNHCR's plans. Firstly, it pointed out that it was only normal for Ethiopia to seek repatriation for its refugees because of the political and material gains that would result from their return (Sudanese Embassy, Addis Ababa to Under Secretary of Foreign Affairs, conf. 1/5/7, 1 September 1983). However, in practice, Ethiopia was clearly incapable of guaranteeing the safe return of sizeable numbers of refugees, if only because it had no control over the areas from which the refugees originated, particularly Eritrea and Tigray. To illustrate this fact, Sudan pointed out that a large scale influx was arriving from Tigray and Eritrea at that time, and more were expected to come from war and famine affected areas (see GPM 1983). As the refugees themselves were not being consulted, and as they were not voluntarily registering for repatriation, the proposals amounted to an attempt to repatriate them against their will. This was likely to result in an international outcry, and as the host country, Sudan, rather than Ethiopia, would be blamed for the violation of human rights.

In spite of the strong and unequivocal position adopted by the Sudanese Government, (particularly the Ministry of Foreign Affairs and COR) (Sudanese Embassy, Addis Ababa to Under Secretary of Foreign Affairs, conf. 1/5/7, 1 September 1983), UNHCR maintained its enthusiasm for 'voluntary' repatriation. According to one observer, this continued enthusiasm was based on the rationale that:

> As the situation within Sudan deteriorates, the government will become increasingly dependent on its donors and aid agencies such as UNHCR and countries such as the USA, both of whom have been promoting the virtues of voluntary repatriation as a 'durable solution' to refugee situations. (Crisp 1984: 20)

In the ensuing months, UNHCR took unilateral action to encourage the promotion of repatriation. A mission chaired by Antoine Noel, Head of the Africa Bureau of UNHCR and himself an Ethiopian, arrived on 20 January 1984 to discuss modalities of voluntary repatriation. Ironically his arrival coincided with EPLF offensives against the positions controlled by the Ethiopian Government. The Eritrean town of Tessenei, which, according to UNHCR was reported to have received returnees from Kassala, was captured on 16 January 1984, and 500 government troops with their arms sought sanctuary in Kassala. The timing of the UNHCR mission appeared to be, as ever, inappropriate. At the same time, the idea of promoting repatriation by limiting material assistance within Sudan (the 'pressure to return' model) was thwarted by the mass exodus in 1984 of refugees from Tigray to Eritrea, which pushed the controversy over durable solutions to the background. The government and UNHCR had to revert to a new phase of relief operations on a massive scale.

The promotion of repatriation was an option devised by UNHCR in the face of persistent Sudanese requests for more financial assistance. It did not offer a solution. It was clearly used to justify the policy of restricting assistance at a time when this was arguably more urgently needed than ever before. Repatriation failed, not only because the government was successful in its campaign to oppose the policy, but also because, faced with the reality of large new influxes from Eritrea and Tigray, UNHCR was unable to sustain its own arguments. For example, given the deteriorating conditions within Sudan, it was hard to maintain that people were being 'lured' by the material conditions in the country of asylum. Nor was it true that this was a 'casual' movement of people who were not refugees in the true sense. Although they were never directly consulted when the repatriation plans were being devised, the victims of the conflict in Eritrea and Tigray made it clear by their actions that, unless the source of the conflict was addressed, repatriation was not a feasible option.

References

Al-Ahmadi, A. M. (1983) to Chief of State Security, No. 35/A/3. 7 September.

Ambassador to Djibouti (1983) 'Who is behind the repatriation of refugees from Djibouti to Ethiopia?' Ambassador to Djibouti to Under-Secretary of Foreign Affairs, No. Djibouti/E/1/2, 12 February.

COR (1983) 'Report on Refugees', No. 57/A/1, 30 November.

Crisp, J. (1984) 'Voluntary Repatriation Programme for African Refugees: A Critical Examination', *Refugee Issues*, BRC/QEH working papers on refugees 1(2).

Cuénod, J., Blavo, E., Prim, G. and Bakhet, O. (1983) 'Assistance Review Mission to the Sudan: 3-18 Nov. 1982', UNHCR, Geneva, January.

ECOSOC (1980) 'Assistance to Displaced Persons in Ethiopia'. E/1980/104, 18 July.

Ethiopian Government Relief and Rehabilitation Commission (1981) 'The Returnee Problem in Ethiopia', Addis Ababa.

GPM (1983) GPM Showak to COR, 'Drought Affected Areas in Ethiopia', Memorandum No. 36/A/4, 23 March.

Hartling, P. (1982) UN Commissioner for Refugees, 'Aide-Mémoire on the Situation of Returnees to Ethiopia', ref. EA/COM8/81-82, 30 April.

Hassan, Z. (1980) Chairman of UNICEF Executive Board, 'Report on Visit to Ethiopia', 13-17 April 1980, Addis Ababa in UNDRO inter-agency report, 27 May-7 June 1980, Annex 11.

Horn of Africa (1984) 'Sudan: Business of Relief' *Horn of Africa* 4(1).

Johnson, L. (1982) Lars Johnson, Programme Officer, UNHCR, Gedaref to R. Muller, UNHCR Representative, Khartoum, 'Suki Socio-Economic Survey: Dec. 1981- Jan. 1982', UNHCR, Khartoum, 1 March.

Johnson, L. and Cree, T. (1982) 'Self-reliance in Refugee Settlements in the Eastern Sudan', UNHCR, Khartoum. Also submitted to the symposium 'Khartoum Refugee Seminar' organised by COR 11-14 September 1982, Khartoum.

Karadawi, A. (1977) 'Political Refugees: A Case Study from Sudan, 1964-1972', M. Phil Dissertation, Reading University.

— (1983) 'Constraints on Assistance to African Refugees', *World Development* 11(6).

Muller, R. (1983) UNHCR Representative, Khartoum to COR: 'Repatriation of Ethiopian Refugees', No. KRT/M/692, 15 March.

UNDRO (1980) Report of UNDRO Mission and Multi-Donor Mission, May-June 1980, Addis Ababa.

US Committee for Refugees (1984) 'When Refugees Won't Go Home: the Dilemma of Chadians in the Sudan', Issue Brief, June.

UNHCR (1981) Report on the Special Programme of Assistance to Returnees to Ethiopia, ref. EA/COM/2/81-82, Report 1.

— (1986) Note on International Protection, Executive Committee, 37th session, No. A/AC.96/680, July.

UNHCR/ILO (1982) 'Income Generating Activities for Refugees in the Sudan' Report of UNHCR/ILO Inter-disciplinary Mission on Employment, Income Generation and Training of Refugees in the Sudan, Geneva.

UNHCR/RRC (1981) 'Short Term Relief and Rehabilitation Needs in Ethiopia', March.

8

Conclusion

Sudan's refugee policy under successive governments had two major concerns: the threat to state security and the socio-economic burden caused by the refugees. The emphasis on the need to contain the threat to state security was maintained throughout the period under study, irrespective of whether a particular Sudanese regime attempted to contain the threat for the sake of stability or to use it to destabilise the regime in Ethiopia. After 1967, with the introduction of a policy which accepted the OAU norms for the treatment of refugees, the latter course of action became the exception rather than the rule. The Sudanese Government's adoption of the OAU norms was intentional, as they provided legitimacy for its attempts to suppress the political activities of the refugees and to contain any threat to the *status quo*. Under the influence of governments which, through their internal policies, had caused the exodus of their citizens, the OAU confirmed the link between refugees and the likelihood of threats to national and international security. Both Sudan and Ethiopia had encountered internal conflict which generated refugees, and each needed to contain the threat posed by their active oppositions in exile. In Sudan, as in Ethiopia, the OAU norms gave credence to what was originally an internal government policy to subdue opposition.

However, governments in the second parliamentary period (1967-1969) failed to impose a total ban on the Eritreans' political activity in Sudan, nor did they succeed in suppressing the southern Sudanese opposition abroad. What these governments succeeded in doing was to make a legal difference between the 'refugees' and the 'political activists'. The first group constituted the pacified and politically inactive; the second group constituted the 'undesirables'. This differentiation helped to separate the refugees from their political cause.

It is argued here that refugee policy evolved as a result of the vulnerability of the governments themselves, particularly with internal conflicts threatening the integrity of their countries. Even in the two instances where Sudanese governments opted for outright support to the Eritrean opposition groups, with no separation in practice between the refugees and their political cause, the attempts were dramatically ended because of the political cost to Sudan itself. For example, the attempt of the radical government of 1964-1965 to provide arms, sanctuary and training for the Congolese Simba helped to intensify the fighting in southern Sudan and the policy had to be abandoned. The second attempt, under Nimeiry's regime, was one in which the president and his security machine tried to destabilise the embattled regime in Ethiopia; but this also had to be abandoned because it was feared that a Sudanese army faced with confrontation with Ethiopia might rise in protest against Nimeiry's policy; and, in 1977, because of the political imperative of national reconciliation with the Sudanese opposition. Whatever the reason for abandoning his designs, Nimeiry failed to repeat the example of Indira Gandhi, who created Bangladesh from a refugee situation in 1970, or Nyerere, who invaded Uganda in support of the Ugandan exiles to overthrow Idi Amin in 1979.

The objective of separating the refugees from the political causes of flight would not have been possible without another complementary policy development. The adoption of the international conventions relating to refugees offered a platform whereby refugees were transformed into a universal category. The 1951 Convention itself evolved from a historically specific situation in Europe, where the links between refugees and security were also recognised. The refugees were considered as victims of persecution rather than as full political actors on a par with governments.

The significance of adopting the international convention was that it helped to transfer the refugees from the political realm to the supposedly nonpolitical or humanitarian realm. It also helped to separate the refugees from their specific context, and to make them a universal category. This not only allowed governments to externalise responsibility for the refugees, but also absolved the regimes in the countries of origin from any direct responsibility. Accordingly, the refugees became powerless victims, and were virtually deprived of any national citizenship rights. Their fate came to be determined not only by the government of the host country, but also by the international community, which had its own priorities.

One basic characteristic of the international regime was that by emphasising a given number of refugees, they paid insufficient attention to the dynamism of the conflict that had generated the refugees.

This approach was not only shortsighted, but amounted to turning a blind eye to the oppression and persecution which was admitted to be the cause of the refugee exodus. In spite of their liberal stipulations pertaining to the basic rights of refugees, the international conventions relating to the refugees fell short of recognising the essential demands expressed by political groups challenging the legitimacy of the regimes ruling their countries of origin. Like the OAU norms, therefore, the international standards were biased towards the status quo and the will of governments.

In the case of Sudan, successive governments found these norms appropriate for two reasons. Firstly, the government was willing to apply the norms to refugees from Ethiopia in Sudan, in return for the guarantee that the political threat to their own regime would also be contained. Secondly, the application of these norms enabled the government to receive financial support from UNHCR for the establishment of rural refugee settlements. In the initial phase, the numbers of refugees were manageable and UNHCR itself conducted negotiations between Sudan and Ethiopia to guarantee the humanitarian nature of the refugee policy. There was therefore a tacit recognition that the willingness of the Sudanese Government to receive the refugees would be matched by the willingness of UNHCR to avail itself of funds to implement the rural settlement policy. These two elements of policy, involving interstate agreements on the one hand, and invitations to international assistance agencies on the other, seemed to offer appropriate solutions to the problems of security threats and economic costs incurred as a result of the presence of the refugees.

The dynamics of the political situation in Ethiopia, and its internal conflicts after 1974, challenged these objectives. In the initial period after the overthrow of the Emperor, the new regime's recognition of the Eritrean question and its pledge to resolve it created an atmosphere of optimism in Sudan that the refugees would at last be able to return home. However, as a result of power struggles within Ethiopia, the regime failed to seek a peaceful solution. As the civil war escalated, accentuated by the Sudanese Government's support for the Ethiopian opposition groups, the nature of the refugee influx in Sudan changed dramatically in terms of numbers, ethnic diversity, and dispersal in urban and rural areas. As a result of the military defeat of the Ethiopian opposition and Nimeiry's shift to seek cordial relations with Ethiopia, Sudan and the refugee aid regime had to face the consequences of the presence of 400,000 refugees. The refugee phenomenon which originated in Ethiopia became part and parcel of the problems within the Sudan.

The ways in which the refugee burden (both real and perceived) created fission within the government and between the government, UNHCR and other aid donors have been discussed. Government authorities, such as local government, state security, the police, and the army, considered the refugees primarily as a cause of security problems. In the absence of programmes to confine refugees in areas away from the towns and border areas, the authorities felt justified in forcing them out of these politically sensitive areas. COR was the lone voice within the government that strove to uphold international standards for the treatment of refugees, or at least to minimise the growing feeling against refugees. However, having neither the political support nor the financial means to reconcile government priorities and the needs of the refugees, COR could only frustrate the decisions to evict refugees by playing off the demands from different levels of the government against each other. No realistic programme could be devised because of the slow responses of UNHCR.

In spite of its stated mandate to protect refugees and to provide material assistance, UNHCR's slow responses to the Sudanese Government's requests were a result of the widening gap in interests between the two. Despite their theoretical agreement on the importance of a partnership to assist refugees, fundamental differences arose at a time when the refugee influx was changing dramatically. This related firstly to the technical difficulties involved in implementing the assistance programme, which subsequently led to differences over fundamental issues. The government considered the role of assistance to be complementary to its overall refugee policy, the management of which was a prerogative of the government itself. UNHCR, on the other hand, felt that as the UN refugee organisation it had a right to influence government policy and, in particular, to guarantee the cost effectiveness of the programmes according to the requirements of international donors. This conflict of interest took shape just at the time, in 1976-1979, when the already large refugee population was beginning to grow. UNHCR resorted to a policy of inaction which it justified in various ways. Sometimes it used arguments that disqualified newcomers from refugee status; sometimes it made any expenditure on financing refugee settlements contingent on extensive research; and often it accused the government of exaggerating the refugee numbers and their needs. This is not meant to suggest that the government was justified in all its demands, but it does show that UNHCR was not doing enough to identify the needs of those who were officially its concern: the refugees themselves.

In fact, as UNHCR reports and other literature have indicated, UNHCR was itself in the throes of defining its own obligations towards refugees and the host countries. One group within the UNHCR bureaucracy considered it to be under no legal or mandatory obligation to help all refugees in every part of the world; the point being that in law, the country of asylum held sole responsibility, even when, as in Sudan after 1978, that country was manifestly unable to discharge that responsibility.

The 1980 international campaign launched by COR to reach donors directly was an unprecedented initiative. It was a clear attempt to break the traditional association between UNHCR and refugee assistance. Arguably, it was COR's only possible alternative in view of the government's declining sympathy for refugees and UNHCR's inaction. The 1980 campaign posed a major challenge to donors in its estimates of the sums of money required. Bypassing UNHCR, COR challenged the long-held view that UNHCR should inevitably be an intermediary between donors and the refugee host countries. The other significant aspect of the campaign was that the request was justified on the principle of international obligation to share the burdens caused by the refugees.

Sudan's appeal superseded the efforts of other poor refugee-affected countries to make their case to the financial donors. Hence the two conferences on Assistance to Refugees in Africa. Between 1980 and 1984, what began as a fundraising campaign for Sudan culminated in a debate about how additional assistance should be given and on what conditions. In the meantime, UNHCR contented itself with what seemed to be a middle position, on a tightrope between the demands of the host countries and the donors. UNHCR's role, as defined, would be to continue to provide relief assistance to refugees. For the provision of additional funds to offset the pressure on the host countries' resources, it would act as a 'catalyst' between the needy countries and the donors. This inevitably reinforced the position of the donors, who accepted responsibility for providing relief, but rejected any notion of obligation to contribute additional assistance in the long term. In other words, the host countries' apparent obligation to receive the refugees was not matched by a reciprocal obligation on the part of the donors. As UNHCR had traditionally adopted a stance which reflected the view of the donors, and had consistently challenged the Sudanese Government's demands for additional assistance, as an intermediary it was likely to act to maintain the *status quo*.

The debate raised by the initiatives of Arusha (1979), Khartoum (1980), ICARA I (1981) and ICARA II (1984) resulted in a situation where additional assistance was made contingent upon commitment by the affected countries to what were called 'durable solutions'.

Durable solutions specifically meant either a commitment of the host country to the eventual integration of the refugees in the host society, or repatriation to the country of origin. As demonstrated, this amounted to a refusal by donors to make concessions to host countries like Sudan. It was almost impossible, given the situation prevailing in 1984, for a government which could not shoulder the burden of the settling refugees to commit itself to allowing them the right to stay on equal terms with its citizens. This was a commitment which the mentors of the 1951 Convention had themselves been unwilling to make, when considering the future of the refugees in Europe after January 1951. Moreover, this solution ignored the other practical reality of the dynamic conflict that was continuing to propel refugees from neighbouring countries to Sudan. It also neglected the fact that Sudan might not be able to guarantee the eventual Sudanisation of the Eritreans, even if it wanted to, because by so doing it would have challenged the Eritrean fronts which had fought for their right to self-determination for twenty-five years. If, for these reasons, a commitment by Sudan to durable solutions was impossible, what remained for the donors was to promote the repatriation of refugees to Ethiopia. In theory, repatriation was the ideal solution. The Sudanese Government had committed itself to encouraging it, and Ethiopia would certainly welcome this solution as it would guarantee both aid and a reputation of political stability.

The problem was that repatriation could not be achieved merely by administrative arrangements, without a strategy that took into account the objectives of the political fronts fighting against the government. Neither UNHCR nor the international community had the mechanisms to address these issues. In spite of this, UNHCR was entrusted with the responsibility for promoting repatriation. Attempts made by UNHCR from 1983 onwards to promote repatriation were aimed primarily to contain the expensive demands of a constantly growing refugee problem, and were not based on a genuine belief in the possibility of repatriation to Ethiopia. UNHCR's review of assistance policy in Sudan, its attempts to persuade the Sudanese Government to sign a tripartite agreement on repatriation, and the despatch of its staff in January 1984 to discuss the modalities of repatriation, all occurred at a time when a new influx from Ethiopia was signalling another crisis. The fact that UNHCR referred to the possibility of repeating the Djibouti repatriation strategy, which had involved simultaneously limiting assistance to the host country, indicates the link between their attempts to cut the costs of the aid programme in Sudan, and the promotion of repatriation to Ethiopia.

In the specific case of refugees in Eastern Sudan, 'integration' or 'repatriation' are not simple strategies for humanitarian assistance; they are fundamentally political issues. Neither the Sudanese Government nor UNHCR was capable of applying either in practice. Repatriation was inconceivable due to the continuing internecine conflict in Ethiopia. The large numbers of refugees militated against a policy of integration in Sudan, not only because this was a politically sensitive issue in Sudan itself, but also because it was resisted by the organised political fronts, who saw the refugees as their political constituency. In the case of the Eritreans, a policy of integration would have been tantamount to undermining their long struggle for self-determination.

A refugee policy that is inspired by external standards and attempts to separate the refugees from the political causes of their flight, is bound to meet with failure. It is an indisputable fact that the refugee assistance programme in Eastern Sudan failed to meet the needs of the refugees.

Epilogue

This book has concentrated on the development of refugee policy in Sudan over the period 1967-1984. A new phase began in 1984-1985, as a massive influx of Eritreans and Tigrayans crossed the border. It resulted in a state of chaos and raised more questions about what the appropriate policy response should be.

A detailed analysis of the problems which arose in that period goes beyond the scope of this study. However, it is arguable that the 1984-1985 tragedy occurred as a direct result of the confusion and conflicts which had characterised the earlier period. In summary, the events which occurred in 1984-1985 and the dramatic problems which arose had their roots in the earlier period, and in many ways resulted from the failure of the government and the aid organisations to devise a satisfactory formula for dealing with the refugees.

Size and Nature of the 1984-1985 Influx

The new influx had a special characteristic; they were mainly starving people from inside Ethiopia who had moved into areas controlled by the TPLF and EPLF. Since 1982, the TPLF had tried to manage its own relief operation for affected people inside Tigray. However, in 1984, not only did people voluntarily move, but the failure of the TPLF and the Ethiopian Government to agree on a truce to facilitate the safe passage of relief provisions left the TPLF with one option; namely, to organise the departure of people from Tigray to the Sudan itself. In October 1984, the Sudanese Government had no other alternative but to deal with the TPLF and its humanitarian organisation, REST. In November 1984, the rate of the influx to Eastern Sudan reached 1,500 per day, adding to approximately 182,000 who were already in COR reception centres in Eastern Sudan.

As the influx from Tigray and Eritrea continued throughout 1985, yet another influx arrived in northern Darfur from Chad. In August

1985, the total number of refugees in the Sudan was estimated by the government to be 1,160,000 (Kidane 1985: 14-15).

Controversy over the Eligibility of the 1984 Influx for Refugee Status

With the deteriorating situation in both Tigray and Eritrea, the TPLF and EPLF argued that the plight of the Tigrayans and Eritreans was the result of a combination of war, drought and starvation. They explained that starvation was caused by the 'cumulative effects of war', as the bulk of the population of Tigray lived in areas controlled by the TPLF. Similarly, much of Wollo and Gondar regions, as well as Eritrea, were effectively administered by the various liberation movements. It was in these areas that the famine was most severe. It was also in these areas that the Dergue had least control. This meant that newcomers to Eastern Sudan were as eligible as any other refugee in the Sudan for legal status. However, both the Sudanese Government and UNHCR initially thought otherwise.

UNHCR justified its position of not treating the new arrivals as refugees on two grounds. Firstly, forgetting the OAU definition, it evoked its own statute, which defines refugees according to the criterion of an individual's 'well-founded fear of persecution'. As fear of individual persecution could not be proved in the case of the 1984-1985 influx, UNHCR did not consider itself to be directly responsible for them. Secondly, UNHCR also considered its role as provider of assistance to be dependent on a government request. As the Sudanese Government had not made this request, UNHCR would not intervene unilaterally. Any dealings with the TPLF were inconceivable, as UNHCR dealt only with governments.

Added to this, the Sudanese Government was at first unwilling to receive yet another influx. Since 1983, attempts to establish reception centres had been strongly opposed by the local authorities. At the central level, a committee representing the Ministry of Foreign Affairs, the Ministry of Internal Affairs, and the State Security recommended a policy of closing the border and denying newcomers the right of seeking asylum. They realised, however, that the decision to close the border did not in itself constitute an effective measure if food could not reach the people. Consequently, it was recommended that the policy should allow food provisions to reach Eritrea and Tigray via the Sudanese border. This suggestion also had its problems as it necessitated cooperation with the TPLF, thereby creating more difficulties with the Ethiopian regime.

The peak of the influx in November 1984 did not facilitate government plans. It was at this point that the President of the Republic asked the Governor of the Eastern Region to declare the official closure of the border, which was, however, impossible not only because of the terrible plight of the refugees, but also in practical terms. The Governor ignored the President's request by referring the issue back to him on the grounds that the closure of international borders was the responsibility of the national rather than the regional government. Subsequently, the government changed its position by arguing that:

> ... the famine situations in both Chad and Ethiopia are compounded by political factors and in both cases the people fleeing to Sudan are considered as refugees under the OAU and UN Conventions. (COR 1984)

Simultaneously, UNHCR changed its mind about the eligibility for assistance of the 1984-1985 influx. Although it did not agree that the refugees fell within the statute, it did admit that the exodus was caused by drought and civil unrest. In an appeal made in April 1985, UNHCR argued:

> While it is difficult to reach categorical conclusions on the possible refugee status of such persons, they must at this time be of proper concern to UNHCR. The office, in cooperation with the governments concerned, is ready to assist with basic emergency care and maintenance within a special programme framework, until such time as climatic conditions for agriculture or actual fund availability in their own countries permit those who can to go.

By taking this middle position of considering the 1984-1985 influx as a special case, UNHCR absolved itself from any permanent commitment and paved the way for future withdrawal.

However, the immediate result was the launching of a massive relief operation. Despite UNHCR's earlier attempts to dismantle COR management in Eastern Sudan, the fact that the office of the GPM remained intact played a crucial role in managing the massive emergency programme (with $33.7 million from UNHCR alone) (COR/GPM 1984). COR and aid organisations were at last working to meet the emergency situation created by the 1984-1985 influx.

The Dilemma of Isolating Refugees from Local Hosts

The widely held assumption that the host population was necessarily better off than the refugees had rarely been put to the test, and few comparative studies had been carried out. Governments argued that there was in fact a relationship between the economic status of the host communities and the economic status of the refugees, and attempted, somewhat unsuccessfully, to quantify the sacrifices made as a result of refugee influxes (see Chapter 6). This, however, was not accepted as a direct concern of UNHCR, and in spite of the ICARA II recommendations, the policy of isolating the refugees from their hosts continued to be applied.

In 1984-1985 the Sudanese communities in Darfur and the Eastern Region experienced severe drought, which led to starvation on a massive scale. Since the famine occurred precisely in those regions where relief was being provided for refugees, it could scarcely have passed unnoticed. Yet, astonishingly, the relief programme ignored the needs of the indigenous community.

Observers subsequently justified donors' belated response to the plight of the Sudanese on the grounds that Nimeiry had never drawn attention to the problem. However, Nimeiry was overthrown in April 1985, as a result of a mass uprising against many causes of discontent relating to the mismanagement of the whole political and economic situation in Sudan. During the backlash against Nimeiry's regime in 1985, the longstanding discrepancy between assistance that had been provided for the refugees and that provided for their hosts became a major issue.

Conclusion

The same theoretical issues which were discussed, for example, at the ICARA I and ICARA II conferences, and never satisfactorily resolved, lay at the heart of the 1984-1985 crisis. Was it justifiable to assist refugees without paying equal attention to the problems faced by the host community? Should African governments be expected to make a permanent commitment to refugees? Could the 'open door' policy be sustained? What responsibility, if any, did UNHCR have to assist internally displaced people? To what extent was it justifiable, and to what extent possible, to influence population movements in one direction or another? Were the new arrivals 'refugees' in the strict sense, and if they were not, what were the policy implications? In the heat of the 1984-1985 crisis, no ready solutions were available, in spite of the fact that these issues had been on the international agenda for nearly two decades.

References

COR (1984) Briefing Document.
COR/GPM (1984) The 1984-1985 Budget, 20/B/1/1, Showak.
Kidane, Y. (1985) *Sudanow* 10(1):14-15.

Bibliography

Published Works

Abdel Karim, A. (1986) 'Wage Labourers in the Fragmented Labour Market of the Gezira, Sudan', *Africa*, 56(1): 54-68.

Abdel Mageed, F. and Ramaga, P. (1988) *Refugee Law: With Particular Reference to Sudan*, COR, Khartoum.

Abdel Rahim, M. (1978) *Changing Patterns of Civil and Military Relations in the Sudan*, Research Report No. 46, Scandanavian Institute of African Studies, Uppsala.

—— (1986) *Imperialism and Nationalism in the Sudan*, Ithaca Press, Khartoum University Press, Atlantic Highlands.

Abdel Rahim, M., Badal, R., Hardallo, A. and Woodward, P. (eds) (1986) *Sudan Since Independence: Studies of Political Development Since 1956*, Gower, Aldershot UK, Brookfield USA.

Abir, M. (1972) 'The Contentious Horn of Africa', *Conflict Studies*, 24: 19.

Abi Saab, G. (1978) *The United Nations Operation in the Congo: 1960-1964*, Oxford University Press, Oxford, UK.

Adepoju, A. (1982) 'The Dimension of the Refugee Problem in Africa', *African Affairs*, 81: 21-35.

Ajaegbo, D. I. (1984) 'The United Nation Development Decade in Africa 1960-1970: A Political and Socio-Cultural Analysis', *Journal of East Africa Research and Development*, 14: 1-8.

Akol, J. (1987) 'Southern Sudanese Refugees: Their Repatriation and Resettlement after Addis Ababa Agreement' in Rogge, J. R. (ed.) *Refugees: A Third World Dilemma.* Rowman and Littlefield, N.J.

Al Assam, M. Mohammed (1983) 'Regional Government in the Sudan', *Public Administration and Development* 3: 111-120.

Al-Gaddal, Mohammed Saeed (1986) *Al-Ḥizb al-Shuyū 'ī al-Sūdānī wa Ingilāb 25 Mayū* (The Sudanese Communist Party and the 25 May Coup) Dar Al-Zahrai, Khartoum.

Ali, A. Ali (ed.) (1985) *The Sudan Economy in Disarray: Essays on the IMF Model*, Ithaca Press, London.

Al-Mushat, A. M. (1984) *National Security in the Third World*, Westview Press, Essex, UK.

Al-Shahi, A. (ed.) (1987) *The Diversity of the Muslim Community*, Ithaca, London.

Aluko, O. (1986) *The Foreign Policies of African States*, Hodder and Stoughton, London.

Amate, C. (1986) *Inside the OAU: Pan Africanism in Practice*, Macmillan, Basingstoke, UK.

Arendt, H. (1967) *The Origins of Totalitarianism*, George Allen and Unwin, London (Revised Edition).

Arlinghaus, B. E. (ed.) (1983) *African Security Issues: Sovereignty, Stability and Solidarity*, Bowker, Epping, Essex, UK.

Arnā'ūt, G. (1986) *al-Lujū 'Fil Taqālīd al arabiya al Islāmiya* (Asylum in Arab Islamic Tradition), UNHCR, Geneva.

Ashami, M. G. (1988) 'The Showak Workshop on the Role of Refugee-Based and Indigenous Sudanese Agencies', *Journal of Refugee Studies*, 1(1): 81-84.

Ayob, M. (1978) *The Horn of Africa: Regional Conflict and Super Power Involvement*, Canberra, Strategic and Defence Studies Centre, Research School of Pacific Studies, National University, Australia.

Azar, E. E. and Moon, C. (eds) (1988) *National Security in the Third World: the Management of Internal and External Threats*, Edward Elgar House, Aldershot, UK.

Barnett, T. (1979) 'Agriculture in the Eritrean Revolution', Norwich School of Development Studies, University of East Anglia.

Baxter, P. T. W. (1978) 'Ethiopia's Unacknowledged Problem: The Oromo', *African Affairs*, 77: 283-296.

Bender, G.J., Coleman, J.S. and Sklar, R.L. (eds) (1985) *African Crisis Areas and US Foreign Policy*, University of California Press, Berkeley, LA.

Bermann (1983) *The Influence of Carnegie, Ford and Rockefeller Foundations on American Foreign Policy: the Ideology of Philanthropy*, University of New York Press, Albany, New York.

Beshir, M.O. (1975) *The Southern Sudan: From Conflict to Peace*, The Khartoum Bookshop, Khartoum.

Betts, T. F. (1967) 'Conference on the Legal, Economic, and Social Aspects of the African Refugee Problems', *Journal of Modern African Studies*, 5(4): 651-664.

—— (1974) The Southern Sudan: *The Ceasefire and After*, Africa Publications Trust, London.

— (1976) 'Development Aid from Voluntary Agencies to the Least Developed Countries', *Africa Today*, 25(4): 44-68.

— (1984) 'Evolution and Promotion of Integrated Rural Development Approach to Refugee Policy in Africa', *Africa Today*, 31: 7-24.

Bolling, L. and Smith, C. (1982) *Private Foreign Aid: US Philanthropy for Relief and Development*, Westview Press, Essex, UK.

Boyd, A. (1966) *United Nations: Piety, Myth and Truth*, (Reprint) Pelican Books, Harmondsworth.

Bramwell, A. (ed.) (1988) *Refugees in the Era of Total War*, Unwin Hyman, London.

Braukamper, U. (1982) 'Ethnic Identity and Social Change Among Oromo Refugees in the Horn of Africa', *North East African Studies*, 4(3): 1-15.

Brooks, H. and Yassin, Al-Ayouti (eds) (1970) *Refugees South of the Sahara: an African Dilemma*, Negro Universities Press, Westport, Connecticut, St John's University, New York.

Brown, G. P. and Henry, S. (eds) (1981) *Boundaries: National Autonomy and its Limits*, Brown and Littlefield, Totowa, New York.

Brown, L. (1977) 'Redefining National Security', *Worldwatch Papers*, 14, Worldwatch Institute.

Brown, R. (1986) 'International Responses to Sudan's Economic Crisis 1978 to April 1985 Coup d'Etat', *Development and Change*, 17: 487-511.

Buehrig, E. B. (1981) 'The Resolution-Based International Agency', *Political Studies*, 29(2): 217-231.

Buzan, B. (1985) *People, States and Fear: The National Security Problem in International Relations*, Wheatsheaf and Chapel Hill, University of North Carolina Press.

Callaghy, T. M. (1982) 'Autonomy of the Political Aristocracy in Zaire', *Journal of Commonwealth and Comparative Studies*, 20: 61-83.

Chabal, P. (ed.) (1986) *Political Domination in Africa: Reflections on the Limits of Power*, Cambridge University Press.

Chackerian, R. and Abdel Rahim, M. B. 'The Sudanese Administrative Elite: Its Development and Orientation', *International Review of Administrative Sciences*, 32: 381-392.

Chaliand, G. (1982) *The Struggle for Africa: Conflict of the Great Powers*, St Martin's Press, New York.

Chambers, R. (1983) *Rural Development: Putting the Last First*, Longman, London.

— (1986) 'Hidden Losers: The Impact of Rural Refugee Programmes on Poorer Hosts', *International Migration Review*, 20(2): 245-263.

Chege, M. (1979) 'The Revolution Betrayed: Ethiopia 1974-1979', *Journal of Modern African Studies*, 17(3): 359-380.

Christensen, H. (1984) 'On Sources and Evaluation', *Journal of East African Research and Development*, 14: 39-46.

Clapham, C. (1969) *Haile Selassie's Government*, Longman, London.

— and Philip, G. (1985) *The Political Dilemmas of Military Regimes*, Croom Helm, London.

Clarke, J. and Kosiniski, L.A. (1982) *Redistribution of Population in Africa*, Heinemann, Portsmouth, New Hampshire.

Cooper, K. (1969) *The Uprooted: Agony and Triumph Among the Debris of War*, Quartet Books, London.

Cottrell, A.J. and Burrell, R.M. (eds) (1972) *The Indian Ocean: Its Political and Military Importance*, Praeger, New York.

Crisp, J. (1984) 'Voluntary Repatriation Programmes for African Refugees: a Critical Examination', *Refugee Issues*, British Refugee Council/Queen Elizabeth House working papers on refugees, Vol. 1(2).

Crummy, D. (ed.) (1986) *Banditry, Rebellion and Social Protest in Africa*, Heinemann, Portsmouth, New Hampshire.

Cumming, D. C. (1937) 'The History of Kassala and Province of Taka', *Sudan Notes and Records*, 20: 1-62.

Cuny, F. C. and Stein, B. (1988) 'Prospects for Promotion of Voluntary Repatriation', in Loescher, G. (ed.) *The Question of Refugees in International Relations*, OUP, London.

Davey, K. J. (1971) 'Local Bureaucrats and Politicians in East Africa', *Journal of Administration Overseas*, 4(1): 268-279.

Dougherty, J. E. (1982) *The Horn of Africa: a Map of Political and Strategic Conflict*, Institute of Foreign Policy Analysis, Cambridge.

D'Souza, F. and Crisp, F. (1986) *The Refugee Dilemma* Minority Rights Group, Report No. 43, London.

Edding, F. (1951) *The Refugees as a Burden, a Stimulus, and a Challenge to the West German Economy*, Martinus Nijhoff, The Hague.

Ellingson, L. (1977) 'The Emergence of Political Parties in Eritrea 1941-1950', *Journal of African History*, 18(2): 261-281.

El-Khawas, E. (1976) 'A Reassessment of International Relief Programmes', in Glantz, M. B. (ed.) *The Politics of Natural Disaster: The Case of Sahel Drought*, Praeger, New York.

Emerson, R. (1972) 'The Fate of Human Rights in the Third World', *International Organisation*, 26 (Winter).

Erikson, L.G., Melander, G. and Nobel, P. (eds) (1981) *An Analysing Account of the Conference on the African Refugee Problem, Arusha, May 1979*, Scandanavian Institute of African Studies, Uppsala.

Falk, R. (1981) *Human Rights and State Sovereignty*, Holmes and Meier, New York, London.

Farer, T. J. (ed.) (1979) *War Clouds on the Horn of Africa: a Crisis of Detente*, Carnegie Endowment for International Peace, New York.

Ferris, E. (1985) *Refugees and World Politics*, Praeger, New York.

Firebrace, J. and Stuart, H. (1984) *Never Kneel Down: Drought, Development and Liberation in Eritrea*, Spokesman, Nottingham.

First, R. (1971) *The Barrel of a Gun: Political Power in Africa and the Coup d'Etat*, Penguin, London.

Forsythe, P. D. (1983) 'The Palestine Question: Dealing with a Long Term Refugee Situation', *Annals of the American Academy of Social Sciences*, 467: 89-102.

Galtung, J., Obrein, P. and Prieswick, R. (eds) (1980) *Self-Reliance as a Strategy for Development*, Bogle l'Ouverture, London.

Gauhar, A. (ed.) (1987) *The Politics of Exile*, Third World Foundation, London.

Gebre-Medhin, J. (1982-1983) 'The EPLF and Peasant Power in Eritrea', *Horn of Africa*, 5(4): 46-50.

— (1984) 'Nationalism, Peasant Politics and the Emergence of a Vanguard Front in Eritrea', *Review of African Political Economy* 30: 48-57.

Glantz, M. B. (ed.) (1976) *The Politics of Natural Disaster: the Case of the Sahel Drought*, Praeger Publishers, New York, Washington, London.

Goodwin-Gill, G. (1983) *The Refugee in International Law*, Clarendon Press, Oxford.

Gordenker, L. (1983) 'Refugees in Developing Countries and Transnational Organisations', *Annals of the American Academy of Political and Social Science*, 467: 62-77.

— (1987) *Refugees in International Politics*, Croom Helm, London, Sydney.

Gordon, C. (1984) *Sudan at the Cross Roads*, Menas Press, Wisbech, UK.

Gorman, R.F. (1981) *Political Conflict in the Horn of Africa*, Praeger, New York.

— (1985) *Refugees in World Politics*, Praeger, New York.

— (1986) 'Beyond ICARA II: Implementing Refugee-Related Development Assistance', *International Migration Review*, 20(2): 283-297.

— (1987) *Coping with Africa's Refugee Burden: a Time for Solutions*, Martinus Nijhoff, Dordrecht.

Gould, W. T. S. (1974) 'Refugees in Tropical Africa', *International Migration Review*, 8(3): 413-430.

Grahl-Madsen, A. (1966) *The Status of Refugees in International Law*, (2 vols) Sijthoff, Leyden.

Green, R. H. (1984) 'Consolidation and Accelerated Development of African Agriculture: What Agenda for Action', *African Studies Review*, 27(4): 17-34.

Gurr, T. (1974) *Why Men Rebel* (4th edn.) Princeton University Press, Princeton, New Jersey.

Habte Selassie, B. (1980) *Conflict and Intervention in the Horn of Africa*, Monthly Review Press, New York, London.

—— (1984) 'The American Dilemma on the Horn', *Journal of Modern African Studies*, 22(2): 249-272.

Hamid, Mohammed B. (1982) 'Confrontation and Reconciliation Within an African Context: the Case of Sudan', *Third World Quarterly*, 5(2): 320-329.

Hamrell, S. (ed.) (1967) *Refugee Problems in Africa*, Scandanavian Institute of African Studies, Uppsala.

Hansen, A. (1981) 'Refugee Dynamics: Angolans in Zambia from 1966-1972', *International Migration Review*, 15(1/2): 175-194.

Hansen, A. and Oliver-Smith, A. (1982) *Involuntary Migration and Resettlement: the Problem and Responses of Dislocated People*, Bowker, Epping, Essex, UK.

Harrell-Bond, B. (1986) *Imposing Aid: Emergency Assistance to Refugees*, Oxford University Press, Oxford.

Hassan, Y.F. (1971) *Sudan in Africa*, Khartoum University Press, Khartoum.

Hende, T. (1983) *From Aid to Recolonisation: Lessons of a Failure*, Harp, London.

Hirschman, A. (1970) *Exit, Voice and Loyalty: Responses to Decline in Firms, Organisations and States*, Harvard University Press, Cambridge, Massachusetts.

Hiwet, A. (1975) *Ethiopia: From Autocracy to Revolution*, Review of African Political Economy, London.

Hodges, T. (1984) 'African Refugees: The Burden of Exile', *Africa Report*, January-February 1984, pp. 4-2 and 36-43.

Holborn, L. W. (1975) *Refugees, a Problem of our Time: The Work of the High Commissioner for Refugees, 1951-1972*, Scarecrow Press, Methuchen.

Hondale, G. H. and Rosengard, J. K. (1983) 'Putting Projected Development in Perspective', *Public Administration and Development*, 3: 299-305.

Horesch, E. (1985) 'Labelling and the Language of International Development', *Development and Change*, 16: 503-514.

Horn of Africa (1981) 'Tragedy in the Horn', A Special Issue on Refugees, 4(1).

—— (1983/84) 'Tigray: Drought, Famine and War', 4(4).

— (1983) 'Eritrea: The Roots of War, Proceedings of Seminar', 6(2).

Howard, A. (1988) 'Refuge or Asylum: A Philosophical Perspective', *Journal of Refugee Studies*, 1(1): 7-19.

Howard, R. (1981) 'The Canadian Government Response to Africa's Refugee Problem', *Canadian Journal of African Studies*, 15(1): 95-116.

Howell, J. (ed.) (1974) *Local Government and Politics in the Sudan*, Khartoum University Press, Khartoum.

Independent Commission on International Humanitarian Issues (1986) *Refugees: Dynamics of Displacement*, Zed Books, London.

Ismail, T. (1970) 'The Sudanese Foreign Policy', *International Journal*, 25: 565-575.

Jacobovici, S. (1984) 'Ethiopian Jews Are Dying: Why Doesn't Israel Help', *International Herald Tribune*, 18 September.

Jackson, R. H. and Roseberg, C. G. (1986) 'Sovereignty and Underdevelopment: Juridical Statehood in the African Crisis', *Journal of Modern African Studies*, 24(1): 1-31.

Jenkins, B. and Gray, A. (1983) 'Bureaucratic Politics and Power: Developments in the Study of Bureaucracy', *Political Studies*, 31: 177-193.

Jundanian, B. (1974) 'Resettlement Programmes: Counter Insurgency in Mozambique', *Comparative Politics*, 6: 519-540.

Kalluniya, K. (1982) 'The Role of the UNHCR in Protecting and Assisting Refugees', *Horn of Africa* 5(1): 19-23.

Karadawi, A. (1983) 'Constraints on Assistance to Refugees: Some Observations from the Sudan', *World Development*, 11(6): 537-547.

— (1987) 'Urban Refugees in the Sudan', pp. 115-129 in Rogge, J. R. (ed.) *Refugees: A Third World Dilemma*, Rowman and Littlefield, Totowa, New Jersey.

Kasfir, N. (1983) 'Relating Class to State in Africa', *Journal of Commonwealth Studies and Comparative Politics*, 20-21: 1-20.

Kelly, M. P. (1985) 'Weak States and Captured Patrons: French Desire to Disengage in Chad', *Round Table*, October 1985, pp. 328-338.

Kennedy, D. (1986) 'International Refugee Protection', *Human Rights Quarterly*, 8(1): 1-69.

Kent, R. C. (1987) *Anatomy of Disaster Relief*, Pinter Publishers, London.

Kessler, D. (1985) 'The Falashas: Meeting the Challenge', *Jewish Chronicle*, 22 November, p. 27.

Khalid, M. (1985) *al-Sūdān wal Nafag al-Muẓlim* (The Sudan and the Dark Tunnel), Edam Publishers, London.

Kibreab, G. (1987) *Refugees and Development in Africa: a Socio-Economic Study of Organised Land Settlements for Eritrean Refugees in Eastern Sudan, 1967-1983*, The Red Sea Press, Trenton, New Jersey.

— (1987) 'Rural Refugee Land Settlements in Eastern Sudan: On the Road to Self-Sufficiency', in Nobel, P. (ed.) *Refugees and Development in Africa*, Scandinavian Institute for African Studies, Uppsala.

Kunz, E. F. (1973) 'The Refugees' Flight: Kinetic Models and Forms of Displacement', *International Migration Review*, 8(2): 125-146.

Kursany, I. (1985) 'Eritrean Refugees in Kassala Province of Eastern Sudan: An Economic Assessment', *Refugee Issues*, BRC/QEH working papers on refugees, Vol. 2(1).

Lamb, G. (1975) 'Marxism Access and the State', *Development and Change*, 2: 119-125.

Lanne, B. 'Rebellion et Guerre Civile en Tchad 1965-1983', *Culture et Développement*, 4(3): 757-81.

Lawless, R. and Monahan, L. (eds) (1987) *War and Refugees: the Western Sahara Conflict*, Pinter Publishers, London.

Legum, C. and Firebrace, J. (1983) 'Eritrea and Tigray', Report No. 4, Minority Rights Group.

Lemarchand, R. (1985) 'The Crisis in Chad', in Bender, G. J., Coleman, J. S. and Sklar, R. (eds) *African Crisis Areas and US Foreign Policy*, University of California Press, Berkeley, LA.

Lemming, G. J. (1982) 'Kassala', *Sudan Notes and Records*, 5: 65-78.

Lesch, A. M. (1985) 'Transition in the Sudan: Aspiration and Constraints', *UFSI Reports*, No. 20.

Levenstein, A. (1983) *Escape to Freedom: the Story of International Rescue Committee*, Greenwood Press, Westport, Connecticut.

Lewis, I. M. (1975) 'The Notion of State and Politics in Somalia', in Smock, D. R. (ed.) *The Search for National Integration in Africa*, New York.

Linden, E. (1976) *The Alms Race: the Impact of American Voluntary Aid Abroad*, Random House, New York.

Lipsky, G. A. (1962) *Ethiopia: Its People, Its Society and Culture*, Harp Press, New Haven.

Lissner, J. (1977) *The Politics of Altruism: a Study of the Political Behaviour of Voluntary Agencies*, LWF, Geneva.

Lobban, R. (1976) 'The Eritrean War: Issues and Implications', *Canadian Journal of African Studies*, 10: 335-346.

Lobban, R. and Fluehr, C. (eds) (1981) 'The Sudan: 23 Years of Independence', *Africa Today*, special issue, Vol. 28(2).

Loescher, G. and Nichols, B. (eds) (1988) *The Moral Nation: Humanitarianism and US Foreign Policy Today*, University of Notre Dame Press, Notre Dame Ind., London.

Loescher, G. and Scanlan, J. A. (1986) *Calculated Kindness: Refugees and America's Half-Open Door*, The Free Press, New York, and Collier Macmillan, London.

Longrigg, S. A. (1945) *A Short History of Eritrea*, Clarendon Press, Oxford.

Lubomyr, Y. L. (1986) 'Unintended Consequences in Refugee Resettlement: Post War Ukrainian Refugee Immigrants to Canada', *International Migration Review*, 20(2): 467-481.

Lundstrom, K. J. (1967) 'North-Eastern Ethiopia: Society in Famine: A Study of Three Social Institutions in a Period of Severe Strain', Research Report No. 34, Scandinavian Institute of African Studies, Uppsala.

—— (1976) *North Eastern Ethiopia: Society in Famine*, Research Note No. 34, The Scandinavian Institute of African Studies, Uppsala.

Machyo, B. O. (1975) 'African Social Scientists Are Incapable of Making Socially Correct Decisions', *African Review*, 5(3): 269-291.

Mahgoub, M. A. (1974) *Democracy on Trial: Some Reflections on Arab and African Politics*, André Deutsch, London.

Makinda, S. M. (1987) *Super Power Diplomacy in the Horn of Africa*, Croom Helm, Sydney, London.

Malwal, B. (1985) *The Sudan: A Second Challenge to Nationhood*, Thornton Books, New York.

Mamdani, M. (1973) *From Citizen to Refugee*, Pinter, London.

Marenin, O. (1975) 'Essence and Empiricism in African Politics', *Journal of Modern African Studies*, 19(1): 1-30.

—— (1982) 'Policing African States: Towards a Critique', *Comparative Politics*, 4: 379-397.

Marrus, M. R. (1985) *The Unwanted of Europe: European Refugees in the Twentieth Century*, Oxford University Press, Oxford.

Mathews, K. (1984) 'The Organisation of African Unity', in Mazzeo, D. (ed.) *African Regional Organisations*, Cambridge University Press, London.

Mazzeo, D. (ed.) (1984) *African Regional Organisations*, Cambridge University Press, Cambridge.

McKowan, R. E. and Zikker, R. (1985) 'Regional Development and Public Policy in Sub-Saharan Africa', *Indian Political Science Review*, December: 103-124.

Mills, R. (1985) 'Population of the Sudan and Its Regions: the 1983 Census', Project Documentation, No. 1, Population Studies Centre, University of Gezira, Sudan.

—— (1985) *Population Policy, Trends, and their Implications In Sudan*, Population Studies Centre, University of Gezira, Wad Medani, Sudan.

Moharir, Y. Y. (1986) 'Decentralised Policy Making and Centre Region Relations in the Sudan with Special Reference to the Eastern Region', in Van Der Wel and Abdel Ghaffar, Mohammed Ahmad (eds) *Perspectives on Development in the Sudan*, DSRC, Khartoum, pp. 239-276.

Morgan, E. P. (1983) 'The Project Orthodoxy in Development: Re-evaluating the Cutting Edge', *Public Administration and Development*, 3: 329-339.

Morris-Jones, W.H. (1983) 'The Politics of Political Science: the Case of Comparative Legislative Studies', *Political Studies*, March: 1-24.

Morrison, E. (1971) *The Southern Sudan and Eritrea: Aspects of Wider African Problems*, Minority Rights Group, London.

Morss, E. R. (1984) 'Institutional Destruction Resulting from Donor and Project Proliferation in Sub-Saharan African Countries', *World Development*, 12(4): 465-470.

Murphy, H. B. M. (ed.) (1955) *Flight and Resettlement*, UNESCO, Lucerne, Switzerland.

Nadel, J. P. (1945) 'Notes on the Beni Amer Society', *Sudan Notes and Records*, 26: 51-94.

Nelson, J. M. (1968) *Aid Influence, and Foreign Policy*, Macmillan, New York.

Nettle, J. P. (1968) 'The State as a Conceptual Variable', *World Politics*, 20: 559-392.

Newland, K. (1981) 'Refugees: New International Politics of Dis-placement', *Worldwatch Papers* 43.

Nichols, B. (1988) *The Uneasy Alliance: Religion, Refugee Work and US Foreign Policy*, Oxford University Press, New York.

Nobel, P. (1982) *Refugee Law in the Sudan*, Research Report No. 64, Scandanavian Institute of African Studies, Uppsala.

Norris, M. W. (1983) 'Local Government and Decentralisation in the Sudan', *Public Administration and Development*, 3: 209-222.

O'Ballance, E. (1977) *The Secret War in the Sudan*, Faber, London.

O'Brien, J. (1986) 'Towards a Reconstruction of Ethnicity: Capital-ist Expansion and Cultural Dynamics in the Sudan', *African Anthropologist*, 88(4): 898-907.

Ohaj, Mohammed A. (1986) *Min Tarikh al-Bija* (From Beja History), Khartoum University Press, Khartoum.

Olufemi, K. (1985) 'Chad: from Civil Strife to Big Power Rivalry', *India Quarterly*, July/December: 376-389.

Orwa, K. D. (1984) 'National Security: An African Perspective', in Arlinghaus, B. (ed.) *African Security Issues: Sovereignty, Stability and Solidarity*, Bowker, Epping, pp. 203-211.

Ottaway, M. and Blackburne, D. (1978) *Ethiopia: Empire in Revolution*, Africana, New York.

Owusu, M. (1975) 'Policy Studies, Development and Political Anthropology', *Journal of Modern African Studies*, 13(3): 367-381.

Oye, O. (1986) 'Qaddafi and Africa's International Relations', *Journal of Modern African Studies*, 24(1): 33-68.

Packenham, A. (1973) *Liberal America and the Third World Political Development: Ideas in Foreign Aid and Social Science*, Princeton University Press, Princeton.

Par, R., Melander, G. and Nobel, P. (eds) (1979) *International Legal Instruments on Refugees in Africa*, Scandinavian Institute of African Studies, Uppsala.

Parfitt, T.V. and Kessler, D. (1985) *The Falashas: The Jews of Ethiopia*, Minority Rights Group, London.

Paul, A. (1950) 'Notes on the Beni Amer', *Sudan Notes and Records*, 31: 223-245.

—— (1954) *A History of the Beja Tribes of the Sudan*, Cambridge University Press, London.

Peperdy, M. (1985) *Tigray, Ethiopia's Untold Story*, REST Support Committee, London.

Permanent People's Tribunal (1985) *A Crime of Silence: The Armenian Genocide*, Zed Books, London.

Pitterman, S. (1984) 'A Comparative Survey of Two Decades of International Assistance to Refugees in Africa', *Africa Today*, 33: 25-54.

Pool, D. (1980) Eritrea, *Africa's Longest War*, Report No. 3, Anti-Slavery Society, London.

Porter, B. D. (1984) *The USSR in Third World Conflicts: Soviet Arms and Diplomacy in Local Wars 1945-1980*, Cambridge University Press, Cambridge.

Ramaga, P. (1985) 'The Limits of Refugee Protection Policy in the Sudan; With Particular Reference to the Yei River District, Equatoria Region', *Refugee Issues*, No. 4, RSP, Oxford.

Robinson, C. J. (1985) 'The African Diaspora and the Italo-Ethiopian Crisis', *Race and Class*, 51-56.

Rogge, J. R. (1975) 'The Qala En Nahal Refugee Settlement Scheme', *Sudan Notes and Records*, 56: 130-156.

—— (1981) 'Africa's Resettlement Strategies', *International Migration Review*, 15(1): 195-212.

—— (1985) *Too Many Too Long: Sudan's Twenty Year Refugee Dilemma*, Rowman and Littlefield, Totowa, New Jersey.

Rogge, J. R. (ed.) (1987) *Refugees: a Third World Dilemma*, Rowman and Littlefield, Totowa, NJ.

Rondinelli, A. D. and Ruddle, R. (1978) 'Coping with Poverty in International Assistance Policy: An Evaluation of Spatially Integrated Investment Strategies', *World Development,* 6: 479-497.

Rose, P. I. (1985) 'Towards a Sociology of Exile', *International Migration Review,* 19: 769-773.

Rubin, N. (1987) 'Africa and the Refugees', *African Affairs,* 73: 291-311.

Rudge, P. (1987) 'Protection and European Asylum Policy', *Third World Affairs,* Third World Foundation for Social and Economic Studies, London, pp 352-357.

Saksena, R. N. (1971) *Refugees: Study in Changing Attitudes,* Asia Publishing House, London.

Salih, H. M. (1980) 'Hadanduwa Traditional Territorial Rights and Inter-Population Relation within the Context of the Native Administration System (1927-1970)', *Sudan Notes and Records,* 61: 118-133.

Schaffer, B. (1975) 'Distribution and Theory of Access', *Development and Change,* 13(2): 13-36.

Schectman, J. B. (1963) *The Refugee in the World; Displacement and Integration,* A. S. Barnes and Co., New York.

Scott, J. (1986) 'Everyday Form of Peasant Resistance', *Journal of Peasant Studies,* 13(2): 5-35.

Seidman, B. R. (1975) 'Law and Development: the Interface Between Policy and Implementation', *Journal of Modern African Studies,* 13(4).

Sen, A. (1984) *Poverty and Famines: An Essay on Entitlement and Deprivation,* Clarendon Press, Oxford.

Shack, W. A. and Skinner, P. (eds) (1979) *Strangers in African Societies,* University of California Press, Berkeley.

Shacknove, A. E. (1985) 'Who is a Refugee', *Ethics,* 95: 274-284.

Shepherd, J. (1975) *The Politics of Starvation,* Carnegie Endowment for International Peace, New York.

Shaw, T. and Ojo, O. (eds) (1982) *Africa and the International Political System,* University Press of America, Washington DC.

Shawcross, W. (1984) *The Quality of Mercy: Cambodia, the Holocaust and Modern Conscience,* André Deutsch, London.

Sherman, R. (1980) *Eritrea: the Unfinished Revolution,* Praeger, New York.

Smock, R. D. (1982) 'Eritrean Refugees in the Sudan', *Journal of Modern African Studies,* 20 (3): 451-465.

Southall, R. (1984) 'Botswana as a Host Country for Refugees', *Journal of Commonwealth and Comparative Politics,* July: 151-179.

Spencer, J. H. (1984) *Ethiopia at Bay: A Personal Account of the Haile Selassie Years,* Reference Publications, Algonac, Michigan.

Stark, F. (1986) 'Theories of Contemporary State Formation in Africa: A Reassessment', *Journal of Modern African Studies*, 24(2): 335-347.

Stein, B. N. (1986) 'Durable Solutions for Developing Country Refugees', *International Migration Review*, 20(2): 264-281.

Stein, B. N. and Tomasi, S. M. (eds) (1981) 'Refugees Today', Special Issue, *International Migration Review*, 15(1).

Stepick, A. (1986) 'Flight into Despair: A Profile of Recent Haitian Refugees in South Florida', *International Migration Review*, 20(2): 329-349.

Stoessinger, J. G. (1956) *The Refugee and the World Community*, University of Minnesota Press, Minneapolis.

Strachan, W. H. (1978) 'Side-Effects of Planning in Aid-Control System', *World Development*, 6: 467-478.

Sulaiman, R. (1984) *Palestine and Modern Arab Poetry*, Zed Books, London.

SUNA (Sudan News Agency) (1981) 'Nemeiry Announces Harsh Measures to Rectify the Economy', *Daily Newsletter*, No. 3940, 10 November.

Sutton, K. (1977) 'Population Resettlement: Traumatic Upheavals and the Algerian Experience', *Journal of Modern African Studies*, 15(2): 279-300.

Sylvester, A. (1977) *Sudan Under Nemeiry*, Bodley Head, London.

Tabori, P. (1972) *The Anatomy of Exile: A Semantic and Historical Study*, Harrap, London.

Trevaskis, G. K. N. (1960) *Eritrea, a Colony in Transition 1941-1952*, Oxford University Press, London.

Trimingham, J. S. (1952) *Islam in Ethiopia*, Oxford University Press, London, New York, Toronto.

Villamil, J. (ed.) (1979) *Transitional Capitalism and National Development in Africa*, Harvester Press, Hassocks, UK.

Vernant, J. (1953) *The Refugee in the Post-War World*, Yale University Press, New Haven.

Wai, D. M. (ed.) (1973) *Southern Sudan: The Problem of National Integration*, Frank Cass, London.

Wai, D. M. (1979) 'Revolution, Rhetoric and Reality', *Journal of Modern African Studies*, 17(1): 71-93.

—— (1983) 'African Arab Relations: Interdependence or Misplaced Optimism', *Journal of Modern African Studies*, 21(2): 197-212.

Waldron, S. (1982) 'Somali Refugees' Background and Characteristics: Preliminary Results from Qorioly Camps', *North East African Studies*, 4(3): 17-24.

Waltz, K. (1970) 'The Myth of Interdependence', in Kindleberg, C. (ed.) *The International Corporation*, MIT Press, Cambridge, Massachusetts.

Warburg, G. (1978) *Islam, Nationalism and Communism in a Traditional Society: The Case of Sudan,* Frank Cass, London.

Warren, H. and Warren, A. (1976) 'The US Role in the Eritrean Conflict', *Africa Today,* 23: 42.

Weis, P. (1972) 'Human Rights and Refugees', *International Migration Review,* 10(1/2): 20-30.

Welch, C. E. (1981) 'The OAU and Human Rights: Towards a New Definition', *Journal of Modern African Studies,* 19(3): 401-420.

Whitaker, B. (1973) *The Fourth World: Victims of Group Oppression,* Schocken Books, Norfolk.

—— (1974) *The Philanthropoids: Foundations and Society,* William Morrow, New York.

—— (1979) *The Anatomy of Philanthropic Organisations,* Penguin Books, Harmondsworth.

—— (1983) *A Bridge of People: A Personal View of OXFAM's First Forty Years,* Heinemann, London.

Whitaker, J. S. (1983) 'Africa Beset', *Foreign Affairs,* 62(3): 746-776.

Wijbrandi, J. B. (1986) *Organised and Spontaneous Settlement in Eastern Sudan: Two Studies of Integration of Rural Refugees,* Work Document No. V-86/1, Faculty of Economics, Free University of Amsterdam, Amsterdam.

Wolde, M. M. (1972) 'Ethiopia and the Indian Ocean', in Cottrell, A. J. and Burrell, R. M. (eds) *The Indian Ocean, Its Political and Military Importance,* Praeger, New York.

Wood, G. (1985) 'The Politics of Development Policy', *Development and Change,* 16: 347-373.

—— (1985) 'Labels: A Shadow Across Reality', *Development and Change,* 16: 343-345.

Woodward, P. R. (1979) *Condominium and Sudanese Nationalism,* Rex Collings, London.

—— (1984) 'Relations Between Neighbouring Countries in North East Africa', Journal of Modern African Studies, 22(2): 273-285.

—— (1985) 'Sudan After Nemeiry', *Third World Quarterly,* October: 958-972.

—— (1985) 'Sudan: the Retreat to Military Clientelism', *The Political Dilemmas of Military Regimes,* Croom Helm, London, pp. 237-254.

—— (1985) *Sudan: Threats to Stability,* Institute for the Study of Conflict, London.

de Zayas, A. M. (1979) *Nemesis at Potsdan: The Anglo-Americans and the Expulsions of the Germans,* Routledge and Kegan Paul, London.

Zetter, R. (1985) 'Refugees: Access and Labelling', *Development and Change,* 16: 249-450.

Zolberg, A. (1986) 'International Factors in the Formation of Refugee Movements', *International Migration Review*, 20(2): 151-169.

Unpublished Material

Abu al-Yaman, H. S. (1980) 'Statistical Report on Refugees in Kassala Province', NCAR, Khartoum.
Abu Sin, al-Hadi, M. (1982) 'The Sudanese Pattern of Population Mobility: A Study in Mobility Transition Process in North and Central Sudan', a paper submitted to the symposium on 'The Impact of Development Projects upon Population Redistribution', Department of Geography, Khartoum University, 8-12 March 1982.
Ageeb, Y. A. I. (1987) 'Income Generating Activities Among Refugees in Eastern Sudan', MA Dissertation, Institute of African and Asian Studies, Khartoum University, Khartoum.
Agha Khan, S. (1981) 'Study on Human Rights and Massive Exoduses', The United Nations Commission on Human Rights, submitted to the UN General Assembly, 34th Session, 31 December 1981.
Ahmed, S. M., al-Tahir, M. and Ali, M. A. (1987) 'Internal Migration in the Sudan: Impacts and Ramifications', paper submitted to the Third Population Conference, Khartoum, 10-14 October 1987.
Akolawin, N. O. (1981) 'Report on the Meeting of the Group of Experts on Temporary Refugee Situations and Large Scale Influxes of Refugees', COR, Khartoum.
al-Amin, B. (1984) 'al-Zirāʿā fi manāṭiq al-lāji'īn: māḍiha hāḍiruha wa Mustaqbaluha' (Agriculture in the Refugee Settlements: Its Past, Present and Future), COR, Khartoum.
al-Bashir, Abd al-Rahman (1976) 'Problems of Settlement of Immigrants and Refugees in Sudanese Society', D.Phil. Thesis, St Antony's College, Oxford.
al-Dawi, T. A. A. (1978) Social Survey on Refugees', UNHCR Project No. 78/AP/SUD/LS/13, UNHCR, Khartoum, April 1978.
Ali, F. al-Sayed (1986) 'Towards Self-Reliance: A Programme of Action for Refugees in Eastern Sudan', First Annual Report, ILO, Showak.
Bakhet, O. (1985) 'Workshop on Future Directions of Assistance to Refugees in Eastern Sudan', Memorandum, UNHCR, MA/SUD/GEN, 592, 16 September.
Bakhet, O. and Gabudan, M. (1984) 'Assessment of the Emergency Situation in the Sudan', UNHCR Report, 84/AP/SUD/LS/10.

Betts, T. F. (1967) 'Zonal Planning for Refugee Integration in Africa', a paper submitted to the Conference on the Legal, Economic and Social Aspects of the African Refugee Problems, No. AFR/REF/Conf./9, Addis Ababa, 9-18 October 1967.

—— (1982) 'Spontaneous Settlement of the Rural Refugees in Africa: Research Project III, Sudan', Euro-Action ACORD, London.

—— (1983) 'The Evolution of the Concept of Development-Orientated Assistance', Discussion paper No. 1 for the OAU/NGOs Meeting of March 1983, Euro-Action ACORD, London.

—— (1983) 'The Evolution of the UNHCR Approach', Discussion Paper No. 2 for the OAU/NGO's Meeting of March 1983, Euro-Action ACORD, London.

—— (1983) 'The Attitudes and Problems of the Governments of Asylum', Discussion Paper No. 3 for the OAU/NGOs Meeting of March 1983, Euro-Action ACORD, London.

—— (1983) 'Planning Implementation and Evaluation: the Possible Roles to be Played by the Governments of Asylum; UNDP; the Specialised Agencies; ILO; and the Voluntary Agencies', Discussion Paper No. 4 for the OAU/NGOs Meeting of March 1983, Euro-Action ACORD, London.

Beyer, G. A. (1976) 'Report on a Mission to Sudan', UNHCR, Geneva.

Birido, O. Y. (1982) 'The International Conference on Assistance to Refugees in Africa (ICARA) and Its Aftermath', paper submitted to the symposium on the Refugee Situation in the Sudan, Khartoum, 11-14 September 1982.

Bulcha, M. (1985) 'Historical and Current Causes Underlying Mass Exoduses in Africa with Special Emphasis on the Ethiopians in Eastern Sudan', paper presented to the Seminar on Refugee Aid and Development, Scandinavian Institute of African Studies, Uppsala, 28-30 October 1985.

—— (1985) 'Sociological and Economic Factors in Refugee Integration in the Host Society: the Case of the Ethiopian Exiles in the Sudan', a paper submitted to the Seminar on Refugee Aid and Development, Scandinavian Institute of African Studies, Uppsala, 28-30 October 1985.

Chambers, R. (1975) 'Rural Refugees in Africa: Observations on UNHCR Policy and Practice', UNHCR, No. 140/18/75 Geneva.

Coat, P. (1978) 'Material Assistance: Some Policy Problems Reviewed in the Light of Robert Chambers's Evaluation Reports', UNHCR, Geneva.

Coles, G. J. L. (1981) 'Temporary Refuge and the Large Scale Influx of Refugees', UNHCR, No. EC/SCP/16/Add.1, Geneva.

— (1985) 'Voluntary Repatriation', Report to the Round Table Conference on Voluntary Repatriation, UNHCR and the International Institute of Humanitarian Law, San Remo, 16-19 July 1985.

COR (1981) 'Projects Presented by the Government of the Democratic Republic of the Sudan to the International Conference on Assistance to Refugees in Africa (ICARA)', COR, Khartoum.

COR/FINNIDA (1987) 'The Project for Mechanisation of Agriculture in Refugee Settlements in Eastern Sudan: A Study of Context and Beneficiaries' (Mikels, G. and Hassan, Y.), a COR/FINNIDA Evaluation Report, COR, Khartoum.

Cree, J. T. (1982) 'Suki Socio-Economic Survey', A Report to UNHCR, Khartoum, No. SOG/202, March 1982.

— (1982) 'Self-Reliance in Refugee Settlements in Eastern Sudan', paper submitted to the symposium on the Refugee Situation in the Sudan, Khartoum, 11-14 September, 1982.

Cuénod, J., Blavo, E., Bakhet, O. and Prim, G. (1983) 'Assistance Review Mission to the Sudan', UNHCR Mission Report, Geneva, January 1983.

Development Studies and Research Centre (DSRC) (1986) 'Socio-Economic Survey of the Spontaneously Settled Refugees in Kassala', Report, COR, Khartoum.

DSRC and The Free University of Amsterdam (1987) 'Eritreans in Kassala: Findings of a Joint Research Project', 3 vols, DSRC, Khartoum University, Khartoum.

Education, Ministry of (1980) 'Report on Education for Eritrean Refugees in Kassala Province', a Report prepared for the 1980 Conference, COR.

US Department of State (1984) 'A Time for Solutions: the US Government Role', ICARA, 11 documents, Geneva.

Dieugues, A.C. (1978) 'Discussion on Evaluation of Rural Settlements', UNHCR, Geneva.

— (1978) 'The Problems of the Phasing-Out of Assistance to UNHCR Organised Rural Settlements', discussion paper, UNHCR, Geneva.

ECA, UNHCR, OAU and The Dag Hammarskjold Foundation (1967) 'Conference on the Legal, Economic and Social Aspects of African Refugee Problems', Final Report, December 1986.

ECOSOC (1980) 'Situation of Refugees in the Sudan', Report of the UN Secretary General, UN/GA/A/35/410, New York, 16 December 1980.

— (1982) 'Situation of Refugees in the Sudan', Report of the UN Secretary General, UN/GA/A/37/178, New York, 15 April 1982.

— (1986) 'Situation of Refugees in the Sudan', Report of the UN Secretary General, UN/GA/A/4/264, New York, 8 April 1986.

EPLF (1982) 'A Second Communiqué on the Ethiopian Prisoners of War', 27 June 1982.

— (1987) 'EPLF Statement on the Famine in Eritrea and Ethiopia and International Relief Effort', Eritrea.

— (1987) 'The EPLF on the Eritrean Refugees', EPLF Commissioner for Refugees, Eritrea, 20 September 1987.

— (1987) 'The Political Report and the Programme for the National Democratic Revolution', Report submitted to the EPLF Second Congress, Eritrea, March 1987.

Ethiopia, Government of (1981) 'Relief and Rehabilitation Activities and Programme', submitted to the UN Conference on the Least Developed Countries, May 1981, (in Refugee Studies Programme, Document No. LE/53, Oxford).

Experiment in International Living (1985) 'Management and Delivery of Refugee Services in Eastern Sudan', Report of a Seminar, Kassala, 30 July-1 August 1985.

Ferris, E. G. (1986) 'Voluntary Agencies and the Politicisation of the Refugee Issue', paper submitted to the seminar series on The Crisis Mass Exodus, RSP/QEH, Oxford, 10 December 1986.

The Ford Foundation (1981) 'Background Memo on Support of Work with Refugees in Africa', Nairobi, 27 May 1981.

— (1984) 'The Impact of Refugees on Poorer Hosts', Khartoum.

— (1985) 'Drought Victims and Refugees in Eastern Sudan', a staff discussion paper, Khartoum, February 1985.

Gaafar, M. and Ramchandarian, V. K. (1982) 'Impact of Development Projects on Population Redistribution: A Case Study of Gedaref Town in Eastern Sudan', Statistics Department, ECA/PD/WP, Khartoum.

Gasarasi, C. P. (1976) 'The Life of a Refugee Settlement: The Case of Muyenzi in Mgala District, Tanzania', a monograph, Dar es Salaam University, Tanzania.

Gaymans, H. (1975) 'Report on Socio-Economic Survey Among Refugees in Wad el Heleiw', UNHCR, Khartoum.

Gilkes, P. S. (1987) 'Conflicts in Ethiopia: Roots, Current Status, and Prospects', a paper submitted to the symposium on 'Crisis in the Horn of Africa, Causes and Prospects', Woodrow Wilson Centre, Washington, 17-20 June 1987.

Goitum, E. (1980) 'Adaptation and Integration: the Case of Eritrean Refugees in the Three Towns', BA Dissertation, Department of Geography, Khartoum University, Khartoum.

Goodwillie, S. (1983) 'Refugees in the Developing World: A Challenge to the International Community', UNHCR working paper submitted to the Meeting of Experts on Refugee Aid and Development, Mont Pélérin, Switzerland, 29-31 August 1983.

Goodwin-Gill, G. (1986) 'Voluntary Repatriation: Legal and Policy Issues', a paper submitted to the seminar series on The Crisis of Mass Exodus, RSP, Oxford, 8 December 1986.

Habte Selassie, E. (1984) 'Eritrea: The National Colonial Question and the National Democratic Revolution', a seminar paper, Institute of Social Studies, The Hague.

Hartling, P. (1984) Statement by the High Commissioner for Refugees to the Second Session of the ECOSOC, Geneva, 16 July 1984.

Hocke, J. P. (1986) 'Beyond Humantarianism: The Need for Political Will to Resolve Today's Refugee Problem', The Joyce Pearce Memorial Lecture, Oxford University, 29 November 1986.

Huntings Technical Services Ltd. (1976) 'Refugee Settlement in East and Central Sudan: Pre-Investment Study', UNHCR Report.

— (1976) 'Refugee Resettlement in Eastern and Central Sudan: Pre-Investment Study', COR/UNHCR Report, Khartoum.

Ibrahim, B. H. and Badran, M. (1984) 'Refugees in the Sudan: Lessons from the Ansar Resettlement Experience', a paper submitted to the Conference on Assistance to African Refugees: Alternative Viewpoints, Oxford.

ICVA (1982) 'ICVA's Mission to Ethiopia to Assess the Situation with Regard to Displaced Persons and Returnees', ICVA, Geneva, 16-30 January 1982 (in RSP Documents, RSP/LE/53).

— (1983) 'Assistance to African Refugees by Voluntary Agencies', Geneva.

— (1984) 'ICVA's Statement to the Second International Conference on Assistance to Refugees in Africa (ICARA II)', Geneva, 9 July 1984.

ILO, UNHCR, COR (1983) 'Organisational Structure for the Promotion of Self-Reliance Among Ethiopian Refugees in the Sudan', Agreement under the Programme of UNHCR, Project No. 83-84/AP/SUD/LS/50/ILO, COR, Khartoum.

Individual Cases Unit (COR) (1982) 'Administrative Assistance for Individual Refugees', a paper submitted to the symposium on the Refugee Situation in the Sudan, Khartoum.

Jaeger, G. (1980) 'A Succinct Evaluation of the 1951 Convention and the 1967 Protocol Relating to the Status of Refugees', a seminar paper, Stuttgart.

— (1980) 'Status and International Protection of Refugees', Protection Division, UNHCR, Geneva.

Karadawi, A. (1978) 'Displacement of Urban Refugees: A Case of Mismanagement', Memorandum, COR, Khartoum.

—— (1979) 'A Note on Urban Refugees in the Sudan 1975-1978', COR, Khartoum.

—— (1980) 'Urban Refugees', a background paper, the 1980 Conference documents, COR, Khartoum.

—— (1982) 'The Relationship between Government and Non-Government Organisations in Refugee Work in the Sudan', submitted to the symposium on the Situation of the Refugees in the Sudan, Khartoum, 11-14 September, 1982.

—— (1984) 'Proposal for the Study of the Integration and Reintegration Processes: The Case of Ethiopian Refugees in Somalia and Returnees to Ethiopia', UNRISD, Geneva.

—— (1985) 'Dynamics of the Refugee Policy in the Sudan', a paper submitted to the Conference on Sudan After Nemeiry, SOAS, London, September 1985.

—— (1982) 'Definition of a Refugee: Changing Concepts', paper submitted to the symposium on the Situation of Refugees in the Sudan, Khartoum, 11-14 September 1982.

Karadawi, A. and Ibrahim, I. (1981) 'Refugee Settlement Programmes in the Sudan: A Country Case Study', submitted to UNHCR Workshop on Rural Refugee Settlements in Africa, Dar es Salaam, 1-11 September 1981.

Kozlowski, A. L. (1982) 'Refugees and Development in Africa', a paper submitted to the symposium on the Refugee Situation in the Sudan, Khartoum, 11-14 September 1982.

Macaulay, S. and Karadawi, A. (1984) 'Income Generating Projects in Refugee-Affected Areas of Sudan: Past Experience and Future Prospects', Report of Survey, COR, Khartoum.

Mahmoud, U.A. (1986) 'Self-Settled Refugees in Gedaref', a UNHCR report, Khartoum.

Michel, T. (1984) 'Psychological Aspects of the Refugee Situation in Sudan: Orientation in New Environments', a paper prepared for the Social and Psychological Research Centre, University of Saar.

The National Committee for Aid to Refugees (NCAR) (1980) Documentation for the 1980 Conference, Khartoum, 20-23 June 1980: Vol.1 Background and Project Summaries; Vol. 2 Economics and Project Implementation; Vol. 3 Project Proposals; Vol. 4 Refugee Settlements in the Southern Region; Vol. 5 The Final Report.

NCAR and UNHCR (1980) 'Planned Settlements in Kassala Province', Report of a Technical Appraisal Mission, NCAR, Khartoum.

Nigli, P. (1986) 'Doubtful Methods in the Struggle Against Famine: Ethiopia's Deportation and Forced Labour Camps', Report, Berliner Missionwerk, Switzerland.

Office of Refugee Affairs, US Embassy, Khartoum (1983) 'Refugee Situation in the Sudan', a Report, US Embassy, Khartoum.
— (1983) 'Sectoral Analysis of the Resource Flows in the Refugee Settlements in Eastern Sudan', US Embassy, Khartoum.
— (1983) 'An Assesment of the Economic Integration and the Impact of Urban Refugees in Port Sudan, Gedaref and Kassala', US Embassy, Khartoum.
— (1984) 'Characteristics of the Ethiopian Refugees Being Resettled in the United States', US Embassy, Khartoum.
Osman, A. M. (1986) 'The Impact of Refugees on Social Services in Refugee-Affected Areas in the Sudan', COR, Khartoum.
Ottaway, M. (1987) 'Foreign Economic Assistance in the Horn: Does it Influence Host Government Policies?', a paper submitted to the symposium on the Crisis in the Horn of Africa, Causes and Prospects, The Woodrow Wilson Centre, Washington.
Palmer, M. (1976) 'The Eritrean Refugee Situation in the Sudan', an ACORD Report, London.
Pezaro, A. (1984) 'Normative Conflict Among Eritrean Women Refugees', Social Psychological Research Centre, University of Saar.
Post, J. (1985) 'Suggestions for the Resettlement Policy Concerning Urban Refugees in Eastern Sudan', Department of Urban and Regional Planning, The Free University of Amsterdam.
Refugee Policy Group (RPG) (1984) 'ICARA II: Burden Sharing and Durable Solutions', Refugee Policy Group, Washington.
— (1985) 'Older Refugee Settlements in Africa', Final Report, Washington.
Relief Society of Tigray (REST) (1981) 'Help the People in Need', REST News Bulletin, Khartoum.
— (1982) Agreement between the Commissioner for Refugees in the Democratic Republic of the Sudan and the Relief Society of Tigray, Khartoum.
— (1985) 'Resettlement or Coercion', Press Release, Khartoum, December 1985.
Rights and Justice (1980) 'Comment on the Report of ECOSOC', A/35/360, on 'Assistance to Displaced Persons in Ethiopia', London.
RRC (Ethiopia) (1981) 'Assistance to the Ethiopian Returnees', Project Proposal, October 1981 (also in RSP Documentation LE/53, Oxford).
— (1981) 'The Returnee Problem in Ethiopia and Assistance Requirements', RSP Documentation LE/53, Oxford.

Schoenmeier, W. H. (1982) 'Psychological Aspects of the Refugee Situation in the Sudan', Social and Psychological Research Centre, University of Saar.

Seyoum, R. M. (1981) 'The Forgotten People', Lecture, St Cross College, Oxford, 6 March 1981.

Seyoum, R. M. and Juel Jensen, B. (1976) 'Investigation of the Problems of Ethiopian Refugees in Sudan', OXFAM Mission Report, April 1976.

Simmance, A. J. F. (1986) 'Durable Solutions', a paper submitted to the seminar series on the Crisis of Mass Exodus, RSP, Oxford.

Sokiri, A. (1972) 'The Social Problems and Political Predicament of Refugees: A Case Study of the Ibuga Refugee Settlement in Western Uganda', Ph.D. Thesis, University of Dar es Salaam, Tanzania.

Spooner, B. C. (1981) 'The Qala En Nahal Refugee Settlement Scheme: Historical Review, Current Status and Programme for Action', Report, Euro-Action ACORD, London.

Sudanese Government (1974) The Regulation of Asylum Act, Presidential Decree No. 45, Khartoum.

al-Tayeb, M. A. (1982) 'Asylum and Sanctuary in Islam', a paper submitted to the symposium on the Situation of the Refugees in the Sudan, Khartoum.

TPLF (1982) 'Birth of a Revolutionary Vanguard', Foreign Relations Bureau, TPLF.

— (1982) 'Aid Used for Uprooting People', statement No. 2, Dec. 1982.

— (1984) 'TPLF Reaction to the Relief Operation in Ethiopia', Press Release, 7 1984.

— (1984) 'A Proposal for the Formation of a United Resistance Force', 8 May 1984.

— (1985) 'Statement by the Central Committee of the Tigray Liberation Front (TPLF) on the Occasion of the 24th Anniversary of the Armed Struggle in Eritrea', Sept. 1985.

United Nations (1951) 'Convention Relating to the Status of Refugees', Geneva, 28 July 1951.

— (1967) 'Protocol Relating to the Status of Refugees', New York, 31 Jan. 1967.

United Nations General Assembly (UNGA) (1950) 'Statute of the Office of the High Commissioner for Refugees', UNGA Res. 428(v), 14 Dec. 1950.

— (1950) The 1950 UN Resolution on Eritrea, UNGA Res. 390(v), 5th Session, 2 Dec. 1950.

— (1983) 'The Infrastructural Burden of Dealing with Large Numbers of Refugees', Report of the UN Technical Team on Sudan's Projects for ICARA II, New York.

—— Resolutions on the Refugee Situation in the Sudan:
  1. UNGA Res. 35/181, 15 Dec. 1980
  2. UNGA Res. 36/158, 16 Dec. 1981
  3. UNGA Res. 37/173, 17 Dec. 1982
  4. UNGA Res. 38/190, 16 Dec. 1983
  5. UNGA Res. 39/108, 14 Dec. 1984
  6. UNGA Res. 40/135, 16 Dec. 1985
—— (1984) 'Declaration and Programme of Action of the Second International Conference on Assistance to Refugees in Africa', A/CNF.125/L.1, 10 July 1984.
—— (1984) 'Detailed Description of Needs, Project Outlines and Background Information on the Refugee Situation', Report of Secretary General, A/Conf. 125/2, 25 March 1984.
—— (1986) 'International Co-operation to Avert New Flows of Refugees', Note by the Secretary General, UNGA 41st Session, No. A/41/327, 13 May 1986.
—— (1986) 'The Role of the Office of the High Commissioner for Refugees in Africa', a Note by the Secretary General, 41st Session, No. A/41/380, 30 May 1986.
—— (1982) 'The International Conference on Assistance to Refugees in Africa', Report of the Secretary General, No. E/1982/76.
UN Co-ordinating Committee for Relief and RRC (Ethiopia) (1981) 'Short Term Relief and Rehabilitation Needs in Ethiopia', a Report.
UNDRO (1980) 'Agency Mission and Multi-Donor Mission to Ethiopia', a Report, 27 May-7 June 1980.
UNDP (1985) 'Note on ICARA II: Status of the Proposals', No. PRO.1/85/189, Khartoum, 29 April 1985.
UNHCR (1979) 'Planning Rural Settlements for Refugees in Africa: Some Considerations', UNHCR PES/326, Geneva.
—— (1980) 'Follow-up on the Various Recommendations of Arusha Conference on Rural Refugees', UNHCR,80/TF/VAR/MA/1/ARU.
—— (1981) 'Port Sudan Sub-Urban Settlement', Agreement between UNHCR and Sir McDonald and Partners, No. 81/AP/SUD/LS/43/DPU, October 1981.
—— (1981) 'Project Management System Handbook', UNHCR/PES/335, Geneva.
—— (1981) 'Managing Rural Settlements for Refugees in Africa', Proceedings of a Workshop on the Follow-up to the Arusha Recommendations on the Rural Refugees in Africa, UNHCR Specialist Support Unit, Geneva.
—— (1982) 'The Office of the United Nations High Commissioner for Refugees', General Information paper, No. HCR/50B/1/82.

—— (1983) 'Refugee Aid and Development', Note by the High Commissioner to the UNHCR/EXCOM, 34th Session, No. A/AC/.96/635, Dec. 1983.

—— (1983) 'A Study of the Issues and Problems Relating to the Question of Additionality in Refugee-Related Development Assistance', No. A/AC.96/635, Annex I.

—— (1983) 'Report of the Meeting of the Non-Governmental Organisations on the Report of Experts on Refugee Aid and Development', No. A/AC.96/635, Annex III, Nov. 1983.

—— (1983) 'Meeting of Experts on Refugee Aid and Development, Mont Pélérin, 29-31 Aug. 1983', a Report, No. A/AC/.96/627, Annex I.

—— (1985) 'Refugee Aid and Development', Note by the High Commissioner to UNHCR/EXCOM, 36th Session, No. A/AC/96/662, Aug. 1985.

—— (1985) 'Voluntary Repatriation', Report of the Round Table on Voluntary Repatriation, Sub-Committee of the Whole on International Protection, UNHCR, Executive Committee, 39th Session.

—— (1985) 'Voluntary Repatriation', Report of High Commissioner to UNHCR/EXCOM, 36th Session, No. AC/SCP/41, 1 Aug. 1985.

—— (1986) 'Statement of Funds Obligated Since 1968', UNHCR, Khartoum.

—— (1986) 'Refugee Settlements: Balos, Bia, Huweig and Qala En Nahal, Kassala, Sudan', Mission Report, UNHCR Technical Support Unit, Geneva.

—— (1988) 'Refugee Aid and Development', No. AC/AC.96/XXXIX/CRP.3, 39th Session of UNHCR/EXCOM, 30 Sept. 1988.

UNHCR and ILO (1982) 'Income Generating Activities for Refugees in the Sudan', Report of UNHCR/ILO Inter-disciplinary Mission on Employment, Income Generation and Training of Refugees in the Sudan, Geneva.

—— (1984) 'Towards Self-Reliance: A Programme of Action for Refugees in East and Central Sudan', Report of UNHCR/ILO Project on Income Generating Activities for Refugees in East and Central Sudan, Geneva.

UNHCR, COR and ILO (1986) 'Workshop on Future Directions of Assistance to Refugees in Eastern Sudan, 14-18 September 1986', Final Report, Khartoum.

USAID (1982) 'Turning Private Voluntary Organisations into Development Agencies: A Question for Evaluation', AID Programme Evaluation paper, No. 12. PN/AAJ/612, Washington, April 1982.

Voll, J. O. (1983) 'Islam and Stateness in the Sudan', a paper presented to the symposium on Religion and Social Change: Islam and Catholicism , discussion paper No. 4, Centre for Developing Areas Studies, Montreal.

—— (1987) 'Major Issues of Governance in Khartoum', a paper submitted to the symposium on the Crisis in the Horn of Africa: Causes and Prospects , the Woodrow Wilson Centre, Washington, 17-20 June 1987.

WFP (1980) 'Report of a Formulation Mission to Sudan to Assess the Medium Term Needs of Food Assistance to the Refugees from Ethiopia, 26 January-15 February 1980', Khartoum.

Wijbrandi, J. L. (1980) 'Organised and Spontaneous Settlement in Eastern Sudan: Two Case Studies of Integration of Rural Refugees', Faculty of Economics, University of Amsterdam.

Woldegabriel, B. (1980) 'Survey of the Sudanese-Ethiopian Relations, Specially Since Freetown Conference', BA Dissertation, African and Asian Studies Institute, University of Khartoum.

Woldegabriel, B. and Karadawi, A. (1987) 'The Role of Indigenous Sudanese and Refugee-based Agencies in Refugee Work in the Sudan', Report of a workshop held at Showak, Eastern Region, 11-14 July 1987.

Primary Sources: Selected Government Documents

(All government documents are confidential)
I provide hereunder the Arabic name and number of the original document. For elaboration of content I also include an English translation in brackets.

File No.	Subject
1/A/1 and 2	Al-Qarārāt al-Jumhūriya, Wa-Qarārāt Majlis al-Wuzarā (Presidential Decrees and Council of Ministers Resolutions)
8/A/1	Lijān al-Ḥudūd (The Borders Joint Committees)
8/A/2	Lajnat al-Ḥudūd al-Mushtaraka M'a Ithiūbya (The Joint Committees on Border Issues with Ethiopia)
17/A/1	Al- Ta'līm (Education)
17/B/2	Ta'līm al-Lāj'in al-Eritriyīn wal Athiūbiyīn (Education of Eritrean and Ethiopian Refugees)
20/F/1	Al Ḥamla al-'Ālamiya Lijam'al-Tabarru'āt (The International Campaign for Fund Raising)
20/F/2	Sundūg Māl al-Lāji'īn (The Refugee Fund)

32/B/1	Mu'tamar Erkwīt (Erkwit Conference)
32/B/2	Al-Mu'tamar al-'Ālamī Limūsa'dat al-Lāj'īn fī Afrīqiya (The International Conference for Assistance to Refugees in Africa)
35/A/1	Shu'ūn al-Lāj'īn Umūmī (Refugees, General)
35/A/2	al-Ittifāqiyāt al Khāṣṣa bi al-Lāji'īn (Agreements Relating to Refugees)
35/A/3	Al Majlis al-Qawmī li-Lāji'īn (The National Refugee Council)
35/A/4	Talabāt al-Lujū' (Application for Refugee Status)
35/A/6	Ihsā'iyāt al-Lāji'īn (Statistical Data on Refugees)
35/A/6	Mashrū'Ḥaṣr al-Lāji'īn (The Refugee Registration Project)
35/A/3 and 4	Al-'Awda al-Ikhtiyāriya Lil Lāji'īn (Voluntary Repatriation)
35/B/3 and 35/C/8	Al-Lāji'īn Bil Sūdān – Umūmī (Ethiopian Refugees in Sudan, General)
36/A/1 (conf.)	Jihāz amn al Dawla (The State Security)
36/A/A/2 (conf.)	Lajnat Ib'ād al-Lāji'īn 'An al-Āṣima (The Committee for Transferring Refugees from Khartoum)
36/A/3 and 36/F/1	Taḥarrukāt al-Lāji'īn (Movement of Refugees)
36/A/4 and 36/B/3	Taqārīr al-Amn'an al-Lāji'īn (The Security Reports
37/A/1/2	Al-'Amal (Employment)
38/A/1	Al-Arāḍī (Land Allocation)
44/A/2	Al-ṣaḥḥa Bi-Mudiriyat Kassala (The Health Situation in Kassala Province)
48/B/1	Al-Tanẓīm al-Maktabī Li Mu'tamad al-Lāji'īn (The Organisational Structure of the Office of the Commissioner for Refugees)
49/B/1	Jawāzāt al-Lāji'īn (Travel Documents for Refugees)
10/A/1	Al-Munaẓamāt al-taṭawu'iya – Umūmī (The Non-Governmental Organisations, General)
10/C/1	Al Umam al-Muttaḥida (The United Nations)
10/C/4	Ijtimā'āt wa-Mudāwalāt al-Majlis al Iqtiṣādi wal-Ijtimā'ī (The Meetings and Deliberations of the UN/ECOSOC)
10/C/5	Ijtimā'āt al-Jam'iya al-'āma Lil-'Umam al-Muttaḥida – Taqārīr al-Majlis (The UN General Assembly – The ECOSOC Reports)
10/D/1	Wufūd wa Mu'tamarāt al-Mandūb al-sāmī (The Meetings of UNHCR)

10/D/2	Ijtimā'āt al-Lajna al-Tanfīdhiya Li-Maktab al-Mandūb al-sāmī Li-shu'ūn al Lāji'īn (The Meetings of UNHCR/EXCOM)
10/D/4	Barāmij al-Musā'adāt Li-Laji'īn (The Programme of Assistance for Refugees)
10/D/5	Ittifāqiyāt Ganaif Li al-Lāji'īn (The 1951 Geneva Convention Relating to the Status of Refugees)
10/D/7	Al-Musūḥ al-ijtimā'iya wa-al Iqtisādiya (COR/UNHCR Socio-Economic Surveys on Refugees)
10/E/2 and 46/D/1	Munzamat al-waḥda al-Afrīqiya (The Organisation of African Unity)
10/E/3 and 46/D/2	Ta'līm wa Tawẓīf al-Lāji'īn al Afāriqa (The Education and Placement of African Refugees)
10/E/4 and 46/D/3	Al-Iḥtifāl Bi-Yawm al-Lāji'al Afrīqī (The African Refugee Day)
10/E/5 and 46/G/1	Ittifāqiat Munaẓamat al-Waḥda al-Afrīqiya li-'ām 1969 (The OAU Convention Governing the Specific Aspects of the Refugee Problem in Africa 1969)
10/E/6 and 46/D/1/1	Mu'tamar Duwali sharq wa-wasaṭ Afrīqiya (The Conference for the East and Central African States)
10/F/1	Jāmi'at al-Duwal al-'Arabiya (The Arab League)
10/K/1	Al-Mu'tamar al-Islāmī – Jiddah (The Islamic Congress – Jeddah)
10/H/1	Al-Bank al-Islāmī Lil Tanmiya (The Islamic Development Bank)
10/H/1-75	Al-Munaẓamāt al-taṭawu'iya (Individual Files on the Non-Governmental Organisations)
12/A and 12/B	Mashāri' wa qurā Iskān al-Lāji'in (The Refugee Settlement Projects)

Al-Mudhakirat (Memoranda)

Ministry of the Interior

Murāj'at Adā'al-Lajna al-Markaziya Li''iadat al-Lāji'īn (Review of the Performance of CCRR) CM/16/9, 28 January 1967

Al-Lāji'ūn al-Iritriyūn wa al-Kunghūliyūn bil Sūdān (The Eritrean and Congolese Refugees in Sudan) 1967

Al-Mashākil Bayn al-Sūdān wa Ithiūbia (The Problems between Sudan and Ethiopia) 6 March 1968

Al-Nashāṭ al Iritrī bil Sūdān (The Eritrean Activities in Sudan) Police Headquarters, August 1968

Al-Iritriyūn: Monaẓamātuhum wa Khilāfātuhum (The Eritreans: Their Organisations and Internal Conflicts) July 1970

Al-Lāji'ūn al Kunghūliyūn fi Jumhūriyat al-Sūdān al-Dimuqrāṭiya, wa al-Lāji'ūn al-Sūdāniyūn fi Jumhūriyat al-Kungu (The Congolese Refugees in Sudan, and the Sudanese Refugees in the Congo), 3 December 1970

Al-Lāji'ūn al Kunghūliyūn fi Jumhūriyat al-Sūdān al-Dimuqrāṭiya (Congolese Refugees in Sudan) 1971

Al-Lāji'ūn al-Iritriyūn fil-Sūdān (The Eritrean Refugees in Sudan) 18 March 1971

Mudhakira'a n al-Lāji'īn al-Ithiūbiyīn bil Sūdān (Memorandum on the Ethiopian Refugees in Sudan) March 1971

Jabhat al-Taḥrīr al Iritriya (The Eritrean Liberation Front) 21 July 1971

The Office of the Commissioner for Refugees

Ib'ād al-Lāji'īn min al-Madīna (Removing the Refugees from Khartoum) No. 36/B/3/2, 25 June 1979

Al Idi'ā'āt al-Ithiūbia bi 'awdat al-Lāji'īn (The Ethiopian Government Allegations on the Repatriation of Refugees) No. 36/B/conf., 4 October 1980

Al-Ḥamla al-'alamia Li Jam' al-Māl Lil Lāji'īn (The International Campaign for Fundraising for Refugees in Sudan) CR/20/F/1, 21 November 1980

Barnāmij tawṭīn al-Lāji'īn bil wilāyāt al-Muttaḥida al-Amrīkya (The United States Resettlement Programme) 10/C/28, 31 December 1981

Malaf al-Lāji'īn bil-Iqlīm al-shargī (A Dossier on the Refugee Situation in the Eastern Region) prepared by the General Project Manager, Showak, 1981

Taqrīr'a n al-Lāji'īn bi-Manṭiqat Karakaun (A Report on the ELF Fighters and their Families in Karakon) No. 35/A/conf. 1983

Al-Lāji'īn bi sabab al-Jafāf (The Refugees caused by Drought) No. 36/A/4, 23 March 1983

Taqrīr Hawl al-Lāji'īn (A Report on Refugees) No. CR/57/A. 20 November 1983

Wufūd wa Tahjīr al-Falāshā (The Influx and Exodus of the Falashas) CR/35/C/1, 18 August 1984

Mushkilat al-Falāshā fi Manṭiqat al-Gedārif: Taṭwurātuha, wa Ḍarūrat Ittikhādh Qarār Min Jihāt'Ulia bisha'niha (The Falasha Problem in Gedaref Area: its Development, andthe Importance of a Decision from the Highest Authority) September 1984

Al-Mu'tamar al-thānī Li-Musā'adat al-Lāji'īn Fī Afrīqiya, Taqrīr
wafd al-Sūdān (The Second International Conference on Assistance to Refugees in Africa: A Report of the Sudan Delegation)
October 1984

Ṣundūq Māl al-Lāji'īn (The Refugee Fund) December 1984

Taqrīr 'an wad' al-Lāji'īn bi Janūb Mudīriyat al-Nīl al Azrag
(Report on the Situation of Refugees in the Blue Nile Province)
GPM/57/A/1, 2 March 1985

Tawajjuhāt al-Siyāsa al-'ama Naḥwa al-Lāji'īn (Guidelines for the
Public Policy towards Refugees) September 1986

Al-Naẓra al-Mustaqbaliya Li-Muwajjihāt al-siyāsa al-'ama Lil-dawla
Tijāh al-Lāji'īn (A Future Outlook of the Government Refugee
Policy) No. 35/A/1 26 October 1986

The National Committee for Review of Refugee Policy March-May 1988, COR, Khartoum

Wad'al-Lāji'īn bil-Sūdān (The Refugee Situation in Sudan)

Muraja'at al-siyāsāt al Rāhina al-Khāṣṣa bi al T'āmul m'a Mushkilat
al-Lāji'īn (A Review of the Current Policy Dealing with the
Refugee Problems)

Al-Athār al-Iqtiṣādiya al-Mutaratiba'A la Tawājud al-Lāji'īn bil-
Sūdān (The Economic Impact of the Refugees)

Ta'thīr al-Lāji'īn 'A la al-sukkān (The Impact of the Refugees on the
Population)

Taqrīr al-Lajna al Qawmiya Li dirāsat awḍa' al-Lāji'īn bil-Sūdān
(The Report of the National Committee on the Refugee Situation in Sudan)

Al-Musa'dāt al-Khārijiya lil-Lāji'īn (External Assistance for Refugees)

Siyāsatunā Naḥwa al-Munaẓamāt al-taṭwui'ya al Ajnabiya (The Policy towards the Foreign Voluntary Organisations)

Al-Haykal al-Tanzīmī wa al-wazīfī Li Maktab Mu'tamad al-Lāji'īn
(The Organisational Structure of the Office of the Commissioner
for Refugees)

The Regional Government of the Eastern Region

Al-amr al-Mahallī al Khāṣ bi Tanzīm taḥarrukāt al-Lāji'īn Dākhil
Mudīriyat Kassala (The Local By-Law Relating to the Regulation of the Refugee Movement in Kassala Province) By-Law No.
75/1980, File No. Exec/16/D/2/3 also 35/B/1/3/Conf., 23
November 1980, Kassala People's Executive Council

Waqā'i'warshat al-'amal 'an al-Lāji'īn wa al-ṣaḥḥa bi al-Iqlīm al-
sharqī (The Proceedings of the Workshop on Refugees and
Health Services in Kassala), January 1984

Dirāsa Ḥawl Mushkilat al Lāji'īn bil-Iqlīm al-sharqī: Māḍihā, wa Haḍiruhā wa Mustaqbaluhā (A Study on the Refugee Problem in the Eastern Region: Its Past, Present and Future), Report of a committee appointed by the Regional Governor, Kassala, March 1986

Gezira Province

Al-wāfidīn wa al-Lāji'īn bi-Mudīriyat al Gazīra (Immigrants and Refugees in Gezira Province) No. 36/B/3/conf., June 1979

The Ministry of Foreign Affairs

Man wara'Ib'ād al-Lāji'īn Min Jibūtī ila Ithiūbya (Who is Behind the Expulsion of Ethiopian Refugees from Djibouti to Ethiopia?) 13 February 1983

Al-Lāji'ūn al Ithiūbiyūn bi Jibūtī (The Ethiopian Refugees in Djibouti) No. FA/Africa/3-1/5, 23 February 1986

Siyāsat al-Sūdān Naḥwa al-Lāji'īn (Sudan's Policy towards Refugees) 16 August 1986

The Security

Al Makhāṭir al-Amniya Li wujūd al-Lāji'īn bil-Kharṭoum (The Security Risks Resulting from the Refugee Presence in Khartoum), No. KPP/41/A/B/4, 1 July 1978

Tarḥīl al-Lāji'īn ila Mu'askarāt Jadīda (The Transference of Refugees to New Camps) The National Security Council, No. 1/B/2/3/549, 17 December 1981

Al-wujūd al-Iritrī bil-Sūdān (The Eritrean Presence in the Sudan), The External Security Unit, 1985

Taqrīr 'an al-wujūd Iritrī bil-Sūdān (A Report on the Eritrean Organisations in Sudan) External Security Unit, 1985

Al-Ittiḥād al-Dimuqrāṭi al-Ithiūbī (The Ethiopian Democratic Union) External Security Unit, 1985

Council of Ministers Resolutions

Al-Lāji'ūn al-Iritriyūn (The Eritrean Refugees) CM/Res 225 Session 212, 15 March 1967

Ittifāqiyat Iskān al-Lājiyīn al-Iritriyīn (The Agreement on the Resettlement of the Eritrean Refugees), CS/RES. 242, Session 32, 20 September 1968

Mashrū' qānūn bi al-Taṣḍīq 'ala Ittifāqiya bi sha'n Inshā' Maktab far'i Li mufawaḍ al-Lāji'īn bil-Khartoum (Approval for UNHCR to Open a Branch Office in Khartoum) CM/Res. 419, Session 59, 19 Janunary 1969

qānūn bi al Taṣdīq 'ala Ittifāqiyat Iskān al-Lāji'īn al-Ithiūbiyīn
bayna Hukumat Jumhuriyat al-Sūdān al Dimuqrāṭiya wa al-
Mandūb al-sāmī Lil Umam al-Muttaḥida, 1970 (Approval of the
Agreement Between the Sudan Government and UNHCR on
Resettlement of Ethiopian Refugees), CM/ Res. 426, 7 April 1970
Indimām al-Sūdān Li-Ittifāqiya al Khaṣṣa bi-wad' al-Lāji'īn wa Bru-
tukūl 1967 al Lāhiq bihā (Accession to the 1951 Convention
Relating to the Status of Refugees and the 1976 Protocol),
CM/Res. 201, Session 101, 10 Oct 1971
Tanẓīm al-Hijra ila al-Sūdān (The Regulation of Immigration)
CM/Res. 1098, 1970
Tawjīh bi-I'dād Dirāsa Mutakāmila wa'ājila 'an al-Lāji'īn (A CM
Directive to Prepare a Study on Refugees in the Sudan), Session
36, 2 November. 1986
Takwīn Lajna Li-Dirāsat waḍ' al-Lāji'īn bil-Sūdān (A Committee to
Conduct a Study on the Refugee Situation in Sudan) 30 January
1988

Presidential Decrees

Tanẓīm al Hijra bil-Sūdān (Decree No. 1098, 1970)
Al-Ittifāqiya al-Sūdāniya al-Nīgīrya al Khaṣṣa bi al Hijra Ghair al-
Mashrū'a (Agreement Between Sudan and Nigeria on Illegal
Immigration), Decree No. 720, 1975
Taqrīr 'an al-Hijra al-Dākhiliya wa-al Khārijiya (A Report on Immi-
gration and Emigration) Decree No. 137, 1977
Mashākil al-Hijra Fī al-Sūdān (The Problem of Immigration in the
Sudan) Decree No. 505, 1978
Takwīn Lajna Li-Dirāsat al-Tawṣiyāt wa al-Khayārat- al Mut'aliqa
bi-Tarshīd wa Tanẓīm al-Hijra (Establishment of a Committee to
Study the Recommendations and Options Relating to the Regu-
lation of Migration), Decree No. 667, 1980
Takwīn al-Majlis-Qawmi Li Ri 'āyat al-Lāji'īn (Establishment of the
National Refugee Council), Decree No. 699, Oct. 1982

The National Defence College Monographs (Khartoum)

Al-Assam, Mohammad Mukhtar (1984) Al-'Alāga Bayn al-Ḥukm
al-Maḥalli wa al-Ḥukm al Iqlīmī (The Relationship Between
Local and Regional Government Systems)
Abdalla, Salih Mohammad (1983) Al-Infāq al-'Askarī fi 'ahd
Thawrat Mayū: Ittijāhātuhu wa Ṭuruq Tarshīdihi (Military
Expenditure during the May Revolution Regime: Its Orienta-
tions and Ways to Improve It)

Abd al-Nabi, Mustafa (1983) Al-Mushkila al-Iritriya: Abʻāduhā wa Inʻikāsatuhā ʻala Amn al-Minṭaqa, bi al-Tarkīz ʻala al-Sūdan (The Eritrean Problem and Its Implications for Regional Security)

Ahmad, Ahmad Idris (1983) Al-Ṣirāʻ fi al-Qarn al-Afrīqī wa-Athārahu ʻala al-Amn al-Qawmī al-Sūdāni (The Conflict in the Horn of Africa and Its Effects on Regional Security)

Allam, Ahmad al-Sayed (1984) Al-ʻAlāqāt al-athiūbiya al-Sūdāniya: al-Māḍi, al-Ḥāḍir, wa al-Mustaqbal (The Ethiopian-Sudanese Relations: The Past, Present and Future)

Ali, Ahmad Mohammad (1984) al-Muskila al-Tshādiya wa Abʻāduhā al-ʻAskariya wa-Athuru dhalikʻala al-Sūdān (The Chadian Problem: The Military Dimension and Its Effects on Sudan)

Al-Sheikh, Al-Sheikh Bashir (1983) Al-Ḥukm al-lāmarkazi fi jumhūriyat al-Sūdān al dimuqraṭiya wa al-murtakazāt al-falsafiya (Decentralisation in the Democratic Republic of the Sudan and its Philosophical Premises)

Fadl al-Sid, Osman al-Sayyid (1984) Al-Qadiya al-Iritriya wa-Inʻikāsātuhā ʻala al-Sūdān (The Eritrean Question and its Consequences for the Sudan)

Gismalla, Zein al-Abdin (1985) Duwal sharq Afrīqiya wa-athāruhā ʻala al-Amn al-Qawmi al-Sūdāni (The East African States and their Influence on the Sudanese National Security)

Hassan, Ibrahim Sulaiman (1987) al-ʻāthār al-salbiya li-nashāt Hayʼāt al-Ighātha (The Negative Effect on the Relief Agency Activities)

Osman, Hashim (1983) Al-Mushkila al-Tshādiya wa Inʻikāsātuhā ʻala al-Sūdān (The Chadian Conflict and its Consequences for the Sudan)

Index

Amin, Idi, 10, 203, 217
Ansar, 18, 57, 203
Anya-Nya, 34, 76
Beja, 15-17, 46, 48
Beni Amer, 16-19, 37, 38, 42, 46, 48, 77, 142
British involvement in determining the Sudanese-Ethiopian border, 12, 48
   occupation of Eritrea, 19
   representations at ICARA II, 185, 186
   support for OXFAM mission, 146
Central Committee for Rehabilitation of Returnees (CCRR), 50-52
Chad, refugee influxes from, 8-10, 203, 223, 225
Church agencies, 53, 69
Commissioner for Refugees (COR), and 1984 influx, 225
   approach to 1975 refugee influx, 69, 74-76, 82-84
   as seen in Huntings report, 154-156
   campaign for international assistance, 162-167, 220
   creation of, 5-6, 52, 54
   decline of role, 193-197, 201-202
   differences with UNHCR over repatriation, 209-211
   evacuation of refugees from Wad el Heleiw, 120-122
   history, 8
   provision of identity cards, 126
   refugee settlements, 49
   relations with central and provincial government, 88-96
   relations with security organisations, 96-118
   relations with UNHCR, 6, 69, 75, 91, 92, 94-96, 127, 137-148

relocation of refugees from Kassala and Gedaref, 128-135
   role in ILO project, 172-3
Committee for Relief, 38, 47, 207
Communists, 32, 46
Congo, 4, 23, 30, 32, 33, 35, 36
Council of Ministers, OAU, policy on refugees, 23, 25
   support for ICARA II, 180
Council of Ministers, Sudan, bans ELF, 43
   COR attached to, 99-101, 110, 111, 163
   granting of refugee status, 46, 93
   Resolution 1225 (1967), 45
   settlement of refugees, 49-52
   urges transfer away from border, 141
Democratic Unionist Party (DUP), 3, 5, 7, 57
Economic Commission for Africa (ECA), 166
Egypt, 2, 7, 11, 12, 16, 17, 32, 60, 85
Eritrea, conflict with Ethiopia, 7, 9, 61-64, 67
   exodus of refugees in 1950s, 4
   geography and links with Eastern Sudan, 12, 16-18, 46, 48, 79
   intensification of war, 157
   policy of Dergue towards, 58
   refugee influx to Sudan, 1967, 10, 37-39
   refugee influx, 1975-1982, 67-73
   refugee influx, 1984-1985, 202, 214, 223-225
   return of refugees to, 208-210
   rise of nationalism, 18-20
   towns of origin of refugees, 84
Eritrean Liberation Front (ELF), 19, 40, 41, 43, 57, 58, 62-64, 71, 73-75, 79, 119, 120, 122, 126, 127, 130, 193

Eritrean Liberation Front/Revolution-
ary Council (ELF/RC), 62, 73
Eritrean People's Liberation Front
(EPLF), 20, 62-64, 66, 71, 74, 75,
78, 120, 122, 193, 213, 223, 224
Eritrean Relief Association (ERA), 78,
116
Ethiopia, 1984-1985 influx from, 223,
225
exchange of refugees with Sudan, 4-
13
migration to Gedaref from, 80, 132
refugee flows from, 70-73, 85, 118
refugee groups in Sudan, 82, 84, 93-
96, 145, 146
relations with Sudan 37, 38, 40-44,
46, 48, 56-67, 88, 98, 119, 122,
159, 216-218
repatriation to, 187-189, 193, 203,
205-207, 209-213, 221, 222
'subversive' activities in Sudan, 125,
126
Ethiopian Democratic Union (EDU), 7,
62-64, 74, 75, 81, 117-120, 122, 124,
125, 128, 145
Ethiopian People's Revolutionary Army
(EPRA), 71
Ethiopian People's Revolutionary Party
(EPRP), 71
Freetown Conference, 66, 177
Frolinat, 10
Gbenye, Christopher, 33, 34
General Project Manager (GPM),
Showak, 96, 97, 120, 121, 125-129,
158, 213, 225
Habre, Hussein, 10, 203
Haile Selassie, 6, 12, 19, 20, 41, 58, 70,
82
Hamdalla, Faroug, 58, 59, 89, 90
Huntings, 141, 142
1976 feasibility study, 150-158
International Conference on Assistance
to Refugees in Africa (ICARA I),
177, 180-185, 220, 226
International Conference on Assistance
to Refugees in Africa (ICARA II),
177, 181, 183-185, 187, 189, 220, 226
International Conference on the Situa-
tion of Refugees in Sudan, 1980,
166-170
International Labour Organisation
(ILO), 190, 206

Technical Mission, 171-173, 200
International Monetary Fund (IMF), 8,
27
Italian rule in Eritrea, 17, 18
annexation of Kassala, 79
invasion of Ethiopia, 80, 82
Italy, agreements over Sudanese-
Ethiopian border, 12
Khashm al Girba, 15, 48, 49, 96, 116,
124, 128-131, 153, 154, 157
Khatmiya, 16-19, 38, 46, 78, 79
Libya, 2, 7, 13, 37, 59, 85
Mahdi, Al-Imam al-Hadi al-, 57
Mahdi, Al-Sadiq al-, 61, 65
Mahdi, Sayed Abdel-Rahman al-, 16
Mahdi, Sayyid al-Sadig al-, 41, 52
Mahdists/Mahdiya, 16-18
Mahjoub, Mohammed Ahmed, 5, 30,
31, 40, 41, 51, 128
Malloum, Félix, 10
Mengistu Haile Mariam, 4, 7, 60, 63,
64, 66, 67
Ministry of Foreign Affairs, 195, 212,
213, 224
Ministry of Interior, 34, 37, 40, 45, 108
Mirghani family, 17, 19, 65, 66, 79
Mobutu, Joseph, 36
Muslim League, 19, 79
Nasser, support for Congolese revolu-
tion, 32
National Council for Assistance to
Refugees (NCAR), 13, 72, 164,
166, 168
National Front, 2, 7, 57, 59-62, 64, 203
National Refugee Council, 164, 175-177,
194, 201
National Security, blocking transfer of
refugees, 122
creation of, 59
policy towards Ethiopia, 64
relocation of refugees, 132
rivalry with Public Security, 65, 97,
100
National Unionist Party (NUP), 3, 46
Nimeiry, Gaafar, 3, 4, 6, 7, 57, 59-67,
90, 106, 110, 111, 119, 166, 168,
176, 203, 217, 226
Organisation of African Unity (OAU), 3-
6, 20-26, 31, 36, 41, 43, 47, 54, 56,
59, 65, 66, 77, 91, 92, 103, 104, 107,
119, 164, 165, 177, 178, 180, 181,
186, 187, 212, 216, 218, 224, 225

October Revolution, 82
Olenga, 33, 34
OXFAM Mission, 69, 70, 144-147
Pan-African Conference, Arusha, 1979,
    164, 165
People's Democratic Party (PDP), 3, 46
Provisional Military Administration
    Council (PMAC), 6, 7
Provincial Commissioner, Kassala, 37, 95
    and ELF, 40
    conflict with central government over
        settlement of refugees, 45-48
    transfer of refugees, 96, 120-122, 128,
        129, 131
Public Security, and EDU, 62
    creation of, 59
    eviction of refugees from Khartoum,
        103, 104, 108
    monitoring of Ethiopian students, 82
    official letters for refugees, 70
    registering of refugees, 98
    rivalry with National Security, 65, 97,
        100
Qala en Nahal, 54, 74, 91, 92, 119-121,
    139-141, 151-154, 156
Refugee Fund, 164, 175, 176, 194, 201
Regulation of Asylum Act, 6, 59, 92, 93,
    101, 103, 110, 114, 159
repatriation, 8, 10, 11, 37, 41, 44, 51-54,
    58, 74, 91, 125, 134, 165, 186-189,
    193, 203-205, 210-214, 221, 222
resettlement, 15, 45, 47-52, 59, 77, 85,
    119, 127, 128, 141, 151, 153-155,
    157, 177, 183, 195, 196, 205
Relief and Rehabilitation Commission
    (RRC), 207-209
shifta, 122-124
Showak, 68, 96, 97, 118, 120, 121, 128,
    129, 131, 141, 142, 151, 153, 156,
    158, 195
Shukriya, 15, 16, 18, 48, 49
Simba, 5, 31, 32, 37, 217
Southern Sudan Liberation Movement,
    58
Soviet Union (USSR), 6, 7, 12, 13, 26,
    57, 60, 61, 71
Sudan Council of Churches (SCC), 98,
    146
Sudanese Communist Party (SCP), 57,
    90
Sudanese Socialist Union (SSU), 67, 95,
    96, 108, 110, 133, 134

State Security, 65, 66, 73, 76, 100-102,
    108, 109, 111, 114-116, 119, 122,
    125-127, 131, 132, 211, 224
Tigray, 2, 7, 62, 63, 68, 70-72, 81, 116,
    123, 145, 146, 173, 202, 206, 210,
    213, 214, 223, 224
Tigray People's Liberation Front
    (TPLF), 63, 71, 73, 74, 81, 117, 118,
    123, 125, 193, 223, 224
Transitional Government, 4, 5, 30, 32-34
Uganda, 1, 2, 4, 8-10, 23, 33, 44, 203, 217
Umma, 3, 5, 7, 31, 57
United Nations Development Pro-
    gramme (UNDP), 140, 166, 181-
    183, 188, 190, 206
United Nations High Commissioner for
    Refugees (UNHCR), and 1984
    influx, 224-226
    appeal by refugees in Wad el Heleiw,
        121
    assistance to refugees, 37, 45, 47, 50,
        53, 54, 59, 74, 102, 107-109, 112,
        114, 133, 168, 169
    follow-up mission, 170, 171
    /ILO Technical Mission, 171-174
    inaction, 8, 76, 162, 166, 219, 220
    influence on government policy, 27,
        193-214
    involvement in ICARA, 178-183, 187-
        190
    involvement in Refugee Fund, 164,
        175, 176
    Master Plan, 153, 154, 158-160
    non-recognition of Ethiopians as
        refugees, 82, 83, 94-96
    policy review, 149-157
    promotion of repatriation, 221
    protest at treatment of refugees, 124,
        129
    relations with COR, 6, 69, 75, 91, 92,
        94-96, 127, 137-148, 158, 159,
    running of Refugee Counselling Ser-
        vice, 98
    Third Follow-up Mission, 174, 175
United States, 12, 165, 166, 177, 178,
    185, 195, 206, 213
World Food Programme (WFP), 112,
    139, 141-144, 166, 176, 182, 199,
    206
World Bank, 15, 27, 182, 190
Zaire, 1, 2, 4, 5, 9, 10, 30, 44, 165